Innovative Assessment for the 21st Century

Valerie J. Shute · Betsy Jane Becker
Editors

Innovative Assessment for the 21st Century

Supporting Educational Needs

Springer

Editors
Valerie J. Shute
College of Education
Florida State University
1114 W. Call Street
32306 Tallahassee, Florida
USA
vshute@fsu.edu

Betsy Jane Becker
College of Education
Florida State University
1114 W. Call Street
32306 Tallahassee, Florida
USA
bbecker@fsu.edu

ISBN 978-1-4419-6529-5   e-ISBN 978-1-4419-6530-1
DOI 10.1007/978-1-4419-6530-1
Springer New York Dordrecht Heidelberg London

Library of Congress Control Number: 2010931400

Printed on acid-free paper

Springer is part of Springer Science+Business Media (www.springer.com)

Acknowledgements

This book was made possible through the generous support of the College of Education at Florida State University. As she describes in the Foreword to this book, Dean Marcy Driscoll initiated a series of annual symposia that bring leading scholars to Florida State. Our symposium focused on new ways of thinking about assessment and served as the springboard for this book. We'd like to acknowledge the outstanding assistance of Soojeong Ingrisone who helped with all aspects of our symposium planning. In addition, we want to thank Kuzey Bilir, Oktay Donmez, and Yanyun Yang for helping us with many of the symposium logistics, and Nash McCutcheon and Emily Keeler for their creative efforts in promoting the symposium.

The quality of the book was enhanced due to the work of our cadre of diligent reviewers: Barbara Davis, Malcolm Bauer, Jill Burstein, Ginette Delandshere, Vanessa Dennen, Oktay Donmez, Rebekah Dorn, Eric Hansen, Dirk Ifenthaler, Tristan Johnson, Yoon-Jeon Kim, Qian Liu, Iskandaria Masduki, Christie Suggs, and Diego Zapata-Rivera. In addition, we are grateful for the exceptional efforts of Yoon-Jeon Kim in helping us format the book chapters. Finally, we want to acknowledge Springer Publishing for their interest in this book.

Foreword

The papers comprising this volume were presented at the 2008 Dean's Symposium sponsored by the College of Education at Florida State University.

The impetus for a symposium series came from a blue ribbon committee that I charged with finding ways to facilitate a culture of inquiry in the college, to promote the exchange of ideas among faculty but also with the constituents of our work. The university's location in the state capital and its proximity to the legislature and state agencies offer us a unique opportunity to partner with constituent groups and influence education policy in the state. To take advantage of this opportunity, the blue ribbon committee suggested an annual symposium that would provide a forum for discussion about topics of keen interest to policy makers and researchers alike, both statewide and nationally.

Our first effort was to sponsor an invited lecture in Spring 2006 that brought teacher educator Marilyn Cochran-Smith to campus. That was a wonderful opportunity not only to hear about the work she's been doing with the Teachers for a New Era project, but also to engage her in conversation with our faculty and doctoral students about teacher education research, practice, and policy.

In Fall 2007, we held our first true symposium, interspersing panel and roundtable discussions with presentations from invited speakers. It was on teacher quality, a topic that is central to education reform efforts in the state of Florida. We were excited to draw educators from around the state and from many sectors— legislative policy makers, superintendents and school leaders, education researchers and administrators. To our great delight, three state legislators also attended and participated in lively discussion.

Our second symposium, held in Fall 2008, resulted in this book. Co-Editors Valerie Shute and Betsy Becker took the lead in organizing a set of presentations and opportunities for discussion around the topic of Assessment. In states like Florida, the concept of assessment tends to evoke strong and often negative feelings because it is most commonly associated with high stakes testing and accountability. Who, after all, *doesn't* have an opinion about the FCAT? Yet Florida is also a leader among states in linking assessment data to instructional intervention. Teachers and principals are expected to monitor individual student progress and ensure that appropriate instructional strategies are employed so that each student can learn. How assessment can go beyond providing numbers to providing insight was the theme of this symposium. It is a critical issue that brings together policymakers, agency officials, school leaders, and education researchers.

The presentations did not disappoint, and I believe the readers of this book will find much to consider. The authors challenge us to think differently, more expansively about assessment and its role in teaching and learning, as well as accountability. They help us to envision what a culture of assessment might look like, incorporating perspectives from teachers and students to state testing personnel. It is our sincere hope that these papers will change the conversations around assessment and lead to advances that will facilitate learning and teaching in the 21st century.

Tallahassee, Florida   Marcy P. Driscoll
June, 2009

Contents

Contributors

Russell G. Almond Research and Development, Educational Testing Service, Princeton, NJ, USA, ralmond@ets.org; almond@acm.org

King D. Beach III International Educational Research and Development Consulting (IERDConsult), Tallahassee, FL, USA, kingbeach108@gmail.com

Betsy Jane Becker Department of Educational Psychology and Learning Systems, Florida State University, Tallahassee, FL, USA, bbecker@fsu.edu

Eric Christesen Department of Educational Psychology and Learning Systems, Florida State University, Tallahassee, FL, USA, emc07c@fsu.edu

Katie A. Clinton New Media Literacies, Annenberg School for Communication & Journalism, University of Southern California, Los Angeles, CA, USA, katherine.clinton@usc.edu

Vincent J. Dean Office of Educational Assessment & Accountability, Michigan Department of Education, Lansing, MI, USA, deanv@michigan.gov

Kris Ellington Accountability, Research, and Measurement, Florida Department of Education, Tallahassee, FL, USA, kris.ellington@fldoe.org

James P. Gee Division of Curriculum and Instruction, Mary Lou Fulton College of Education, Arizona State University, Tempe, AZ, USA, James.Gee@asu.edu

Daniel T. Hickey Learning Sciences Program, Indiana University, Bloomington, IN, USA, dthickey@indiana.edu

Michelle A. Honeyford Department of Literacy, Culture, & Language Education, Indiana University, Bloomington, IN, USA, mhoneyfo@indiana.edu

Allan C. Jeong Department of Educational Psychology and Learning Systems, Florida State University, Tallahassee, FL, USA, ajeong@fsu.edu

Joseph A. Martineau Office of Educational Assessment & Accountability, Michigan Department of Education, Lansing, MI, USA, martineauj@michigan.gov

Jenna M. McWilliams Learning Sciences Program, Indiana University, Bloomington, IN, USA, jenmcwil@indiana.edu

Mari Pearlman Pearlman Education Group LLC, Lawrenceville, NJ, USA, mapearlman@comcast.net

Alysia D. Roehrig Department of Educational Psychology and Learning Systems, Florida State University, Tallahassee, FL, USA, aroehrig@fsu.edu

Mark D. Shermis College of Education, The University of Akron, Akron, OH, USA, shermis@uakron.edu

Valerie J. Shute Department of Educational Psychology and Learning Systems, Florida State University, Tallahassee, FL, USA, vshute@fsu.edu

Vincent Verges Test Development Center, Florida Department of Education, Tallahassee, FL, USA, vergesv@leon.k12.fl.us

Lynn Wicker Florida State University Schools, Inc., Tallahassee, FL, USA, lwicker@admin.fsu.edu

Chapter 1
Prelude: Assessment for the 21st Century

Valerie J. Shute and Betsy Jane Becker

Abstract We recently hosted an assessment symposium at Florida State University which served as the basis for this book and focused on how to integrate assessment and instruction to improve student learning and education. The chapters in this book address the general issue of integrating assessment and instruction, and additionally provide innovative solutions to hard questions such as: What would an assessment, suitable for the needs of the twenty-first century, look like? How could it be standardized? Should it be standardized? How could it satisfy the current obsession with "metrics"? What is the role of the professional teacher in making twenty-first century assessments possible? What constraints would be faced by those who would implement such innovations in assessment practice?

Keywords Assessment · Education · Learning · Measurement

1.1 Introduction

> Measurements are not to provide numbers but insight. Ingrid Bucher

The quote above inspired the title of the assessment symposium at Florida State University which served as the basis for this book. The symposium—*Assessment for the Twenty-First Century: Insight*—focused on how to integrate appropriate assessment and instruction to improve student learning and education, especially to suit the needs of the twenty-first century. We were motivated by the belief that the goal of assessment should shift from obtaining numbers and rankings to providing insight—on learners and learning, as well as on instructors and instruction.

V.J. Shute (✉)
Department of Educational Psychology and Learning Systems, Florida State University,
Tallahassee, FL, USA
e-mail: vshute@fsu.edu

V.J. Shute, B.J. Becker (eds.), *Innovative Assessment for the 21st Century*,
DOI 10.1007/978-1-4419-6530-1_1, © Springer Science+Business Media, LLC 2010

The symposium had two intertwining tracks: (a) innovative assessment ideas and technologies to support twenty-first century educational needs, and (b) specific educational and assessment issues and needs (e.g., teacher and student testing and accountability). Florida State University's College of Education hosted the 2-day symposium as a part of the college's annual Dean's Colloquium Series. Keynote speakers included James Gee of Arizona State University, Russell Almond of Educational Testing Service (Princeton, NJ) and Mari Pearlman of Pearlman Education Group, LLC. Our keynote speakers were innovative researchers who have written on assessment for twenty-first century skills, and who understand broad policy implications and the challenges of educational reform. Additional speakers, broadly comprising educational researchers, policy makers, and practitioners, presented assessment-related research, and others responded to the invited speakers' presentations, to connect their ideas to the context and concerns of researchers and of state education departments. All speakers' and respondents' papers are included in this book.

This book covers a range of topics. It does not just focus, for instance, on the policy issues of large-scale assessment. Instead the book expounds upon the provocative forward-thinking proposals of the keynote speakers and serves as a launching pad for careful analyses of practical problems of implementation of assessment, technical psychometric issues, and policy issues.

Our goal for the symposium was to bring together groups who don't normally convene. We wanted policymakers and educational professionals to have the opportunity to learn about the latest research by scholars from across the nation; and also wanted educational researchers to learn about critical educational issues important to the states and to practitioners. The symposium successfully opened up lively discussions among speakers, respondents, and attendees.

We now examine why we believe that this type of conversation—begun at the symposium and continued with this book—is important. After identifying some problems that may benefit from new thinking about assessment, we spend a little time defining key aspects (and terms) of assessment, as well as describing different types of assessment, to provide a basis for understanding subsequent chapters. Finally, we close with an overview of the chapters in this book, as well as our own thoughts on moving forward with assessment.

1.2 The Big Problems

> Knowledge is no longer an immobile solid; it has been liquefied. It is actively moving in all the currents of society itself. John Dewey

This presentient quote by Dewey (1916, p. 40), nearly 100 years ago, is particularly relevant now. The world is evolving and effectively shrinking, due mainly to the interconnections made possible via the Internet and other communication technologies. Our twenty-first century existence confronts us with problems of enormous complexity (e.g., meltdowns on Wall Street, nuclear proliferation, pharmaceuticals in the water supply, and poverty). Those who confront these issues in the twenty-first century (e.g., policy makers) need to think critically, to identify and examine relevant research, and to understand how systems in general work, because solutions will be highly complex and interconnected. When confronted by problems, especially new issues for which solutions must be created out of whole cloth, the ability to think creatively, critically, and collaboratively, and then communicate effectively is essential.

Learning and succeeding in a complex and dynamic world is not easily measured by the well-worn, multiple-choice response formats on simple knowledge tests. We need to re-think assessment, identify new skills and standards relevant for the twenty-first century, and then determine how to best assess students' acquisition of the new competencies—which may in fact involve *others* doing this assessment (e.g., the community of peers suggested in Chapter 2 by Gee, this book). Moreover, the envisioned new competencies should include not only cognitive variables (e.g., critical thinking, reasoning skills) but also noncognitive variables (e.g., teamwork, tolerance, tenacity) as the basis for new assessments to support learning. Each of these may be embedded and supported within valued domains—such as mathematics and science.

Learning is an important part of everyday life, and is a lifelong endeavor. This is especially true for knowledge workers in both developed and developing countries. Avoiding lifelong learning and training is not an option for most people who work in areas where rapid change is a norm in terms of how people work, what they are expected to do, and the tools and information with which they work. For instance, people working in information technology (IT) areas need to constantly acquire new knowledge and skills about new products and ideas, and to perform new tasks. People may change their careers multiple times before retirement, requiring new learning for new work contexts, as well as new social networks and contacts (e.g., Higgins, 2001). Indeed, all of us face complex problems both at work and in our daily lives. The complexity of these problems and the huge quantities of available information require substantial learning and continuing education as well as the development of learning management capabilities over our lifetimes (Georghiades, 2004; Sungur, 2007).

With all of these changes taking place in the world, it might be comforting that education has changed little in the past several decades. We don't see it that way. "Old school" (pun intended) philosophies and approaches are often inappropriate in today's rapidly changing and information-rich world. Students need to develop new competencies that are quite different from those needed by earlier generations in order to deal successfully with the deluge of data and information in the twenty-first century (e.g., information communication and technology skills). Many educationally valuable skills that are potentially suitable for success in the twenty-first century are not currently being acknowledged, let alone assessed. Toward this end, we must agree on what skills we value and promote these skills for a society requiring knowledge workers, not simply service workers. Then we must determine how best to measure those skills.

In addition to needing to identify a new set of skills for "twenty-first century competencies," we believe that the very nature of assessment should be changing. Over a dozen years ago, the National Research Council (NRC, 1996) made a similar plea, which has yet to be adequately addressed. Table 1.1 presents a modified version of the NRC call for changes in the focus on assessment needed to support educational reform for the twenty-first century.

Table 1.1 Changing assessment foci

Less focus on assessing	More focus on assessing
Learning outcomes	Learning processes
What is easily measured	What is most highly valued
Discrete, declarative knowledge	Rich, authentic knowledge and skills
Content knowledge	Understanding and reasoning, within and across content areas
What learners do *not* know	What learners understand and can do
By teachers alone	By learners engaged in ongoing assessment of their work and that of others

1.3 Defining Assessment Ideas and Terms

Assessment should not merely be done *to* students; rather, it should also be done *for* students, to guide and enhance their learning. NCTM (2000)

In this section we briefly define and disambiguate important assessment terms that often get confounded. For instance, what exactly is the difference between "measurement" and "assessment"? Let's start with the basic idea of measurement. Whenever you need to measure something accurately, you probably grab an appropriate tool to determine how heavy, light, tall, short, fast, slow, hot, cold, bright, dark, straight, or curved something is. We measure to obtain information (data), which may or may not be useful, depending on the accuracy of the tools we use, as well as our skill at using them. Measuring things like a person's height, a room's temperature, or a car's speed is technically not an assessment and is instead simply collecting information relative to an established standard. How does this relate to education?

1.3.1 Educational Measurement

Educational measurement, in the context of this chapter, refers to the application of a measuring tool (or standard scale) to determine the degree to which educationally-valuable knowledge, skills, and other attributes have been, or are, being acquired.

It thus entails the collection and analysis of data from learners. According to the National Council on Measurement in Education Web site (http://www.ncme.org/), this includes "theory, techniques, and instrumentation available for measurement of educationally-relevant human, institutional, and social characteristics." A *test* is education's equivalent of a ruler, thermometer, or radar gun. But note that a test does not improve learning any more than a thermometer cures a fever; both are simply tools. Tests alone can't enhance educational outcomes. Rather, tests can guide improvement (presuming they are valid and reliable) if they motivate adjustments to the educational system. Examples of educational adjustments include providing the basis for bolstering curricula, ensuring support for struggling learners, guiding professional development opportunities, and distributing limited resources fairly.

Again, we measure things to get information, which may be quantitative or qualitative.[1] How we choose to *use* the data is a different story. For instance, back in the early 1900s, students' abilities and intelligence were extensively measured. However, this wasn't done to help them learn better or otherwise to progress. Instead, the main purpose of testing was to track students into appropriate paths, based on the belief that their aptitudes were inherently fixed. That is, a dominant belief during that period was that intelligence was part of a person's genetic makeup, thus testing was aimed at efficiently assigning students into high, middle, or low educational tracks according to their supposedly innate mental abilities (Terman, 1916). In general, a fundamental shift to practical education occurred in the country during the early 1900s, countering "wasted time" in schools and abandoning the classics as useless and inefficient for the masses (Shute, 2007). Early educational researchers and administrators inserted into the national educational discourse the metaphor of the school as a "factory" (Kliebard, 1987). This metaphor is no longer apt.

1.3.2 Assessment

Assessment involves much more than just measurement. That is, in addition to systematically collecting and analyzing information (i.e., measurement), it also involves interpreting and acting on information about learners' understanding and/or performance in relation to educational goals.[2] Measurement, then, can be viewed as a precursor to or special case of assessment. Assessment information may be used by a variety of stakeholders (e.g., teachers, administrators, students, parents) and for a variety of purposes, such as to help improve learning outcomes, programs, and services, and also to establish accountability. Furthermore, an assortment of procedures

---

[1] For a fuller, more balanced perspective on educational measurement, see Messick (1989) and Oosterhof (2009) which extend educational measurement beyond statistical conceptualizations and numbers to include qualitative information as well.

[2] Others, such as Guion (1998), see assessment as including less formal means of evaluating individuals.

is associated with the different purposes. For example, if your goal was to enhance an individual's learning, and you wanted to determine her progress toward an educational goal, you could: (a) administer a quiz; (b) view a portfolio of her work; (c) ask the student (or peers) to evaluate her progress; (d) watch the person solve a complex task; (e) review her lab reports or journal entries, and so on. You'd then need to use the information gathered via these assessments to help guide her further learning activities.

Finally we consider who is doing the assessing. Very often, it is the teacher. However, *self-assessment* may be a viable option, as well as an important skill, especially if a valued educational goal is to produce self-directed and productive lifelong learners. Promoting learners' self assessment in relation to setting reasonable learning goals involves supporting (assessing) knowledge of specific goals and learners' progress toward them. It also involves supporting learners' metacognitive skills of reflection and revision. Alternatively, *peer assessment* involves individuals collaborating with one another to solve, explain, or understand a problem or task. A variety of benefits (e.g., cognitive, social, motivational) accrue from encouraging learners to work collaboratively. An effective teacher should emphasize a high and equal level of interaction among group members, giving all an opportunity to negotiate meaning, acquire new strategies and skills, and develop higher-order thinking skills. However, as collaboration becomes an increasingly important aspect of twenty-first century learning, it introduces not only opportunities, but also serious challenges for assessment which will need to be resolved with innovative research (e.g., Jeong, 2005; Macdonald, 2003; Shute, Jeong, Spector, Seel, & Johnson, 2009).

1.3.3 Determining Assessment Quality

Because assessment is a process by which information is obtained relative to a known objective, and since inferences are made about what a person knows (unobservable) on the basis of responses to assessment tasks (observable), there's always some uncertainty in inferences made on the basis of assessments. So, an important goal in educational measurement is to collect really good information about the learner(s) and to minimize uncertainty or error. Consequently, key aspects of assessment quality are consistency and validity.

The broad term *consistency* is used here rather than the more familiar term *reliability* because it includes not only the quantitative aspects of reliability (e.g., correlations between parallel forms of tests), but also qualitative aspects of assessment (e.g., consistency in a teacher's description of a learner's performance on two comparable tasks). To illustrate, consider the produce scale at your local grocery store. If you weigh two pounds of carrots in the morning, and the scale is consistent, the same scale should register the same weight for the carrots an hour later. Similarly, classroom tests and standardized exams should be stable, and it shouldn't make much difference whether a learner takes the assessment at 10:00 AM or 11:00 AM. Another measure of consistency (i.e., internal consistency) relates to the items within a test. For instance, if you create an Algebra 1 test, you'd assume that if a learner correctly solves a difficult linear equations problem, then he should solve other linear equation problems correctly. Similarly, the notion of generalizability is often used with performance assessments and portfolios, and addresses the adequacy with which you can generalize from a sample of observations to the universe of observations from which it was randomly sampled.

As with consistency, there are a number of different types of validity; but in general, *validity* refers to the extent to which the assessment accurately measures what it is supposed to measure and the accuracy of the inferences made from test results. For instance, if you wanted to assess learners' math problem solving skills, but you gave them a personality questionnaire to complete, that would not be a valid assessment of their math skills. Regarding the relationship between validity and consistency, even if an assessment is judged to be consistent and stable (see above), it may not, in fact, be a valid measure. Let's use a scale analogy again, only now it's your bathroom scale. Suppose that you step on your scale 10 times in a row and your scale, without fail, indicates that you weigh 150 pounds. The *consistency* of your scale may be very good, but it may not be accurate (valid) if you actually weigh 165 pounds. Because teachers, parents, school districts, and so on currently make decisions about learners based on assessment results (e.g., grades, retention, graduation), the validity inferred from the assessments is essential, and it's even more crucial than the consistency. So, consistency is a prerequisite for validity. That is, inconsistency in observations always threatens their validity. On the other hand, simply having consistency in what is observed does not ensure the validity of those observations.

1.4 Kinds of Assessment

> When the cook tastes the soup, that's formative; when the guests taste the soup, that's summative. Robert Stake

Different types of assessment are often presented in contrast to one another. The two most familiar types of assessment are summative and formative, and the choice and use of a particular type of assessment depends on the educational purpose. Schools generally make heavy use of summative assessment (also known as assessment *of* learning). These can be quite useful for accountability purposes (e.g., assessments for grading and promotion purposes) but only marginally—if at all—useful for supporting individual learning. In contrast, learner-centered measurement models rely mostly on formative assessment, also known as assessment *for* learning. Formative assessments can be very useful in guiding instruction and supporting individual learning, but not for overall high-stakes decisions. Also, the assessment-for-learning model is often implemented in a non-standardized and hence less rigorous manner than summative assessment, and thus may have more limited validity and consistency (Shute & Zapata-Rivera, 2010). This is not to say such assessments don't have value. Rather, the less standardized, informal nature of formative assessment can be seen as a call for researchers to develop new techniques to capitalize on these assessments' value and utility (e.g., a synthetic approach using many formative assessments might provide an aggregate picture that cannot be seen in single individual assessments). Strong formative assessment research is urgently needed given changes in the types of learning and learning outcomes we are valuing as twenty-first century competencies as well as the new, broader, complex and integrated set of contexts in which learning is taking place and applied.

Summative assessment reflects a more traditional approach to assessing educational outcomes. This involves using assessment information for high-stakes, cumulative purposes, such as for grades, promotion, certification, and so on. A summative assessment is usually administered after some major event, like the end of the school year or marking period; or before a big event, like college entry. Benefits of this approach include the following: (a) it allows for comparing learner performances across diverse populations on clearly defined educational objectives and standards; (b) it provides reliable data (e.g., scores) that can be used for accountability purposes at various levels (e.g., classroom, school, district, state, and national) and for various stakeholders (e.g., learners, teachers, and administrators); and (c) it can inform educational policy (e.g., curriculum or funding decisions).

Formative assessment involves using assessments to support teaching and learning. Formative assessment is incorporated directly into the classroom curriculum and uses results from learners' activities as the basis on which to adjust instruction to promote learning in a timely manner. A simple example would be a teacher giving a "pop quiz" to his students on some topic or lesson, immediately analyzing their scores, and then re-focusing his lesson to straighten out a misconception shared by a substantial number of students in the class. This type of assessment is administered more frequently than summative assessment and has shown great potential for harnessing the power of assessments to support learning in different content areas and for diverse audiences (e.g., Black & Wiliam, 1998; Hindo, Rose, & Gomez, 2004; Schwartz, Bransford, & Sears, 2005). In addition to providing teachers with evidence about how their class is learning so that they can revise instruction appropriately, formative assessment directly involves learners in the process, such as by providing feedback that will help them gain insight about how to improve.

1.5 Discussion

Our symposium was organized to explore the many possible faces of future assessment—and asked hard questions, such as: What would an assessment, suitable for the needs of the twenty-first century, look like? How could it be standardized? Should it be standardized? How could it satisfy the current obsession with "metrics"? What is the role of the professional teacher in making twenty-first century assessments possible? What constraints would be faced by those who would implement such innovations in assessment practice?

This book strategically brings together views on innovation in assessment along with perspectives concerning the opportunities and barriers presented by the innovative ideas from those involved in research and large scale assessment. The two main themes are represented, respectively, by our invited speakers, and by respondents from state departments of education and university researchers involved in research on assessment issues. Our keynote chapters focus on innovation in three different realms—authentic assessment in contextualized environments (Jim Gee), evidence centered assessment design (Russell Almond), and the role of teachers and the connection between teaching and learning in assessment (Mari Pearlman). These three realms represent three fundamental areas of promise for future assessment systems. Each keynote chapter is followed by a response paper.

Additional chapters focus on more specific issues, as well as barriers and potentials for implementation of innovative assessment options. For instance, the chapter by Mark Shermis addresses important research concerning automated essay scoring and its potential for widespread use in statewide testing systems. Joseph Martineau and Vincent Dean describe their ideas for making assessment relevant to students, teachers and schools by explicitly considering transparency, standards, and measures/scales. Alysia Roehrig and Eric Christesen summarize their research on designing and developing a reliable and valid tool for assessing the quality of teaching in grades K-12. Their tool can be used in the professional development of teachers to foster students' literacy achievement and motivation. Allan Jeong describes an innovative tool he developed called jMAP that can be used to externalize and assess learners' mental models. In his chapter, he presents findings from two studies that illustrate how jMAP was used to support the assessment of causal understanding, and to identify areas for future research and development. And finally, Dan Hickey and colleagues discuss important issues relating to the assessment of new media and technology proficiencies. In their chapter, they introduce a design-based "participatory assessment framework" comprised of multiple levels of increasingly formal outcomes, and urge researchers to focus first on defining the contexts underlying social participation before attempting to assess individual proficiencies.

Each kind of assessment has a role to play in improving teaching and learning, and needs to be part of a total, balanced and blended assessment system. Using different kinds of assessment will allow us to discern learners' knowledge, skills, and other attributes from multiple perspectives, providing a clearer and more complete picture of each learner (Fletcher, 2007). And the more we know about learners, the better we can provide them with optimal support at the time they really need it. Moreover, it's crucial to involve learners in the assessment process through peer- and self-assessment. These alternative assessment approaches stimulate the use of higher-order thinking skills and help learners to understand more deeply (Shute, 2008).

We conclude with a set of principles of good assessment based on merged recommendations from Kellough and Kellough (1999), Mislevy, Steinberg, and Almond (2003), and Shute (2008):

- Understand and specify in advance of teaching the achievement targets (i.e., competencies) that learners are supposed to attain.
- Inform the learners, simply and clearly, about the competencies (as well as the associated rubrics), from the very beginning of the teaching and learning process.
- Use classroom assessments to bolster learners' confidence and help them assume responsibility for their own learning, toward the goal of engendering lifelong learners.
- Translate assessment results into frequent, descriptive feedback (not judgmental, subjective, or norm-referenced feedback), providing learners with specific insights on how to improve.
- Continuously adjust instruction (whether classroom- or computer-based) relative to the results of the formative assessments.
- Engage learners in regular self-assessment with standards held constant so that they can watch themselves grow over time and feel empowered.

We posit that the most important and powerful feature of assessment is the use of results to make improvements and decisions. This is true whether the assessment is used to support personal learning or for accountability purposes. Another important feature of assessment is to make learning—processes and products—visible to all stakeholders. That is, a person's knowledge (and other mental states and traits) is invisible to others, and sometimes to oneself (e.g., tacit knowledge). Using an evidence-based assessment can contribute toward improved teaching and learning (see Chapter 4 by Pearlman, this book), as well as help explicate evidentiary arguments supporting claims about that knowledge (see Chapter 6 by Almond, this book).

Knowing when to use a particular type of assessment and how to interpret the results is not easy. Similarly, designing assessments using an evidence-based approach is non-trivial. But consider the potential end result: i.e., assessments that exert substantial influence on the quality of information provided to teachers and learners to support instructional decision-making and meaningful learning. This chapter has briefly touched on different assessment topics and approaches, calling for a rational understanding of what we value in terms of competencies to be instructed and assessed. Knowing what a learner knows comes from obtaining quality evidence, which in turn is obtained from carefully designed assessments. The ideas herein, but more importantly, throughout this book, are intended to support teachers, learners, and policy makers, and perhaps even inspire educational researchers toward new, exciting projects.

References

Black, P., & Wiliam, D. (1998). Assessment and classroom learning. *Educational Assessment: Principles, Policy and Practice, 5*(1), 7–74.
Dewey, J. (1916). *Democracy and education*. New York: Simon & Shuster.
Fletcher, G. (2007, October 19). *Assessing learning from a holistic approach: Creating a balanced system of learning assessment*. Paper presented the Congreso Internacional Evaluacion Factor de Calidad Educativa, Queretaro.

Georghiades, P. (2004). From the general to the situated: Three decades of metacognition. *International Journal of Science Education, 26*(3), 365–383.

Guion, R. M. (1998). *Assessment, measurement and prediction for personnel decisions.* Mahwah, NJ: Erlbaum.

Higgins, M. C. (2001). Changing careers: The effects of social context. *Journal of Organizational Behavior, 22*(6), 595–618.

Hindo, C., Rose, K., & Gomez, L. M. (2004). Searching for Steven Spielberg: Introducing iMovie to the high school English classroom: A closer look at what open-ended technology project designs can do to promote engaged learning. In *Proceedings of the 6th international conference on learning sciences* (pp. 606–609). Mahwah, NJ: Erlbaum.

Jeong, A. (2005). A guide to analyzing message-response sequences and group interaction patterns in computer-mediated communication. *Distance Education, 26*(3), 367–383.

Kellough, R. D., & Kellough, N. G. (1999). *Secondary school teaching: A guide to methods and resources, planning for competence.* Upper Saddle River, NJ: Prentice Hall.

Kliebard, H. (1987). *The struggle for the American curriculum, 1893–1958.* New York: Routledge and Kegan Paul.

Macdonald, J. (2003). Assessing online collaborative learning: Process and product. *Computers and Education, 40*(4), 377–391.

Messick, S. (1989). Validity. In R. L. Linn (Ed.), *Educational measurement* (3rd ed., pp. 13–103). New York: Macmillan.

Mislevy, R. J., Steinberg, L. S., & Almond, R. G. (2003). On the structure of educational assessment. *Measurement: Interdisciplinary Research and Perspective, 1*(1), 3–62.

National Council of Teachers of Mathematics (NCTM). (2000). *Principles and standards for school mathematics.* Reston, VA: NCTM.

National Research Council (NRC). (1996). *National science education standards.* Washington, DC: National Academy Press.

Oosterhof, A. (2009). *Developing and using classroom assessments* (4th ed.). Upper Saddle River, NJ: Pearson.

Schwartz, D. L., Bransford, J. D., & Sears, D. L. (2005). Efficiency and innovation in transfer. In J. Mestre (Ed.), *Transfer of learning from a modern multidisciplinary perspective* (pp. 1–51). Greenwich, CT: Information Age Publishing.

Shute, V. J. (2007). Tensions, trends, tools, and technologies: Time for an educational sea change. In C. A. Dwyer (Ed.), *The future of assessment: Shaping teaching and learning* (pp. 139–187). New York: Lawrence Erlbaum Associates, Taylor & Francis Group.

Shute, V. J. (2008). Focus on formative feedback. *Review of Educational Research, 78*(1), 153–189.

Shute, V. J., Jeong, A. C., Spector, J. M., Seel, N. M., & Johnson, T. E. (2009). Model-based methods for assessment, learning, and instruction: Innovative educational technology at Florida State University. In M. Orey (Ed.), *2009 educational media and technology yearbook* (pp. 61–80). Westport, CT: Greenwood Publishing Group.

Shute, V. J., & Zapata-Rivera, D. (2010). Educational measurement and intelligent systems. In E. Baker, P. Peterson, & B. McGaw (Eds.), *Third edition of the international encyclopedia of education* (pp. 75–80). Oxford, UK: Elsevier Publishers.

Sungur, S. (2007). Modeling the relationships among students' motivational beliefs, metacognitive strategy use, and effort regulation. *Scandinavian Journal of Educational Research, 51*(3), 315–326.

Terman, L. M. (1916). *The measurement of intelligence.* Cambridge, MA: Riverside Press.

Chapter 2
Human Action and Social Groups as the Natural Home of Assessment: Thoughts on 21st Century Learning and Assessment

James Paul Gee

Abstract This paper argues that formal systems of assessment have their origins in the everyday circuit of human action. Assessment is an integral part of all human learning. This is its "natural home". Social groups have always lifted assessment out of the circuit of human action and partially formalized it as a way of both "mentoring" and "policing" (norming) newcomers and members alike. This aspect of assessment is more prevalent today than ever thanks to the proliferation of interest-driven groups on the Internet. Finally, I discuss the further formalization of assessment in systems of assessment used in schools. The more "natural" and social forms of assessment hold out keys for improving school-based assessment, as well as indicators about core ethical issues.

Keywords Assessment · Learning · Testing · Digital media · School · Society

2.1 The "Natural Home" of Assessment: Human Action and Social Conventions

In this paper I start with learning and assessment as they occur in everyday action, which is, I argue, their "natural" home. I then discuss how social groups lift assessment out of everyday action in order to formalize it as a way of mentoring and policing newcomers. Then I take up the issue of the yet more formalized forms of assessment we use in our schools and other institutions. I argue that this latter enterprise has much to learn (including ethically) from the previous two settings. I will also discuss the role new forms of digital learning can play in making learning and assessment deeper in school and society.

J.P. Gee (✉)
Division of Curriculum and Instruction, Mary Lou Fulton College of Education,
Arizona State University, Tempe, AZ, USA
e-mail: james.gee@asu.edu

V.J. Shute, B.J. Becker (eds.), *Innovative Assessment for the 21st Century*,
DOI 10.1007/978-1-4419-6530-1_2, © Springer Science+Business Media, LLC 2010

Assessment is today largely associated with institutions and the word carries the connotation of institutionally sanctioned assessors and methods. I want to argue, however, that assessment, as a "natural" practice, has its original home in human action and learning. I will argue that good and fair institutional assessments must be grafted onto that base and grown from it.

To make the case for this claim let's think about a woman—named Mary, say—engaged in action. Assume she acts based on a goal. She then must reflect on whether her action has moved her closer to her goal or not. She must ask herself: Was the result of my action good for my purposes or not, or somewhere in between? She must make a judgment. Once she has answered this question, then she acts again, revising, adjusting, or advancing in some fashion her earlier action, unless her goal has already been reached. Then she reflects and judges again about whether this new action is good or not.

Through action, Mary is basically probing the world. She is asking the world a question. Then she sees if the answer (the world's response) is adequate, acceptable, correct, or good for her purposes. She is assessing the quality of her actions, a form of "self-assessment". Of course, in getting and considering this answer from the world, Mary can, as one of her possible moves, rethink and revise her goal.

I do not want to engage in a philosophical theory of action here. Let me just say that the pattern of "goal/probe/response from world/reflect/new revised probe" is one basic and important pattern of human action (Gee, 2003/2007, 2004; Schön, 1983). Formalized, it is also a basic procedure of experimental science, where the goal becomes a hypothesis.

When Mary asks whether her action is good or not, how does she know the answer? She must have a *value system* in terms of which she can make such a judgment. Research in neuroscience (Damasio, 1995, 1999, 2003) has made it clear that such a value system is driven both by cognitive factors and emotional ones. Unless Mary cares in some fashion about her possible choices of action, it is hard or impossible for her to make a choice as how to act next, no matter what "reason" alone tells her. It is here, of course, that we touch on the foundations of such things as "motivation", "interest", and "engagement".

This value system, the system that tells Mary whether the result of her action/probe is adequate, acceptable, correct, or good or not, is what I will call, following Donald Schön, her *appreciative system* (Gee, 2004, 2007; Schön, 1963; Vickers, 1973, 1983). I call it this because it is the system through which she appreciates the results of her actions/probes.

But where does Mary's appreciative system come from? How did she get it? Does she just make it up herself? Usually the answer is "no". Imagine I wanted to make a drought resistant garden in my back yard. If I start knowing little about the matter, I could do this through a long process of trial and error. What I would normally do is find out what other more expert people have done, what they have learned from their communal history in making such gardens.

Thus, when Mary acts/probes and then reflects on the result/response from the world, it is usually not Mary alone who determines what "counts" as acceptable, adequate, correct, or good. What often determines this is some social group that has developed *conventions* for what counts as acceptable, adequate, correct, or good and how to go on, a social group that has informed Mary.

Whether playing baseball, courting a mate, doing a proof in mathematics, engaging in a business deal, or creating a drought resistant garden, some social group (sometimes a group as large as a "culture") has conventions—has learned things—about what counts as acceptable, adequate, correct, or good and what counts as a way to successfully go on in a trajectory of action to accomplish certain sorts of goals. These conventions, of course, vary across different groups and situations as to how rigid or open-ended they are, and how much room they leave open for choice, variation, and adaptation.

The conventions are often based on a shared social history of discovering and passing on what works. If Mary is engaged in science, for instance, the conventions are connected to "theories" or "methods", as well as normative practices. If she is engaged in designing and uploading clothes for *the Sims* to the Internet (a video game), then we don't always use elevated terms like "theory" and "method", though all social groups have their theories and methods and "tried and true" favored ways of proceeding.

The word "convention" here may offend some. Some groups, of course, have conventions about favored ways of proceeding that are not very effective from the point of view of reality testing (e.g., astrology) or conventions that lead to evil (e.g., Ku Klux Klan or neo-Nazis). But all this shows is that choosing a social group and its conventions is often a moral choice.

Back to Mary: In many cases, Mary must know the conventions in order to know how to go on. She may well discover many things for herself, but she is unlikely, in most cases, to discover everything for herself. Her appreciative system is her internalized version of the conventions with whatever personal variation can, in a given case, be added. So, then, too, it becomes relevant to ask how Mary learned the conventions. This amounts very often to asking what her relationship is to the social group whose conventions these are. The best way to learn a group's conventions is to participate in the group, but one can learn such conventions through observation and study, as well.

The argument I have developed so far—as readers will have noted already—is an amalgam of the ideas of Schön (1983) and Ludwig Wittgenstein (1953/2001). Let me call the "goal/probe/get a response from the world/reflect based on an appreciative system/new revised probe" cycle a "basic circuit of human action". I will add one more element to this circuit below—namely, identity.

In this circuit, learning and assessment are not separate, but, rather, part and parcel of each other. Mary learns something from the world's response to her probe, in terms of which she revises her next action/probe. She learns through "assessing the situation" via her probe, the world's response, and her reflection on that response using her appreciative system. Learning and assessment are here really inseparable as part of this basic circuit of human action.

Mary's learning and assessment are not, as we have seen, just individual. Her appreciative system reflects, in part at least, the conventions she has gained from interactions with, or observations of, some social group. Her appreciative system, in fact, does not have to be entirely in her head. Appreciative systems are not just "mental". Mary can make use, if need be, of other people and various tools (including texts) that also participate in those conventions, in order to supplement what is in her head. Appreciative systems are represented out in the world as well as in heads. They are, in that sense, "distributed" across other peoples' heads, texts, tools, technologies, and practices.

By the way, Mary can transform the conventions if her actions vary from them in some way, just so long as her variation catches on with some social group that uses those conventions. If people who use those conventions recognize and accept what Mary has done—with the variations she has added—as falling under those conventions (as being acceptable, adequate, correct, or good) then she has transformed the conventions in a small or big way. This is, of course, the key source of innovation (Gee, 1990/2007).

This rather arid philosophical discussion about action, learning, appreciative systems, and social norms or conventions is motivated, in part, by the reality that today digital media allow people to engage with more social groups and their conventions than ever before. If I want to engage in drought resistant gardening today I can readily find not just texts, as I could at an earlier time in a library, but whole communities on the Internet ready to share their knowledge and conventions with me.

But, for now, we will leave Mary and move on to a real situation. This will allow me to give a concrete example of what I have been trying to get at and bring in one more crucial notion—the notion of identity—so far left out.

2.2 Becoming a SWAT Team Member: Identity and Domains

When people act, they are usually acting in accord with their appreciative systems, which, in turn, are usually connected to the conventions of some social group. Furthermore, social groups and their conventions always operate in a given *domain* (Gee, 2003/2007). Their conventions are not about everything, but about some specific domain of knowledge and practice.

Domains are almost infinitely variable and new ones arise all the time. Academic areas are domains, but so are popular culture practices like *Yu-Gi-Oh* or video gaming (and within it specific types of games and gaming practices). Domains arise any time a social group creates conventions about how to act and value in regard to some particular and characteristic set of beliefs, knowledge claims, and practices.

Domains are crucial to assessment. Since domains—actually the social group whose domain it is—define what counts as the "right way(s)" to "go on" in a chain of action to accomplish goals, it is problematic to engage in assessment outside any domain whatsoever. Where would one's appreciative system come from? How would one know how to "go on"? Of course, in rare cases, someone may have, through trial and error, made up everything by him or herself. But in the case of most sophisticated domains, this is unlikely.

In order to move to a concrete example, let's reflect on the domain of a SWAT (Special Weapons And Tactics) police team. As I talk about SWAT, readers may want to replace SWAT with their favorite science domain, for example—they will see that things work much the same way in SWAT and in science. Though we don't usually think about science, especially as a school subject, in the ways in which I am going to talk about SWAT, I argue we should.

Let's think about someone trying to take an action as a member of a SWAT team. One issue that we did not discuss with Mary is this: How does one begin to act when one is just a beginner, a newcomer? A newcomer has not yet developed an appreciative system by which to "assess the situation" after he or she has acted/probed.

Lots of times—especially if we are thinking about schools or workplace training—we think of learning in terms of someone learning facts or skills, what we might broadly call "content". However, since both acting and learning are usually tied to a social group that gives the learner an appreciative system, both acting and learning must start not with facts or skills, but with an *identity*.

Our SWAT team newcomer must start with the identity of being a SWAT team member. Why? Because it is this identity that tells newcomers in the first place what goals they should have and how, in general, they should "appreciate" or "assess" their actions towards those goals.

The word "identity" is used in many different ways, so what do I mean by it specifically here? I mean a "way of being in the world" that is integrally connected to two things: first, characteristic *goals* (namely, in this case, goals of the sort a SWAT team has); and, second, characteristic *norms* and *values* by which to act and evaluate one's actions (in this case, these norms and values are those adopted by SWAT teams). "Identity", in this paper, means the goals and norms/values that flow from a given social group and its conventions.

The norms and values amount to a value system. For example, in regard to SWAT, some of the norms and values are: don't shoot people, even if they have a gun, until you have warned them you are a policeman; don't ever enter a room in a way that unduly risks the safety of your team or innocent people in the room; secure any situation before moving on; never lag in vigilance; and other much more specific recipes for action, adjustments to action, and the repair of action, down to specifics like "what I just did left my back facing an unlocked door; that is bad, I need to revise my action and quickly"—see my discussion on rubber doorstops below.

Now, of course, to accomplish goals within certain norms/values, the SWAT team newcomer must master a certain set of skills, facts, principles, and procedures ("content"). But only after he or she has some understanding of—and has accepted, if only provisionally—what I have called an "identity" (here as a SWAT team member) does such "content" make sense or become useable.

So our basic circuit of human action has to be revised a bit. It is: "identity/goal/probe/get a response from the world/reflect based on an appreciative system /new revised probe" (iterated).

As newcomers begin to master "content" (facts/information and skills) in an enterprise like SWAT, they are given tools and technologies that fit particularly well with their goals and norms/values, and that help them master the content by using these tools and technologies in active problem solving contexts. [Too often in school content is introduced without identity or tools/technologies or simply with the identity of being a "good student" "doing school"].

These tools and technologies have an interesting property. They mediate between—help explicate the connections between—the newcomer's identity (goals, norms/values), on the one hand, and the content the newcomer must master, on the other. They tie goals, norms/values, and content together—i.e., integrate them.

Something as simple as the SWAT team's doorstop device is a good example (it's just a rubber doorstop, nothing special). This little tool integrally connects the team's goal of entering rooms safely and norm/value of doing so as non-violently as possible with the content knowledge that going in one door with other open doors behind you can lead to being blindsided and ambushed from behind, an ambush in which both you and innocent bystanders may be killed. Of course, the SWAT team has many pieces of equipment and technology more sophisticated than the doorstop.

We can think about such tools and technologies in quite expansive ways. In SWAT, tools and technologies include types of guns, ammunition, grenades, goggles, armor, lightsticks, communication devices, door stops, and so forth. But they also include one's fellow SWAT team members, who model correct skills and knowledge for the newcomer and mentor newcomers. Such modeling and mentoring almost always integrate goals, norms/values, and content—for example, in stories experienced members tell newcomers or in after-action reviews (debriefings) teams do with each other.

Some will be bothered by the way in which I treat people as tools for helping other people act and learn. However, in today's global world, being able to use and be a part of "distributed knowledge systems" is a crucial twenty-first-century skill. In such a system, knowledge is stored, spread, and networked across people, their environments, tools, and technologies.

Taking inspiration from Latour (2004), we could call the human members of the SWAT team, as well as their tools and technologies, and even objects in the environment that the SWAT team members use as tools (e.g., corners to hide behind), "actants" (Callon & Latour, 1992; Latour, 2004). From this perspective, not just humans are "actors" (effective agents involved in causing things to happen) and so we name them all—humans, tools, technologies, and objects—"actants". Of course, human beings have forms of intentionality and desire that objects, tools, and technologies don't. But, in turn, objects, tools, and technologies have their own "affordances" that we ignore at our peril and that help us to be effective in the world when we honor them.

We can see the real "team" as composed of all these things, and not just humans all by themselves, and call it an "ensemble" [of humans, objects, tools, and technologies] (Latour, 2004 uses the term "collective" and Latour, 2005 uses the term "actor-actant network"). All these things—people, tools, technologies, and objects—have to "dance" with each other if coordinated action is to be pulled off.

It is a dance in which humans have to learn both to lead and follow; to coordinate other people, tools, and objects, but to get coordinated by them, as well (Knorr

Cetina, 1992). Humans have to be active and passive both, to get into synch with others, with tools, with technologies, and with objects and the environment. This is why, for example, activity theory (Engeström, 1987) stresses evaluating learning not in terms of individuals, but in terms of "systems", something like what I have called an "ensemble" here. Learning becomes about forms of participation and engagement with others and with objects, tools, and technologies in "systems".

Keep in mind that this is how Latour describes science—really the work of the sciences (Latour, 2004)—as well. Furthermore, I intend my SWAT example to be generalizable. Other enterprises work in similar ways, whether it is a branch of science or being a *Yu-Gi-Oh* fanatic. It should be noted, as well, than even were a SWAT team member to operate alone, he or she would still be operating by the social goals and norms/values of the group. So, too, with scientists and *Yu-Gi-Oh* fanatics. For us humans, individual action is also social action.

Of course, humans belong to many different social groups. Their membership in each group—and the characteristic goals, norms, and values they have as actors in those groups—can affect how they act within each other group. Thus, each individual's actions are never totally predictable or the same as other people's actions within any group.

What I have said about SWAT could be said about other domains, e.g., gardening, cooking, video gaming, biology, Catholic theology, law, dentistry, street gangs, blogging, bird watching, and many specific types within each of these. Each of these is a domain (there are domains within domains: for example, real-time strategy video gaming within video gaming). Domains are not, of course, separate from each other. They exist within a larger social, political, and economic structure that imposes other rules, conventions, norms, and values on them. Some domains are closer to others and they all exist in a complex web of relations of similarity and difference, affiliation and opposition.

So I have introduced a variety of terms that I argue are central to assessment in its most indigenous, natural state as part and parcel of human action and learning: identities, domains, goals, norms/values, probes, responses from the world, reflection, revised action, revised (rethought) goals, appreciative systems, conventions, social groups, actants, tools, technologies, objects, and ensembles (of humans, objects, tools, and technologies). These are not the terms of art in current work on formalized systems of assessment (in schools, for instance). But I will argue that they should be if we are interested in learning that leads to participation, production, and problem solving. Of course, the real "proof" of this claim will only come when we develop concrete examples of new assessment systems that are built around these "terms of art" and not our current ones.

It is pretty clear that it would be silly to formalize assessments (made, say, by some institution) of SWAT team members outside the terms of art above. Silly, too, to formalize assessments of, say, scientists outside these terms of art. Even if one was to make up a "fact test"—instead of, say, a performance-based assessment— for a SWAT team member or a scientist of a certain sort, the facts chosen would certainly be selected against the background of the characteristic identities, values, norms, goals, conventions, and collaborations and actions with other people and with tools and technologies in these domains. At least they would if we cared about "authenticity" and "transfer" to real problem solving. Formal assessments that are authentic and transfer are made relative to deep knowledge of a domain.

2.3 Lifting Assessment Out of the Basic Circuit of Human Action: The First Step

So far I have argued that assessment has its "natural" home in human action. But I have also argued that human action involves an identity and an appreciative system, both of which are tied to some domain and the social group whose domain it is. So it is not surprising that assessment (and, of course, learning too) can be and is lifted out of the basic circuit of human action and "formalized" by these groups themselves.

SWAT teams, scientists, and *Yu-Gi-Oh* fanatics want to know how newcomers are faring. They want to know this both in order mentor newcomers and in order to police them and, in the act, defend the group's norms/values. Assessment at the group level (beyond an individual's appreciative system) for most social groups is both a form of mentoring and policing (Latour, 2005). In some cases this means being sure that norms are adhered to. In other cases, it may also mean that newcomers and others are encouraged also to improve the "rules of the game"—as we hope happens in science domains at their best.

Mentoring and policing are not as opposed to each other as it might at first seem (and as they often are in school). Newcomers usually want to "live up to" their new identity and, since this is an identity they value, they want that identity "policed" so that it remains worth having by the time they gain it more fully. They buy into the "standards". Surely this is how SWAT team members, scientists, and *Yu-Gi-Oh* fanatics feel. This is, of course, a significant condition to state. Students in school may not "buy in" enough to have this condition met.

Of course, if people are being forced to take on an identity they do not want, then there often is a real opposition between mentoring and policing for these forced newcomers. This is a practice that I would count as violence towards the basic circuit of human action (because it either substitutes not caring for caring or fear for caring in the newcomer's use of an appreciative system—remember emotions and not just reason are crucial). Again, this is a dilemma for schools.

We need to ask how different groups (SWAT teams, biochemists, *Yu-Gi-Oh* fanatics) take assessment out of the basic circuit of human action (its natural home) and "formalize" it through mentoring and policing. To answer this question we would have to engage in specific ethnographies, since different groups do different things. This would, indeed, be a worthwhile and important project, since such social group assessments are closer to the natural home of assessment than are assessments run by institutions (like schools) removed from these groups (I am leaving schools aside for now, though, of course, they constitute themselves quite distinctive social groups).

However, one important thing that social groups have in common when they assess their newcomers and members is this: Whatever practices they engage in, these must, for the most part, end up forming and influencing the newcomer's appreciative systems. That is, more formalized assessments must, in some way, become internalized into the learners' appreciative systems (or, at least, be useable by the learner through texts, tools, and other people). The learner must become a self-assessor. Learners must learn to mentor and police themselves. So, then, too, the question arises as to how people go from group assessment to self assessment. I would offer a largely neo-Vygotskian account of this in terms of development within a "zone of proximal development", but must leave the matter aside for now.

Another important thing that social groups have in common when they assess their newcomers and members is this: At least some of this assessment (mentoring and policing) is done when the learner is part of what I called an ensemble above and is, in fact, an assessment of how the learner behaves as a member of the ensemble. This is "in situ" assessment, but of a special type: it is assessing how the learner can coordinate and get coordinated by other people, tools, technologies, and objects in the "dance" (sometimes called the "mangle", see Pickering, 1995) of practice. [If you want to know whether someone is a good birdwatcher, you want to assess how they "dance" with birds, bird books, binoculars, environments, and other birders].

Let us call this "ensemble assessment"—keeping in mind that "ensemble" has a special meaning here (we could call it "dance assessment" or "mangle assessment" as well). Needless to say, such assessment requires the presence (in reality or virtually, as we will see below) of other people (who share identities and appreciative systems), tools, technologies, and objects.

2.4 "Sim Domains": Simplified Simulations of a Domain

The reader may well wonder why I chose SWAT as my example. Here is the reason: I have played the video game *SWAT4*. *SWAT4* is a simulation of a SWAT team in which the player is a virtual SWAT team member commanding three other team members (Gee, 2007). Such games/simulations (or related ones) are used in training real policemen. In real training, however, sooner or later, the real world becomes the training space. Such games are also used by everyday people who have no intention of becoming a SWAT team member (like me).

In terms of learning, assessment, and acting, a game like *SWAT4* operates in many ways like actual SWAT teams. However, much real-world complexity is removed in such a game. The game is a simplified and idealized simulation. Simulations are a type of model. For my purposes here, models are simplified representations of real objects or systems where the representation is similar in some ways to the object or system it represents. Think, for example, of a model plane used either in play or in a simulated wind tunnel for scientific tests, or of various sorts of diagrams, graphs, and blue prints—more abstract models. Simulations (which these days are often virtual worlds) are just large and intricate models that seek to represent relationships in a system.

Models and simulations enhance learning by creating a well designed learning space that controls complexity and orders what is to be learned in effective ways. Learning of this type does not, of course, have to be a game. We can use models and simulations of a great many different types to simplify a domain and render understanding and problem solving more tractable.

From the standpoint of learning, games like *SWAT4*, and simulations more generally, do several things: First and foremost, they give players/learners an "empathy" or "feel" for a complex domain, a domain initially too complex or dangerous to confront directly.

Second, such games prepare players/learners for future learning in the domain should they want or need to engage in more such learning, including in the real world (Bransford & Schwartz, 1999). Third, such games give players/learners some facts (information) and skills, acquired through participation in the practice, thus, acquired as meaningful, not as "decontextualized".

It should be said that not just young learners use simulations for these purposes. They are used for just these purposes by scientists, as well. Even for scientists, the real world is often too complex to confront directly, without simplification and ordering.

While not everyone will think that SWAT is an important "educational" domain, we could imagine using digital media to do the same thing for domains more closely connected to common educational goals (see Shaffer, 2007), for example, urban planning, engineering, chemistry, space science, law, the courts, and many other such domains. For instance, an urban planning game could engage even young learners with empathy for the complex domain of urban planning and in the act teach skills from a variety of "academic" areas like sociology, economics, ecology, and even the mathematics of flow for traffic (for an actual example, consider the commercial game *Sim City,* or the educational urban planning "epistemic game" made by David Shaffer, 2007).

2.5 Play

Games like *SWAT4* are used as forms of play, as well as, in more professional versions, forms of workplace learning for policemen. A chemistry game could be used as a form of both play and learning for students in school, reaching the same learning goals as *SWAT4*, but in a domain we think of as more educational. Play, in this sense, is not necessarily antithetical to learning, even in school.

But there is another sense of play that, at first sight, seems not at all at home at school. This is play in the sense of "being playful" and "playing around with things". I have in mind here imaginative play, play like what a child does in a sandbox or with a doll house.

When young children are playing house, or children or adults are playing with the *Spore* creature creator (where you make colorful and weird fantasy creatures), they are in a fantasy space where they are using their imaginations and where failure need not be an issue. This is why some people talk about this sort of play as being done from within a "magic circle" (Huizinga, 1950) that shuts out the harsher aspects of reality (e.g., sorting, consequential failure, and harsh competition).

We have long known that children can learn important things and ready themselves for life through such imaginative play (much as young animals practice adult activities in play). Some also believe that older children and adults can, through such imaginative play, develop creativity that can eventually lead to innovation in more serious domains (Gee & Hayes, 2010). Even professionals and scientists sometimes just "play around" and try things out away from the strictures of professional activities and duties.

This type of play I will label a domain (though of course it is a very special type of domain) and call it the "domain of play", but by "play" right now I mean only imaginative play of the sort I have been talking about. As the child or adult plays— say, makes a creature in the *Spore* creature creator—the person is outside real world academic, professional, and specialist domains. No social group is directly norming or policing the child or adult. Indeed, if it is a scientist playing around, the scientist may be engaging in such play precisely to free him or herself up from such norms.

However, norms and values—and appreciative systems—do play a role in such play. Even in play—when a child role-plays a mother or when I make a creature that tickles me in the *Spore* creature creator—in order to act I usually have to ask myself if I like the outcome of my action and whether I want to change that action in some way to get another outcome. That is just to say that even when I play I often have to have an appreciative system. There may be exceptions, but clearly in many cases, when people are playing, in the sense I am now using the term, they often revise what they are doing based on whether they like the outcome or not—in fact, children playing house, for instance, often debate such things.

But where in such play does the appreciative system come from? It comes from the appreciative systems of real world domains—e.g., the domain of parenting for the child playing house or the science domain the playful scientist knows. However, in imaginative play I am free to play with these domains' conventions.

In such play, we can ask questions like: What happens—how would I "go on"—if children ordered their parents around or fathers stayed home? What happens—how would I "go on"—if I thought about this problem in sociology the way gardeners think about gardening? Of course, such play has, in history, had real consequences later on in the world, though we can never tell when such play might have such consequences.

In reality, such play is, in fact, play with—being fast and loose with— appreciative systems in a space where the domains whose appreciative systems you are playing with can't "get you", can't enact any bad consequences on you for breaking or varying their conventions. But note that in such play you cannot break all the conventions all at once, since if just "anything goes", then nothing goes, and you would not even know you were playing house. The fun, of course, is in keeping some conventions and breaking others and seeing what happens, how things fit together or don't, what it feels like to have changed the domain or combined different domains in new ways.

The play domain is a source of creativity and innovation. It is important for very young children in their early socialization in life (e.g., consider children playing school). It is important, too, for people who have become adept at and comfortable with—perhaps too comfortable with—the norms and values of real-world domains.

Play, in the sense I am using the term here, disallows evaluative sorts of assessment from the outside (the player is, of course, assessing in the sense of appreciating from the inside). If we start to "grade" people for their play, we destroy it. We could of course watch our children playing in order to give them better dolls or dolls that afford different forms of play—this is what Will Wright did when he created *the Sims*.

Can we imagine—beyond kindergarten—young people playing in schools? College students? There could not be any grades. We could only resource their play. And one resource we could give them is lucid understanding and engagement with real-world domains that they can then "play with". I have seen this happen in schools in programs that were not graded, admittedly at the periphery of the curriculum. In one striking case, the teacher could not tell which kids were "Special Ed" and which were not, since all the kids were quite creative—and the teacher attributed this to the fact that she did not grade.

So, in the end, free play involves appreciative systems and domains, just as do more formal learning and work. We cannot exit appreciative systems and domains; we do not normally live in situations where just "anything goes"—because we would then not know how to "go on".

2.6 Five Learning Environments

The *SWAT4* example is useful because it allows us to distinguish different ways of setting up learning environments. In order to discuss these learning environments I need first to introduce a few technical terms.

First, it is crucial—or nothing but confusion will ensue below—to see that a domain (as I am using the term) is *not* defined by a set of facts, skills, and principles ("content") but by the *uses* people make of certain sorts of facts, skills, and principles. One and the same fact, skill, or principle—or word, for that matter—may be used quite differently in different domains. So, for example, when I call physics a "domain", I do not mean physics as a set of facts (that one might find in a textbook). I mean physics as certain sorts of activities, practices, norms, and values engaged in by people who use certain sorts of facts and skills in certain ways to carry out these activities and practices and instantiate these norms and values.

It is useful to distinguish between specialist domains and what I will call the "life-world" domain (Habermas, 1981). Domains like SWAT, biochemistry, law, video gaming, and *Yu-Gi-Oh* are "specialist" in the sense that people in these domains take on specialized identities and specialized forms of language. But we humans also all often live and act just as "everyday" people, not as specialists of any sort.

Of course, different cultures have different ways of enacting (in words and deeds) being an "everyday person". When we are acting as "everyday people", I will say we are acting in the domain of the "lifeworld". People learn what it means to be a culturally distinctive "everyday person" through their initial socialization in life and in their later interactions with their "local" communities. They do not need school for this.

It is useful to point out, as well, that among specialist domains, one is particularly important and special. Most humans live in societies where there are identities, appreciative systems, and skills that integrate people into something "bigger" than the various family and community sub-cultural and class identities they start learning as children. I will call this the "public sphere" (Habermas, 1989), the place where one is a citizen of a larger society (or even the global world).

The public sphere is a specialist domain because it involves dealing with institutions and practices that incorporate specialist language and practices (think about going to the motor vehicles department, getting a passport, or going to court). Most people pick up such language and practices after their socialization early in life has started them well on their way to their lifeworld identities.

Now I want to distinguish five learning environments, or five "spaces" where learning occurs. These provide ways in which people learn beyond their lifeworlds, so schools are relevant here, since that is one of their purposes. Of course, people learn in these environments outside of school as well.

1. Actual Environment Learning: Such learning involves actually joining—and being mentored and policed by—the social group that forms one's identity and appreciative system in a given specialist domain (like becoming a SWAT team member, a biochemist, a *Yu-Gi-Oh* fanatic, or a "citizen").
2. Pretense Environment Learning: Such learning involves going through the actual real world learning processes in a given specialist domain (as in 1 above), but with no intention of actually joining and staying in the social group whose domain it is. A journalist undergoing SWAT training to write about it would be an example. So would a spy. So would some forms of ethnographic research. I do not here mean anything invidious by the term "pretense", only that we are here involved with a certain type of "pretending".
3. Sim Environment Learning: Such learning involves gaining empathy for a domain's identity and appreciative system through a simplified and/or idealized version of the domain via a simulation. The learner need not actually join the social group whose domain it is. Sim Learning does not have to be in a virtual world, of course. A teacher can set up a simulation in her classroom of what it means to be a scientist of a certain sort and do science of that sort. Such learning is not "Pretense Learning", since the simulation will not be the actual real-world situations in which scientists learn to be scientists of that sort. Further, such simulations do and should simplify the actual domain in various ways to focus on important aspects in ways that are fruitful for learning—that is the point of simulations. Many so-called "inquiry" approaches to science learning fall under the heading of Sim Environment Learning, though not all are coherent (see below).

When we engage in Sim Environment Learning, what is going on is "real" or "authentic". But it is also simplified and puts a premium on trying things (probing and reflecting) and not on failure and the cost of failure (as can happen in the "real world" when a physicist fails to get tenure, say).

4. Play Environment Learning: Such learning involves imaginative play with appreciative systems and different domains' conventions, safe from bad real-world consequences.

5. Generic Environment Learning: Such learning is tied in the here and now to no specific domain (remember, a domain is not defined by content, but by uses of content), but deals with information and skills that have historical ties to specific domains and might eventually apply to any, all, or some specific domain in the future. It is a sort of domain promissory note.

Readers who do not remember that a domain is not defined by its content alone, will immediately object: Why can't a kid just learn (memorize) a fact or principle from physics? Isn't that learning physics in some non-generic way? Why bother with social groups, like physicists? Why can't we just have physics as facts?

This to me is still generic learning. The student has just memorized something. If he or she tries to act on that knowledge, the whole issue of an appreciative system will immediately come up (how to decide what is a "good" result; how to go on). That will, in turn, immediately bring us to specific social groups and their identities, conventions, goals, norms, and values. Until then the fact learned is generic, because it is just waiting around to see if it ever gets applied or used in a domain or a simulation of one. And, of course, often the student cannot use it and it remains forever generic or becomes forgotten.

If the student is to act (probe the world), that student must have internalized some appreciative system tied to physics as a social group and activity in the world. Thus, the student—if he or she is to act—must have learned more than a fact, skill, or principle in isolation from identities, conventions, goals, norms, and values connected to physicists and physics as a practice.

Of course, someone will say: "Wait a minute, kids in school cannot all be expected to do physics in the sense of living by the actual norms and values of real adult physicists". Well, they certainly can engage Sim Environment Learning and play by the rules in just the way I played by the SWAT rules when I played *SWAT4*. In this case, they will at the very least gain an appreciation for physics as a "form of life" (Wittgenstein, 1953/2001) and see how physics "facts" are tools for doing things and solving problems.

One can immediately see the problem with schools here. There really are only five choices and Actual Environment Learning and Pretense Environment Learning are often impracticable or impossible in school (though I will discuss important exceptions below). Generic Environment Learning is a mainstay of schooling, but is not always very motivating or effective. Sim Environment Learning is today more practicable than ever before, thanks to new digital media that allow us to make games and simulations.

School does often engage in Actual Environment Learning and Pretense Environment Learning, but in an odd way: It creates a specialized domain we might call "doing school" (that is being good at school in and of itself, even when school practices have no important tie to any other domain), and apprentices people to that domain. Some students are just engaged in pretense when they engage with this apprenticeship, others take it "for real". Some people find something useful in "doing school"—and it probably fits one for being a quiescent participant in society and the workforce—but I have no particular brief for it. It is odd to think that so much of our standardized testing apparatus, and preparation for such tests in school, is a form of this "doing school", even when called "science" or "mathematics". In any case, the old literature on the "hidden curriculum" in school is replete with discussion and critique of "doing school" (which usually serves as a "sorting device") and I don't have anything more to say about it here.

2.7 Generic Environment Learning

At times Generic Environment Learning is necessary or useful. A good example would be learning to decode print. Learners will most certainly use decoding in lots and lots of specific domains later on. But as we move on in reading, there comes a limit to the usefulness of generic learning.

Some substantive generic comprehension strategies apply to almost all domains that require reading, but much in comprehension and vocabulary growth (necessary for comprehension) requires integration and embedding in specific domains. Generic comprehension and vocabulary strategies will not by themselves allow a student to comprehend natural science, say, as against social science or literary criticism.

Because generic learning has grave limits, we get a phenomenon like the so-called "fourth-grade slump" (see Gee, 2008 for discussion and citations) when we overdo it. The fourth-grade slump is the phenomenon whereby many children do all right learning to read early on in school—often through generic learning—but cannot read well to master academic content later on with its own distinctive forms of complex language that require more than generic language and literacy skills.

There may be some point in young people learning "content" (facts, skills, and principles) connected to a domain like physics without actually engaging with the real domain or a Sim version of it. Perhaps there are "facts" everyone should know and, surely, knowing lots of such facts facilitates reading "content area" texts or, at least, textbooks. But, again, there are grave limits here. Such facts are retained in only a superficial form, at best, after schooling ends if they are never connected to acting and appreciating in a domain. One certainly cannot make decisions using such facts—even as, for example, an "informed citizen" using science facts—since such decisions would require some hold on a domain's appreciative system (otherwise how would one know if the decision's results were "good" or "bad"?).

However, when schools try to leave generic learning and enter another environment devoted to non-generic learning, they run onto trouble. They immediately face arguments about what to teach since there are so many specific domains. They face problems, as well, with delivering either a real domain or a lucid Sim version of one in the classroom. We have seen that it can be done, but it often requires substantive change in the "grammar of schooling".

2.8 Non-lucid Pseudo-Domain Learning in Schools

Many educational approaches claim to be engaged with domain learning. Such approaches sometimes use the term "inquiry", though this term covers many different approaches— some good, some bad. In some cases, these approaches engage students in some potpourri of science or math facts and activities, for example, with no worry about how these actually tie to any real domain, its appreciative system, and the uses made of such facts.

We could call this another form of generic learning or we could just recognize it as non-lucid pseudo-domain learning. This is learning where no one is really clear what the domain is or how the classroom learning relates to any real domain.

I don't want to discuss specific cases here. So let's just take an example not based on any specific curriculum. Imagine we are told that children will study a pond. The children are told that they are going to be "investigators". They will ask questions of the residents around the pond; they will count the birds in the area; and they will test the water in the pond to see if it is affected by local construction.

But we can now ask: Where does the identity the children are supposed to adopt come from? Where do they get the norms and values that will form their appreciative systems? What are the "rules" here, what conventions should they follow? Where did these conventions come from? What domain or domains in the real world are the answers to these questions tied to?

If the answers to these questions are not clear to the teachers and the students, then this is non-lucid pseudo-domain learning. Just because kids are taking samples of water and testing for things like acidity does not mean they are engaged in science. After all, people who own pools regularly test their pool water, but they are not engaged in any domain of science.

It is not enough just to have a goal, hypothesis, or question, such as "Is local construction near the pond impacting water quality?". Learners need to know where the goal or question came from, why it is part of the domain from which it came, and how to assess the results of each action (probe) in an ongoing trajectory of activity towards accomplishing that goal. They need to form an appreciative system and to do this they need mentoring and policing (for real or within a simulation) in the conventions, goals, norms, and values of a domain (one or more).

Different domains count birds and count them in different ways for different purposes. A number of domains in the world might call their members "investigators" or, at least, say they are engaged in "investigations". None use the term generically. So, too, many scientific domains exist, none of which calls itself just "science".

The point of domain-centered learning should be to achieve lucidity so that learners understand what they are doing and why, and so that they contextualize their learning in terms of meaningful practices and ways of being in the world. Of course, in any number of jobs in the world—certainly many service jobs, but even some professional ones—people just follow rote rules and use technologies they do not understand. But the purpose of school, in my view, is understanding, and in particular, understanding of how knowledge is built and debated in practice. Such understandings are also important, I believe, for the development of informed citizens, especially in our crisis-filled, high-risk, global world replete with interacting and potentially dangerous complex systems.

2.9 Pro-Am Communities

As I have said, it is sometimes hard to bring an actual real-world domain into school, though it is, of course, possible to bring in a Sim version of the domain. However, popular culture today gives us important examples of significant Environment 1 (Actual Environment) learning that could go on in school, but almost never does.

Today young people are using the Internet and other digital media outside of school to learn and even become experts in a variety of domains. We live in the age of "Pro-Ams": amateurs who have become experts at whatever they have developed a passion for (Anderson, 2006; Leadbeater & Miller, 2004).

Many of these are young people who use the Internet, communication media, digital tools, and membership in often virtual, sometimes real, communities of practice to develop technical expertise in a plethora of different areas. Some of these areas are digital video, video games, digital storytelling, machinima, fan fiction, history and civilization simulations, music, graphic art, political commentary, robotics, anime, and fashion design (e.g., for Sims in *The Sims*). In fact, there are now Pro-Ams in nearly every endeavor the human mind can think of.

These Pro-Ams have passion and go deep rather than wide. At the same time, Pro-Ams are often adept at pooling their skills and knowledge with those of other Pro-Ams to bring off bigger tasks or to solve larger problems. These people don't necessarily know what everyone else knows, but do know how to collaborate with other Pro-Ams to put knowledge to work to fulfill their intellectual and social passions.

We do not know how pervasive this Pro-Am phenomenon is among less privileged young people, though many community programs are seeking to offer less privileged kids the opportunity to engage with digital communities of practice. We know is that this is a promising space where we can work to involve more and more young people in ways that will lead to twenty-first-century skills (Gee & Hayes, 2010).

Let me give one specific example: A young rural girl, quite unaffiliated with school, is in an out-of-school program to encourage girls' interest in technology (Hayes, 2008). In the program she has learned that she can use Photoshop to turn real clothes into fashions for her Sims in the game *The Sims*, though this is something of a technical feat. Nonetheless, this is something she wants badly to do. She has learned that she can do it, but not how to do it. This she has to learn on her own— actually not on her own because much help is available on the Internet—because the people who run the out-of-school program do not themselves know how to do it.

After much effort, the girl eventually designs virtual clothes from real clothes for her friends (her status in her peer group goes way up) and then discovers she can upload her clothes on the Internet so that people across the world can see them and use them. Soon hundreds of people are using her designs and heaping her with praise (she now has "global" status).

This girl originally did not sell her clothes, but gave them away. But soon she opened a shop in *Second Life* (a virtual world built by its own "players"), a shop which she constructed herself. She started selling her clothes there for Linden dollars, which can be traded for real money. She has become a classic example of what the Tofflers (Toffler & Toffler, 2006) call a "prosumer," a consumer who produces and transforms and does not just passively consume.

Such prosumers produce originally for off-market status and as part of a community of likeminded experts. But, as the Tofflers point out, such prosumer activity often impacts markets when people like this little girl eventually sell their goods or services. In fact, the Tofflers believe such activity, though unmeasured by economists, is a big part of the global economy and will be a yet bigger part in the future.

This young girl is engaged in Actual Environment Learning. She has actually joined several Pro-Am communities or what we could also call "passion communities"—non age-graded social groups that mentor and police domains dealing with things like designing clothes for *the Sims* or designing and selling in *Second Life* (Gee & Hayes, 2010). The standards are high here. Others in these passion communities have mentored her, but they hold her to very high standards if she is to be accepted as an "insider".

I like this example and not just because of how it shows so clearly the connections among identity, skills, and domains with their conventions and standards. It also shows some of the limitations of current so-called "liberal" approaches to education. Many educators confronted with this example would say how horrible it was to entice this girl to be interested in fashion, since this is such a gendered stereotype (many of these educators are the same people who say, however, that we need to bridge to minority students' interests).

However, when this girl was asked how this experience had made her think differently about her future, she did not say that she wanted to become a clothes designer, but rather that she wanted to "work with computers" because she had seen that they are source of "power." She saw working with computers, too, as a source of innovation and creation. We do not know what identity transformations are happening to people as they engage with real standards in real domains unless we ask.

In designing and selling her clothes, the girl has learned some important twenty-first century skills, ones taught more commonly today out of school than in. She has learned how to use a technologically sophisticated product like Adobe Photoshop; how to think about the visual system (e.g., color, hue, texture), a mainstay of research in cognitive science; how to design clothes; how to upload her clothes to the Internet; how to build her own website; how to communicate with people across the world about her designs; how to use *Second Life*'s building tools to design a store; how to manage the store and become an entrepreneur; and how to be a member of and move across various passion communities and, in the act, "transfer" her learning and knowledge from one place (domain, institution) to another (an important sense of "transfer").

However difficult it might be for schools to engage with Actual Environment Learning in some domains (say, nuclear physics)—and here Sim Environment Learning should be available—schools can engage young people in Actual Environment Learning in regard to "Pro-Am communities" ("passion communities") that incorporate important twenty-first century skills. This would mean helping young people actually to join and become "Pro Ams" in such communities. Of course, this would require wholesale reform in school attitudes and practices (otherwise kids will know they are being duped into "doing school").

2.10 Twenty-First Century Skills

There is a lot of talk today—and lots of lists—devoted to twenty-first century skills, that is, skills important for success in our high-tech, high-risk, global world (Jenkins, Clinton, Purushotma, Robison, & Weigel, 2006). I don't intend to offer another list here. Rather, I want to make two claims about twenty-first century skills.

First, we should not ask about skills first and foremost. Rather, we should ask first about domains. We should ask what domains in our twenty-first century world are worth learning. And "learning" here means gaining an appreciation for these domains' appreciative systems. We should debate domains first. Then we can talk about the skills these domains impart. Why talk about domains first? Because skills are only meaningful—and really only acquired well and retained long—when they are connected to the goals, norms, values, and conventions of a domain.

Second, the ever present question of transfer (does a given skill learned in one area—e.g., *Yu-Gi-Oh* math or fan-fiction writing—transfer to another area—e.g., school math or writing in school?) needs to be changed. First of all, who cares whether a skill learned in the real world (say in a Pro-Am community) transfers to school if school is only about "doing school" and does not itself transfer to the real world? But also, we need to talk about domains first and skills later.

The crucial transfer question is this: once we have settled on what domains we think are worth learning in the twenty-first century, we should then ask which domains are particularly good preparation for future learning of other domains (Bransford & Schwartz, 1999), domains we value equally or more. What is a good

trajectory of domains (say for science) such that each domain in the trajectory creates good preparation for learning in later domains (and not all the domains in this
trajectory need to be "science" domains)? After all, after school, all real learning is
centered in domains and, in our fast changing global world, people have to be good
at learning new domains throughout their lives.

DiSessa (2000) has argued, for example, that his tinkering with things like quartz
radios as a kid was good preparation for learning physics later on. This was not
because he actually learned a lot of physics facts while tinkering, but because such
tinkering gave him an identity that prepared him to be unafraid and undeterred in
learning a technical domain like physics later on.

I believe that *Pokémon* is a great domain to prepare one to learn in *Yu-Gi-Oh* and
Yu-Gi-Oh helps prepare one to learn in *Magic the Gathering*. All of them are great
preparation for learning *Dungeons and Dragons*, which is really a rather different
domain. And *Dungeons and Dragons* is great preparation for learning creative writing in a variety of domains, though my 13 year old used this trajectory to prepare
himself for learning to be an actor in Shakespeare plays (fantasy, strange language,
face-to-face role playing all combined) in a Young Shakespeare theater (though of
course he did not know he was on that trajectory when he began). Different kids take
different trajectories and it is time we studied these pathways in and out of school.

Let me close this section by making it very clear that a person does not have to
learn skills, facts, or tools identified with a given domain only via that domain. So,
for example, if people build (design) virtual places and objects in *Second Life*, using
Second Life's building tools, they use tools and ways of thinking from geometry, but
not directly by being in the domain of geometry, but rather, by being in the domain
of being a *Second Life* builder (designer).

Such learning in *Second Life* is a good preparation for future learning in the
domain of geometry, as well as in other domains that use tools from geometry.
One does not have to learn "geometry" (skills, facts, tools) in "geometry" (the
domain), so to speak. But one has to learn geometrical skills, facts, and tools
in some domain whose appreciative system makes them meaningful and tells the
learner how to "go on" in using them for action and problem solving (as *Second
Life* building does for some geometrical skills, facts, and tools). Otherwise, we
just have Generic Environment Learning. Learning "geometry" in *Second Life* is
Actual Environment Learning, since one is actually joining the domain of *Second
Life* builders (designers)—a rather demanding lot, by the way.

2.11 Formalizing Assessment Beyond the Basic Circuit of Human Action and Social Groups that Form People's Appreciative Systems

We have seen that social groups "in charge" of various domains lift assessment out
of the basic circuit of human action (its natural home) and "formalize" it in terms
of mentoring and policing practices. I have argued that we ought to study these
practices in various domains (including Pro-Am domains).

We as a society have lifted assessment out of these social groups themselves and formalized it yet further. We have set up practices and institutions whose goal is to assess facts, skills, and knowledge—such as in reading, geometry, or science— outside the indigenous workings of the domains that use these facts, skills, and knowledge in particular ways.

However, I argue that our formal standardized assessments of facts, skills, and knowledge are, in a sense, backwards. Often such tests are interested in what learners have learned "in general" from their education. For example, many such tests do not want to assess the geometry embedded in building in *Second Life* or in any other specific application of geometry in given school project using geometry. They want to know whether students can generalize their knowledge of geometry beyond specific applications.

There are two problems with this approach. First, such tests of general knowledge do not necessarily show that learners can actually apply their knowledge—of geometry, say—to specific problem solving applications. And, second, knowledge grows ground up from specific applications and generalizes only after people have had deep experience with a number of different applications. Generalized formal assessments often cannot distinguish between students who have learned their more abstract general knowledge through lots of experience with applications and those who have memorized facts and procedures, but not learned them on the ground of problem solving applications.

DiSessa's (2000) work in science education is very illuminating on this issue. He has successfully taught children in sixth grade and beyond the algebra behind Galileo's principles of motion by teaching them a specific computer programming language called Boxer. The students write into the computer a set of discrete steps in the programming language. For example, the first command in a little program meant to represent uniform motion might tell the computer to set the speed of a moving object at 1 m/sec. The second step might tell the computer to move the object. And a third step might tell the computer to repeat the second step over and over again. Once the program starts running, the student will see a graphical object move 1 m each second repeatedly, a form of uniform motion.

Now the student can elaborate the model in various ways. For example, the student might add a fourth step that tells the computer to add a value a to the speed of the moving object after each movement the object has taken (let us just say, for convenience, that a adds one more meter per second at each step). So now, after the first movement on the screen (when the object has moved at the speed of 1 m/sec), the computer will set the speed of the object at 2 m/sec (adding 1 m), and, then, on the next movement, the object will move at the speed of 2 m/sec. After this, the computer will add another meter per second to the speed and on the next movement the object will move at the speed of 3 m/sec. And so forth forever, unless the student has added a step that tells the computer when to stop repeating the movements. This process is obviously modeling the concept of acceleration. And, course, you can set a to be a negative number instead of a positive one, and watch what happens to the moving object over time instead.

The student can keep elaborating the program and watch what happens at every stage. In this process, the student, with the guidance of a good teacher, can discover a good deal about Galileo's principles of motion through his or her actions in writing the program, watching what happens, and changing the program. What the student is doing here is seeing in an embodied way, tied to action, how a representational system that is less abstract than algebra or calculus (namely, the computer programming language, which is actually composed of a set of boxes) "cashes out" in terms of motion in a virtual world on the computer screen.

An algebraic representation of Galileo's principles is more general than what diSessa's students have been exposed to. Basically it is a set of numbers and variables that do not directly tie to actions or movements. As diSessa points out, algebra doesn't distinguish effectively "among motion ($d = rt$), converting meters to inches ($i = 39.37 \times m$), defining coordinates of a straight line ($y = mx$) or a host of other conceptually varied situations". They all just look alike. He argues that "[d]istinguishing these contexts is critical in learning, although it is probably nearly irrelevant in fluid, routine work for experts," who, of course, have already had many embodied experiences in using algebra for a variety of different purposes of their own.

Once learners have experienced the meanings of Galileo's principles about motion in a situated and embodied way, they have understood one of the situated meanings for the algebraic equations that capture these principles at a more abstract level. The equations take on a real meaning in terms of embodied understandings. As learners see algebra spelled out in more such specific material situations, they will come to master it in an active and critical way, not just as a set of symbols to be repeated in a passive and rote manner on tests.

At an institutional level we need authentic assessments that tell us both where and how people can apply knowledge, and when and how far they can generalize it based on those applications. Such authentic assessments should, in my view, be focused on learners' appreciative systems. They would tell us whether learners, faced with a complex problem, know how "to go on", how to probe, reflect, assess, and re-probe on a trajectory of action to a goal. Such assessments would require that we be sure, before we assessed individuals, that they had the opportunity to engage in domain-centered learning in ways that gave them an emerging appreciative system.

Such assessments would assess how well learners' actions and reflections express the conventions of the domain. They would assess whether learners can articulate their knowledge of these conventions and articulate how these conventions guide their probes, reflections, and goals. However, not all knowledge can be articulated and such assessments would have to honor tacit knowledge, as appropriate.

Such assessments would also assess the extent to which learners can transfer their knowledge to new problem solving applications. They would assess whether learners can innovate in a domain—that is, engage in actions that both reflect conventions in the domain and vary from them in ways that are both acceptable and creative.

Finally, such assessments should always be clearly related to a developmental trajectory through a domain. Any rich domain—academic or Pro-Am—has various and different trajectories to mastery. These are often recognized by insiders to the domain and can be researched (in part through the copious moment-by-moment data digital media make possible). An assessor should know on which trajectory a learner's performance resides, how this trajectory relates to other trajectories through the domain, and even know if this particular trajectory is one that leads to the capacity for innovation in the domain. Assessments should let a learner and other stakeholders in the learner's learning know on which trajectory to mastery his or her performance resides, how this compares to other trajectories, including innovative ones, and how the learner can be helped to proceed further on this trajectory or on another one.

So I am arguing that more authentic assessments—ones that go beyond assessing facts, skills, and knowledge apart from domains and applications—should be centered on appreciative systems and developmental trajectories. Such a system of formal assessment has, perhaps, not been practical on large scale in the past, but digital tools and virtual worlds will make it more practical in the future.

There is another role for formal assessment, one that sometimes, maybe often, can replace its role in regard to assessing individuals altogether. To see this other role, let us ask this question: Do we need to assess the girl making clothes for *the Sims* and selling clothes in *Second Life*, the girl we discussed above as an emerging Pro-Am? Can't we just accept the judgments of the Pro-Am or passion communities she has been part of? They have, after all, held her to high standards. Members of these communities have clear viewpoints on how she stands in the community in regard to these standards. They have given her (a multifaceted) "grade" that is, however, always in progress as she continues to grow.

If we did want to accept the indigenous judgments of such Pro-Am communities for more public credentialing purposes, then our more formal systems of assessment would need only to serve a validating role. We would use assessments to check that the group's judgments aligned with the standards we wanted to apply. If they did, we could stop assessing individuals and let the group do its work and make its judgments. Achieving a certain standing in the group would itself earn a "credential".

The same principle would apply if we wanted to create such communities ourselves, in or out of school—communities organized like Pro-Am communities—but devoted to more "academic" concerns. We would need to get them up and running with social mentoring and policing; internally and mutually defended standards; clearly transmitted appreciative systems; and interactions with the ensemble and ensemble assessments (or mangle assessments or dance assessments, whatever we want to call them). We would then want to validate that they worked to the standards we desired. And then we would need to get out of the way.

On this approach, as we set up Environment 1 (Actual) and Environment 3 (Sim) learning, assessment would be seen not as something that involves "judging" individuals, but as something that is validating that a certain social organization of learning works for certain purposes. The social organization then would make judgments internally that we would stand by externally as well. There would be no need for any "final exam" or one shot "big test".

Let me be clear what I am saying here: on a good "fan fiction" site, for example, no one needs to give each writer a formal test (Black, 2008). Thanks to the social organization of the site—its ways of coaching, mentoring, reviewing, and giving feedback, as well as determining members' reputations and standing in the community—everyone knows where everyone else stands.

Of course, there are subtleties, negotiations, and even differing judgments about such matters. So the "assessments" here are multifaceted with multiple "scores" and they are ongoing in terms of members' trajectories of learning. But that is as it should be. A single decontextualized "score" is meaningless against such nuances. We can organize academic learning we care about in such ways as well.

The validating role of assessment here would apply to transfer as well. Instead of giving each individual some test of transfer, we would use assessment instruments to validate that some domain—organized in some way—is, in general, good preparation for learning for specific future domains we care about. Then we would let the indigenous workings of the social group do its work.

All this is to say that one of the jobs of twenty-first century assessment ought to be validating social organizations of learning. The job of twenty-first century educators ought to be designing such social organizations and then letting them run. As they run, members themselves may well find new ways to enhance learning and judgments about learning. We can, in turn, validate these as they arise.

Of course, formal institutionalized systems of assessment thrive on schools, since schools so rarely call on or create the sorts of indigenous domain-centered forms of mentoring and policing we have discussed above. And, indeed, formal institutionalized forms of assessment seem required if we are to assess Generic Environment Learning, since there appear to be no "natural" practices to draw on here.

2.12 Conclusion

I have argued, then, that twenty-first century assessment needs to be centered on appreciative systems both when we assess individuals and when we validate learning communities. This means, at a minimum, the following:

1. We need to study the indigenous mentoring and policing practices (the learning and assessment practices) embedded in domains and the social groups that operate them, especially ones that young people can join on their own (such as Pro-Am communities). Our studies here may tell us, as assessors, that we need to leave things alone and trust the indigenous assessment practices. Or they may tell us that we need—if we are to use these domains for educational purposes (broadly speaking)—to tweak things a bit, to improve and extend the indigenous practices. Either way, once we have "officially" validated the indigenous practices (tweaked or not), we can just let things run.
2. We need to study Pro-Am communities and academically relevant domains, as well as Sim versions of them, to see how they prepare (or can be best made

to prepare) learners for future learning in other domains. We then need to pick Pro-Am communities and academically relevant domains that are highly fruitful not just for the skills they give learners, but for the future trajectory of learning on which they can set the learner in terms of other Pro-Am communities and domains.

3. We need to create educationally relevant (again, broadly speaking) Pro-Am communities in schools and other educational settings and design their mentoring and policing systems along the lines of the best practices we have found in such communities out in the world with whatever improvements (again from the inside) we can make.

4. We need to use digital media (and other approaches) to engage in learning in schools, and in out-of-school programs with educational goals. This means bringing real domains or Sim versions of them to school—for example, chemistry as a domain modeled or simulated as well as *SWAT4* does for SWAT. Assessment in regard to much learning needs to be developed in terms of seeing that learners have developed appropriate appreciative systems and are developing them on a trajectory towards mastery (i.e., making and revising probes in more and more "appropriate" and "good" ways by the standards of the domain or the Sim version we have introduced). We should be assessing how learners reflect on probes and how they make judgments about how to "go on" and how they can discuss and argue over this. This is what people do in a real domain.

5. To accomplish 4 above we need to know for any domain we have introduced into education what are the trajectories to "mastery" (there are almost always more than one). These trajectories will be ones successful learners and members have taken through the domain (or Sim versions of it). Assessment of any individual—beyond the validating role I have discussed above—should always have one major purpose: to tell the learner and other stakeholders in the learner's learning where in one of these trajectories he or she is, and how he or she can develop further along that trajectory or another fruitful one.

6. For twenty-first century learning, we need to know for any domain we have introduced into education what some of the innovative ways are to move along a trajectory to mastery—what have turned out to be innovative solutions to problems and techniques for innovation in the domain. Assessments should tell the learner and other stakeholders in the learner's learning how he or she is developing in terms of not just a trajectory to mastery, but one that involves some degree of innovation (and, perhaps, this is done on a second or subsequent "play through"—curricula, like good video games, should be re-playable).

7. Finally, all assessments that assess Generic Environment Learning should have to validate that when people pass, they can later recruit the assessed skills in a real or Sim domain. This means demanding that all Generic learning assessments must be validated in terms of "preparation for future learning" (Bransford & Schwartz, 1999). Otherwise they are pointless, other than as an assessment of "doing school".

References

Anderson, C. (2006). *The long tail: Why the future of business is selling less of more*. New York: Hyperion.

Black, R. W. (2008). *Adolescents and online fan fiction*. New York: Peter Lang.

Bransford, J. D., & Schwartz, D. L. (1999). Rethinking transfer: A simple proposal with multiple implications. In A. Iran-Nejad & P. D. Pearson (Eds.), *Review of research in education* (Vol. 24, pp. 61–100). Washington, DC: American Educational Research Association.

Callon, M., & Latour, B. (1992). Don't throw the baby out with the bath school! A reply to Collins and yearly. In A. Pickering (Ed.), *Science as practice and culture* (pp. 343–368). Chicago: University of Chicago Press.

Damasio, A. R. (1995). *Descartes' error: Emotion, reason, and the human brain*. New York: Quill.

Damasio, A. (1999). *The feeling of what happens: Body and emotion in the making of consciousness*. Orlando, FL: Harvest Books.

Damasio, A. (2003). *Looking for Spinoza: Joy, sorrow, and the feeling brain*. Orlando, FL: Harvest Books.

diSessa, A. A. (2000). *Changing minds: Computers, learning, and literacy*. Cambridge, MA: MIT Press.

Engeström, Y. (1987). *Learning by expanding. An activity theoretical approach to developmental research*. Helsinki: Orienta Konsultit.

Gee, J. P. (1990/2007). *Sociolinguistics and literacies: Ideology in discourses* (3rd ed.). London: Taylor & Francis.

Gee, J. P. (2003/2007). *What video games have to teach us about learning and literacy* (2nd ed.). New York: Palgrave/Macmillan.

Gee, J. P. (2004). *Situated language and learning: A critique of traditional schooling*. London: Routledge.

Gee, J. P. (2007). *Good video games and good learning: Collected essays on video games*, learning, and literacy. New York: Peter Lang.

Gee, J. P. (2008). *Getting over the slump: Innovation strategies to promote children's learning*. New York: The Joan Ganz Cooney Center at Sesame Workshop.

Gee, J. P., & Hayes, E. R. (2010). *Women and gaming: The Sims and 21st century learning*. New York: Palgrave/Macmillan.

Habermas, J. (1981). *The theory of communicative action*. London: Beacon Press.

Habermas, J. (1989). *The structural transformation of the public sphere: An inquiry into a category of bourgeois society* (pp. 183–194). Cambridge, MA: MIT Press.

Hayes, E. (2008). *Girls, gaming, and trajectories of technological expertise. In* Y. B. Kafai, C. Heeter, J. Denner, & J. Sun (Eds.), *Beyond Barbie and Mortal Kombat: New perspectives on gender, games, and computing*. Boston: MIT Press.

Huizinga, J. (1950, org. 1938). *Homo ludens: A study of the play element in culture*. Boston: Beacon Press.

Jenkins, H., Clinton, K., Purushotma, R., Robison, A. J., & Weigel, M. (2006). *Confronting the challenges of participatory culture: Media education for the 21st Century*. Chicago: MacArthur Foundation.

Knorr Cetina, K. (1992). The couch, the cathedral, and the laboratory: On the relationship between experiment and laboratory, in science. In A. Pickering (Ed.), *Science as practice and culture* (pp. 113–137). Chicago: University of Chicago Press.

Latour, B. (2004). *Politics of nature: How to bring the sciences into democracy*. Cambridge, MA: Harvard University Press.

Latour, B. (2005). *Reassembling the social: An introduction to Actor-Network-Theory*. Oxford: Oxford University Press.

Leadbeater, C., & Miller, P. (2004). *The pro-am revolution: How enthusiasts are changing our society and economy*. London: Demos.

Pickering, A. (1995). *The mangle of practice: Time, agency, and science*. Chicago: University of Chicago Press.

Schön, D. A. (1983). *The reflective practitioner: How professionals think in action*. New York: Basic Books.

Shaffer, D. W. (2007). *How computer games help children learn*. New York: Palgrave/Macmillan.

Toffler, A., & Toffler, H. (2006). *Revolutionary wealth: How it will be created and how it will change our lives*. New York: Knopf.

Vickers, G. (1973). *Making institutions work*. London: Associated Business Programs.

Vickers, G. (1983). *Human systems are different*. London: Harper & Row.

Wittgenstein, L. (1953/2001). *Philosophical investigations* (3rd ed.). Oxford: Blackwell Publishing.

Chapter 3
Growing Learning and Assessment in the 21st Century

King D. Beach III

Abstract This response begins with an exegesis of four key aspects of Gee's approach to learning and assessment in Chapter 2. Learning-assessment events in Pemapur, a Himalayan village with a short history of formal schooling and a long history of agriculture are used for illustration. It ends with a brief exploration of two issues that deserve greater attention by Gee. How might we "grow" educational assessment beyond the specifics and idiosyncrasies of moment-to-moment learning without stripping it of its relation to the identities, norms, values, and knowledge of the domain? And related to this, how can we assess learning "transfer" across domains without stripping assessment of the specifics of the domains, historical relations between domains, or of the trajectories people choose across them?

Keywords Assessment · Learning · Transfer · Sociocultural · Nepal

My response begins with a critique and extension of several key aspects of Gee's approach to issues of learning and assessment. This will lay groundwork for my concluding discussion of two related aspects of Gee's chapter that I find to be the most challenging for current educational assessment practices—challenges that deserve further exegesis.

I will craft my response using empirical illustrations from fieldnotes of my own research on the transitions that people make between in- and out-of-school systems of learning activities (Beach, 1990, 1995, 1999, 2003, 2005, 2006). My hope is that the reader will find the richness of the detailed descriptions of observed behavior conducive to exploring several of the key aspects of Gee's chapter. My fieldnotes originate from a series of studies in a small village in the mountains of Western Nepal that I will call Pemapur, that not coincidentally is where I am drafting this response.

K.D. Beach III (✉)
International Educational Research and Development Consulting (IERDConsult),
Tallahassee, FL, USA
e-mail: kingbeach108@gmail.com

V.J. Shute, B.J. Becker (eds.), *Innovative Assessment for the 21st Century*,
DOI 10.1007/978-1-4419-6530-1_3, © Springer Science+Business Media, LLC 2010

Prior to 1963 there were no schools in Pemapur. No electricity. No roads. No shops. Subsistence agriculture with family and friends equaled life. Today I can visit dozens of shops, overhear a mobile phone conversation, borrow a friend's motorcycle, and teach at a high school with over 400 students. Thus, Pemapur is a perfect place for examining some of the learning and educational assessment issues that Gee raises—a place where there is a clear "before and after" to the introduction of schooling and formal assessment. Not incidentally, Pemapur has also been the site for some of my research (Beach, 1990, 1995, 1999, 2003, 2005, 2006).

I begin with a discussion of four key aspects of Gee's approach to issues of learning and assessment. Each is introduced and explored within the context of a particular event or set of events occurring in Pemapur relevant to the issue at hand.

Learning and assessment are naturally-occurring aspects of most domains and are integral to their sustenance.

Here in Pemapur I watch a father and his son (probably 11 or 12 years old) plow a paddy behind my house in preparation for planting. Simultaneous with the son's water buffalo trampling an irrigation barrier dividing the terraces while said son remains oblivious, the father shouts that he needs to anticipate and not steer so close to the field edge. Several minutes later his son reacts too late and struggles mightily to avoid taking out another part of the barrier. Still the buffalo drags plow and son across the field edge, but this time the father says nothing. His son's next dozen or so passes with the plow are perfect, albeit with many early fine adjustments to their collective trajectory.

The father's and eventually the son's performance assessments are clearly integral to the sustenance of this domain, not to mention the family's irrigation system. Assessment is a part of plowing and the father-son relationship, and shifts seamlessly from father to son in the performance. Mentoring and policing assessment functions as Gee describes them and they both operate simultaneously in the father's shout to his son. Because of this the mentoring function exists in the silence of the father the second time the irrigation barrier is breached, and the policing function has dropped out altogether. For the son there is never a separation of the two functions in his increasingly focused self-assessment of his performance.

Whether one cares to call it policing, summative, or high stakes, it never contradicts the mentoring or more formative aspect of the father's assessment of his son's plowing. The summative high stakes assessment is just as integral to plowing as the more finely tuned and nuanced formative aspect. Thus, I would argue, consistent with Gee I believe, that there is no *logically necessary* separation between the ongoing in-classroom formative assessment that teachers do with their students, and high stakes state wide assessments of student achievement, for example. Looking at assessment in this way helps us ask a highly productive question: if there is no logically necessary separation between the two forms of assessment, exactly what are the socio-political (not necessarily psychometric) circumstances that have lead us to an impasse between the two in formal education? Though Gee does not directly formulate this as a productive question, he should. His argument for taking human action in context as the natural starting point for developing learning assessments into practice will be subject to the same socio-political forces that created a sharp distinction between formative and summative learning assessment.

Becoming a successful participant in a particular domain involves contributing to and maintaining the norms and values of the domain, as well as identity craftwork.

I am buying some soap, two packs of biscuits, and 250 grams of tea from a high school student helping out in his grandfather's shop after school. More customers arrive as the teen meticulously writes down the cost of my soap, then biscuits. He weighs the tea, writes down the weight, and asks grandfather (who is waiting on other customers) how much tea costs. Grandfather replies that tea is 758 rupees a kilo. The teen writes that down too, pulls out his calculator, and spends the next 10 minutes meticulously calculating what the total should be. I am amused, but grandfather is not. Grandfather, who has never been to school, tells his grandson he should put down the paper and the pen and the calculator and think quickly—do the math in his head or on his fingers. Grandson appears horrified and refuses. This is not merely resistance to change, but to giving up an important public display of what it means to be an educated person in Pemapur.

Here some of the norms and values of shopkeeping are made transparent: serve the customer not only by accurately calculating the total amount of money to be requested, but also by doing it *quickly*. We also see what Lave (1996), has called identity craftwork coming into play. The teen has spent 11 long years in school learning how to do written arithmetic and use a calculator. He is being asked to give up that which symbolizes what he has been working hard to become—a formally literate and highly educated person—by his grandfather, who has never attended school and is illiterate.

What is at issue here is not merely or even largely the grandson's knowledge of mathematics, but rather a conflict between the demands of two domains—shopkeeping and schooling—and his identity craftwork, something that both grandfather and grandson eventually resolve. The larger challenge this presents is not to educational assessment per se, but rather to how to create learning environments where people can do identity craftwork as part of knowledge construction within domains such as schools that partially borrow norms and values from other domains not formally tasked with education. Assessing the learning of those traversing the domains necessarily involves an assessment of the domains and their relationship to who the learners are and who they hope to become.

Gee's playful, simulated, and pretense learning environments are not entities so much as ways of thinking about how we might construct relations between schooling and other domains of practice, but avoid simply reducing one to the other, or assuming some form of generic or promissory relationship. Play, simulation, and pretense environments where identity craftwork is integral to learning accomplish this precisely *because* of their tentative relation to other "actual" domains. Because of this tentative relationship there are both built-in means of assessment and the freedom to modify the built-in means to meet some of the unique demands of formal schooling.

Learning environments that expand extend peoples' learning and its assessment beyond any day-to-day existence and routine functioning.

The wife of a teacher began the very first shop in Pemapur when their oldest daughter was old enough to look after the younger children. Located beside the school, the shop provided tea and freshly made snacks for students and teaching staff. Her shop opened the same year the high school opened, and 9 years after Pemapur had its first elementary school students. Today Pemapur has two main bazaars and over a hundred shops. Shopkeeping that began as an extension of a teacher's family and the school is now a major, far more formal enterprise. Shopkeepers have supplanted former Ghurka soldiers with British pensions as Pemapur's wealthiest.

It is not only that learning domains extend people such as the teacher's wife beyond their routine functioning; the domains themselves are extended to cover new previously uncharted territory. Engeström (1996) and van Oers (1988) have studied this in considerable depth within working environments and school, respectively.

This opens up a new area to consider for educational assessment—the capability of a domain to be extended by its participants into new territory. Gee's chapter foregrounds assessment relative to learners' participation in different forms of learning environments. If we are to take the proposition of creating more opportunities for play-, sim-, and pretense-like participations in school seriously, however, we should consider ways to assess the expansive potential of such opportunities as a part of schooling. Without such assessment we run the risk of turning a promising set of pedagogical intentions into something analogous to the word problem that attempts to bring some version of the "real world" into the school untouched—something that Gee himself would strongly argue against. A follow-on piece where Gee details the historical-developmental aspects of several of the sim domains and pro-am communities expansion to include new territory and people would provide a nice base from which to consider the shape of an assessment of the expansive learning potential of a domain.

Educational assessment for the twenty-first century needs to accept the challenge of assessing relations between persons and domains through a focus on appreciative systems.

School was the first organization in Pemapur to group large numbers of same-age persons together for a common purpose. Prior to schooling, all activities in Pemapur involved multiple ages and generations. The first group of teenagers to drop out or graduate from Pemapur's high school formed a dance club. The concept of a club was entirely new to the village and extended similar age activities from the school out into the broader organization of the community. Today there are sports clubs, political clubs, community development clubs, and cultural clubs. They are an integral part of life in Pemapur. All contain similar-aged groups of villagers.

A unit of assessment here could be changes in individual students' dancing abilities among those who do and do not participate in the dance club after leaving Pemapur's high school. However, this presupposes the existence of a dance club. Another unit of assessment could be the genesis of the dance club itself. This presupposes similar-aged individuals who like to dance, want to continue to do something together, and have sufficient collective motivation to create a new type of social organization and identity in Pemapur. Neither would be consonant with assessment that is integral to learning in school, or in the dance club, but then how could it be if we are concerned with learning/assessment across the domains?

Gee's concept of an appreciative system as an iterative "identity/goal/probe/get a response from the world/reflect based on an appreciative system/new revised probe" gets us part of the way towards units of educational assessment for how people and circumstances create, learn, and grow a new social form and trajectory that is nothing less trivial than culture itself. If the role of education is to quite literally help people become more productive of culture, then this is important. What is missing is that "the world" is more than a static entity to bounce probes off of, something that Gee clearly believes as well when he suggests that appreciative systems are distributed across other people, texts, tools, technologies, and practices. However, this suggestion does not resolve the issue of what appropriate units for educational assessment could be for how people and circumstances create, learn, and grow new social forms and trajectories across them.

An appropriate and valid unit of educational assessment for this necessarily shifts us away from the learner or the domain per se to their developmental relation, over time. This is a relation that exists not in a gap or vacuum between the two, but rather in systems of symbols, artifacts, values, texts, and norms that are produced and circulate between them—sometimes personal and private, and at other times public and collectively debated and standardized. This is the ground from which both the cultural person and domains are produced.

These four excursions lead us to two of the challenges that Gee's paper presents for educational assessment in the twenty-first century. As they are closely linked, I will discuss them together.

How do we "grow" educational assessment beyond the specifics and idiosyncrasies of moment-to-moment learning without stripping it of its relation to the identities, norms, values, and knowledge of the domain? And related to this, can we address the issue of learning "transfer" among domains without stripping assessment not only of the specifics of the domains, but also of the historical relations between domains and the trajectories people choose across them.

Gee discusses several ideas that have the potential to move assessment closer to the actualities of learning in school for a necessarily indeterminate future, such as Bransford's and Schwartz's (1999) concept of assessing learning in school *as* preparation for future learning. He also describes Pro-Am communities as promising examples of organized groups of amateur experts where learning has built-in forms of assessment. Depending on the nature of the particular Pro-Am community, it can support some individuals in discovering and transitioning into related actual-world activities. Schooling as preparation for future learning requires a new form of assessment that tethers it not only to the specifics of learning in school, but also to the potentials for future learning. Pro-Am communities contain built-in means for keeping assessment tethered to the ongoing flow of their learning activities.

However, neither of these approaches, in and of themselves, allows us to "grow" assessment to a level that might satisfy those who are concerned with, say, how we might assess learning mathematics at school in preparation for running small businesses in Surkhet district, where Pemapur is located. It would definitely not satisfy those who want a statewide assessment of student learning in Florida. My purpose here is not to satisfy everyone so much as to acknowledge the importance of large-scale assessments for some purposes; and to ponder for a moment how we might get a bit closer to that scale of educational assessment without divorcing it from the flow of activities it is assessing.

For this I will return to the example of assessing learning mathematics in Surkhet's schools as preparation for running small businesses, such as shops, throughout the district. Note that educational assessment would serve no certifying function here. It is possible to become a shopkeeper without receiving much or any formal education, though that is much more unusual today than it was a decade ago. Today a lack of any formal education will limit what one can do as a shopkeeper.

Rather than thinking about how to assess learning math in school for its potential to help students later learning one of a wide range of business activities including shopkeeping, we might consider "growing" a new system of learning activity, one that gradually "lifts" assessment along with it to a level beyond particular schools, shops, and students. Consider for a moment the afterschool program, an activity system that Cole (1996) and others have developed in a wide variety of national and international contexts. Further consider the idea of afterschool programs in communities such as Pemapur that serve a syncretic purpose—improving students' understandings of mathematics in school and simultaneously supporting them in learning how to create and run small business enterprises by helping them create and run several village shops.

Assessment of participation in such a syncretic system of activity, would be more "general," or more accurately, at a higher level of social organization than either learning mathematics for school or learning how to use math in a particular business, if that syncretic activity is carefully designed. Educational assessment under these circumstances is necessarily "lifted" above the specific identities, norms, values, and knowledge associated with schooling, and also those invoked in creating one's own small business. But assessment would be integral to and a necessary part of the ongoing flow of participation in this syncretic activity system.

References

Beach, K. (1990). From school to work: A social and cognitive history of mathematics in a Nepali village. *Himalayan Research Bulletin*, 5(2), 46–52.

Beach, K. (1995). Activity as a mediator of sociocultural change and individual development: The case of school-work transition in Nepal. *Mind, Culture, and Activity*, 2(4), 285–302.

Beach, K. (1999). Consequential transitions: A sociocultural expedition beyond transfer in education. In A. Iran-Nejad & P. D. Pearson (Eds.), *Review of research in education* (Vol. 24, pp. 101–139). Washington, DC: American Educational Research Association.

Beach, K. (2003). Learning in complex social systems meets information processing and mental representation: Some consequences for educational assessment. *Measurement: Interdisciplinary Research and Perspectives*, 1(2), 149–154.

Beach, K. (2005). Consequential transitions: A developmental view of knowledge propagation through social organization. In T. Tuomi-Gröhn & Y. Engeström (Eds.), *Between school and work: New perspectives on transfer and boundary-crossing* (pp. 39–62). New York: Pergamon.

Beach, K. (2006). A socio-cultural approach to the generalization of knowledge, skill, and identity. In M. Nobu & K. Takahashi (Eds.), *Sociocultural approaches to learning and education* (pp. 56–84). Tokyo: Iisimi Publishers.

Bransford, J. D., & Schwartz, D. L. (1999). Rethinking transfer: A simple proposal with multiple implications. In A. Iran-Nejad & P. D. Pearson (Eds.), *Review of research in education* (Vol. 24, pp. 61–100). Washington, DC: American Educational Research Association.

Cole, M. (1996). *Cultural psychology: A once and future discipline.* Cambridge, MA: Harvard University Press.

Engeström, Y. (1996). Development as breaking away and opening up: A challenge to Vygotsky and Piaget. *Swiss Journal of Psychology, 55,* 126–132.

Lave, J. (1996). Teaching, as learning, in practice. *Mind, Culture, and Activity, 3*(3), 149–164.

Van Oers, B. (1998). The fallacy of decontextualization. *Mind, Culture, and Activity, 5*(2), 135–142.

Chapter 4
Aiming at Learning: Assessment as the Critical Link

Mari Pearlman

Abstract Inequities in educational opportunity in the United States and variability in individual states' standards for student achievement have been amply demonstrated by the intensive focus on standardized test results over the past few years. The call for higher educational attainment for U.S. students has intensified even as test results indicate persistent performance gaps. In order to effect real changes in the achievement of students in U.S. public schools, particularly the learning achievement of children in poverty, we need to think differently about assessment, and recognize its rightfully central place in the education enterprise. To do this, however, we need also to recognize that we can make no progress without some common set of assumptions and benchmarks by which we gauge such progress. What we need is an assessment that is worth teaching to, one that allows for meaningful comparisons across states, and one that is connected with instruction in fundamental ways. One way to accomplish these goals would be to use the National Assessment of Educational Progress (NAEP) to create benchmark assessments at 4th, 8th, and 12th grade levels to assess the achievement of all students in U.S. public schools against common standards for learning and performance.

Keywords Accountability · Assessment · Common standards · NAEP · NCLB · Performance benchmarks

No part of the public education enterprise has received more attention and engendered more rhetoric over the past 8 years than student assessment. The pressures brought to bear on educators through the enforced implementation of high-stakes annual testing of children and publication of the results have suggested that testing alone can change educational outcomes for children, a position somewhat akin to a belief that a really good thermometer can cure a fever.

We have an opportunity in the next 2 or 3 years, with a new administration in Washington responsible for the reauthorization of the Elementary and Secondary

M. Pearlman (✉)
Pearlman Education Group LLC, Lawrenceville, NJ, USA
e-mail: mapearlman@comcast.net

V.J. Shute, B.J. Becker (eds.), *Innovative Assessment for the 21st Century*,   49
DOI 10.1007/978-1-4419-6530-1_4, © Springer Science+Business Media, LLC 2010

Education Act, home of the No Child Left Behind legislation and attendant education policy, to focus on what really matters, which is learning. In order to effect real changes in the achievement of students in U.S. public schools, particularly the learning status of children in poverty, we need to think differently about assessment, and recognize its rightfully central place in the education enterprise.

To do this, however, we need also to recognize that we can make no progress without a common set of assumptions and benchmarks with which to gauge such progress. We need an assessment that is worth teaching to, one that allows for meaningful comparisons across states, and one that is connected with instruction in fundamental ways. One way to accomplish these goals would be to use the National Assessment of Educational Progress (NAEP) to create benchmark assessments at 4th, 8th, and 12th grade levels to assess the achievement of all students in U.S. public schools against common standards for learning and performance. A number of challenges must be met to implement this idea: NAEP assessments would need to be designed for the reporting of individual student results, the NAEP content frameworks and performance standards would need intensive review and revision, and a great deal of conversation across state boundaries about the benefits of such an approach would need to occur.

In order to explore a better alternative, it is important to understand the current state of testing in U.S. education and review the path that led to our current situation. We are currently mired in the confusion created by the supposedly democratic practice of allowing each of the 50 states to decide its own educational standards and practices. I argue that it is absolutely necessary to create some common understanding of what student achievement across all U.S. public school students at selected grade levels should be. Further, I argue that it is unlikely that such a welter of practices, standards, and tests as currently exists can support any real change in learning outcomes for children.

Recent economic events make it clear that such a shift in student performance is imperative for everyone's future in the U.S.: the U.S. must earn its way back to solvency and economic power. It cannot do this without serious commitment to educating children to be thinkers and learners, not merely test takers. And right now, we do not even have the means to make progress on this front because we have no agreement about what and how to teach children at each level of their K-12 education, about what expectations for demonstrating learning should be common across all U.S. school children at each level, and about how we should use assessment to help ensure this common standard of content and performance.

I have used the gnomic utterances of Yogi Berra to introduce the major sections of the chapter. These seemed appropriate not only because of what they say, but because the game of baseball is not entirely unlike the enterprise of education. It is absolutely dependent on team effort, it is leisurely in both its individual games and its very long season, it has very long periods of apparent inactivity (non-fans call this unbearable tedium) interrupted by moments of great drama, money for players does not guarantee outcomes and winning, and some surprisingly stolid and consistent efforts result in victory. In addition, the enterprise of baseball is preoccupied with data about individual and team performance, and with interpretations of those data to increase positive outcomes. The differences in the use and agreed-upon purposes of these data between baseball and education are salient: in baseball, everyone agrees on what success looks like, and everyone acknowledges that 100% success for everyone in the enterprise is impossible. Perhaps more important, in baseball using the data for specific purposes of improvement in specific areas is quite sophisticated and disciplined. I think educators could learn a great deal from reading a book like *Moneyball: The Art of Winning an Unfair Game*, by Michael Lewis (2003), which details the ways in which consistent and persistent interpretations of data can yield surprising performance gains even when the raw material—players and salary resources—are unpromising.

4.1 Part I: Current State

We made too many wrong mistakes

–Yogi Berra

In the spring of 2010, 8 years after the passage of No Child Left Behind—the most far-reaching testing legislation in the history of U.S. education—where are we in terms of awareness of and more effective deployment of connections between teaching and learning as a result of increased student testing? My answer would be, "No farther down the path than we were in 2002." Indeed, we may be substantially more distant from the goal of improving children's learning outcomes, because across the nation educators have focused so narrowly on testing outcomes as an end in themselves.

To be sure, we now have empirical evidence of systematic differences in the ways children of poverty, color, and disability and more advantaged children perform on standardized tests, regardless of which tests are employed in which geographies. This is not a startling new fact for educators. However, its undeniability, given the disaggregated NCLB test results is, perhaps, a positive outcome, because it makes it more difficult for even the most self-serving politician to avoid the results of the virtually universal differentiation of educational results that is tied to these different subgroups' performances. And the spotlight NCLB has focused on achievement for *all* students, and particularly those students who have persistently occupied the lowest levels of achievement, is positive and important.

However, the imposition of unrealistic goals through Adequate Yearly Progress (AYP), the culture of punishment of schools and teachers that such target shooting creates, and the persistent refusal to recognize the disparity of expectations, standards, and test rigor across different states has led to perverse results[1] that have weakened the links between assessment and learning.

---

[1] For example, the labeling of schools as "failing" in states like Florida, which has been working systematically to implement standards-based instruction and assessment, with rigorous expectations for student achievement, while schools in states with exceptionally low standards all achieve AYP.

How did we get so mired in this confusing and ultimately destructive use of assessments? It is useful to step outside the cloud of argument that shrouds any discussion of NCLB for a moment and ask a simple question: "What is the point of testing children using standardized testing tools?" It is instructive to review the history of answers to this question, as they are revealed by testing practice in public education in the United States. As Robert Linn recounts in his 1995 William Angoff Lecture at Educational Testing Service, the links between externally mandated assessments and teaching have a long history. In 1992, the Office of Technology Assessment (OTA) report, *Testing in American Schools: Asking the Right Questions* reviewed the history of testing in American School from the nineteenth century (when Horace Mann introduced written examinations) to the present. Linn quotes the OTA report summary of the view that tests are a tool that could support education reform:

> The idea underlying the implementation of written examinations... was born in the minds of individuals already convinced that education was substandard in quality. This sequence— perception of failure followed by the collection of data designed to document failure (or success)—offers early evidence of what has become a tradition of school reform and a truism of student testing: tests are often administered not just to discover how well schools or kids are doing, but to obtain external confirmation—validation—of the hypothesis that they are not doing well at all (Linn, 1995, p. 7).

While it may be important to use test results as evidence of the failures of class-room instruction, they have been seen as not merely messengers of the need for reform, but agents of reform itself. Why is this the case? Linn gives the following reasons:

1. Tests and assessments are relatively inexpensive. Compared to changes that involve increases in instructional time, reduced class size, attracting more able people to teaching, hiring teacher aides, or programmatic changes involving substantial professional development for teachers, assessment is cheap.
2. Testing and assessment can be externally mandated. It is far easier to mandate testing and assessment requirements at the state or district level than anything that involves actual change in what happens inside the classroom.
3. Test and assessment changes can be rapidly implemented. Importantly, new test or assessment requirements can be implemented within the term of office of elected officials.
4. Results are visible. Test results can be reported to the press. Poor results in the beginning are desirable for policy makers who want to show they have had an effect. Based on past experience, policymakers can reasonably expect increases in scores in the first few years of a program (Linn, 2000) with or without real improvement in the broader achievement constructs that tests and assessments are intended to measure. The resulting overly rosy picture that is painted by short-term gains observed in most new testing programs gives the impression of improvement right on schedule for the next election. (Linn, 1995, pp. 7–8)

For more than 25 years, beginning with minimum competency testing in the 1970s and continuing with standards-based reform efforts through the 1990s and attendant test uses, education policy makers in the United States have advocated testing as a means to demonstrate how seriously they are taking raising student achievement. Certainly some of that focus was directed at identifying individual teachers and even schools that were "failing," but much of it was directed sincerely at efforts to improve the overall status of student learning in the United States. And from 1969 forward, the federal government, through its development and administration of the NAEP, invested in the assessment of student learning across the developmental span of public schooling (sampling at grades 4, 8, and 12), critical curriculum areas (mathematics, reading, science), and—most important—time. NAEP is the only source of long-term trend data on student learning in the United States over the last four decades.

By 1995, when Robert Linn delivered the lecture quoted above, there was a new focus in states on the nexus of performance-based assessments, content standards, and performance standards, as a result of the Clinton administration's *Goals 2000* education initiative. Lauren Resnick led the performance-based assessment charge, articulating three basic premises that ground advocacy for this kind of assessment as truly contributing to learning:

- WYTIWYG, a play on the then-new "What You See Is What You Get" description of computer screen presentation: What You Test Is What You Get.
- "You do not get what you do not assess."
- (Assuming that some kind of testing for accountability will be a permanent feature of the education enterprise) "Make tests worth teaching to." (Resnick & Resnick, 1992, p. 59)

Concomitant with the Resnick "new standards" approach to assessment was a national focus on the creation of content standards. The National Council of Teachers of Mathematics (NCTM) led the way, and by the end of the decade of the 1990s, national and state content standards existed in almost every field. For teachers, the National Board for Professional Teaching Standards articulated in its field by field examination of accomplished teaching the knowledge standards in virtually all fields of teaching, and these teacher content knowledge standards were coordinated with content knowledge standards across the various disciplines, such as mathematics, science, and language arts.

Then there was a preliminary skirmish with the vexing issue of performance standards. If content standards—often negotiated political settlements among warring factions in a given field of study—covered the "what" of learning, performance standards were intended to wrestle to the ground the issue of "how much." Given the mandates of NCLB, it is instructive to review some basic characteristics of performance standards. As Linn says,

> There are at least four critical characteristics of performance standards. First, they are intended to be absolute rather than normative. Second, they are expected to be set at high, "world-class" levels. Third, a relatively small number of levels (i.e., advanced, proficient)

are typically identified. Finally, they are expected to apply to all, or essentially all, students rather than a selected subset such as college-bound students seeking advanced placement. (Linn, 1995)

In the context of our current challenges, the issue of performance standards is a critical one. The performance standards established for NAEP reporting have been roundly criticized as unrealistically high (see, for example, Pellegrino et al., 1999; Shepard et al., 1993). They are, however, consistent across geography, cohorts of students, and time. One of the pressing issues raised by NCLB concerns the enormous differences among states' performance standards, particularly the standard of "proficient" that matters for AYP. And it should be noted that setting performance standards is by no means a settled issue in the measurement community—there are multiple methods and no agreement about which works best. It is not incidental to this problem that the search for psychometric methods that would allow comparison of the results of different tests has resurfaced in the past 5 years, and with no silver bullet solutions.[2]

Finally, and significantly given what has happened in the first decade of this twenty-first century, the 1990s era of standards-based reform explicitly acknowledged the importance of Opportunity-To-Learn (OTL) standards. First introduced as a critical component of any accountability legislation by the National Council on Education Standards and Testing in 1992, this was by far the most controversial part of the *Goals 2000* legislation. These standards were voluntary in the legislation, a response to the controversy the topic engendered among those who believed passionately that equity concerns should be paramount, and those who vigorously resisted the incursion of the federal government into local control of education. Andrew Porter summarized it this way:

> To proponents, OTL standards represent the age-old problems of equity in education. In particular, advocates of OTL standards see them as an appropriate antidote to the potentially negative effects of high stakes testing on students who, through no fault of their own, attend schools which provide an ineffective education. To opponents, OTL standards evoke all their worst fears about federal intrusion into local control of the quality and nature of education. (Porter, 1994)

As we know now, *Goals 2000* morphed into No Child Left Behind. The importance of test scores to teachers and schools, and particularly, rapid improvements in test scores against an absolute standard, increased exponentially. Measurement experts, with Robert Linn in the lead, have repeatedly explained why the provisions of the legislation cannot work mathematically—there is no hope of 100%

---

[2] See Robert Linn (2005a) for the latest account of the difficulties and confusion that attend the effort to make mathematical models bridge gaps in content, difficulty, and methodology in different assessments. Also Barton has described the challenges in the late 1990s to performance standard setting activities (Barton, 1999, pp. 19-20).

proficiency among any large country's student population, and certainly not a country with 55 million students in its public schools[3] —and do not lead to any coherent and useful body of information about student learning that can inform educators' practice and work to the betterment of student learning. And, indeed, a flood of information shows disparities between "success" as measured by NCLB rules and by many other metrics that educators, parents, and policy makers have used to assess schools, such as a child's civic and community engagement, what children seem to know and be able to do in the world outside the standardized test, and the like.[4]

What all of the focus on testing has done is create a culture of testing that confuses what we might call diagnosis and treatment. In fact, over the past six years, even the "diagnosis" nominally available from test results has become suspect: the work of aligning assessments to content standards, and adjusting curriculum and instruction to support both content and assessment of its mastery was only just begun by 2000. It is a long and arduous process to move a state's education enterprise—curricula, teacher practices, assessments of learning, teacher preparation—to a new platform of integrated content and performance standards, particularly if the expectations are significantly higher for student learning than they have been in the past. The frenzy created by the national mandate for annual testing in reading and mathematics in every grade from 3–8 has created a devolution in assessment quality, and has made the systematic work of standards-based alignment and adjustment much more difficult to accomplish.

Norm-referenced shelf tests have been decorated in criterion-referenced (read standards-based) ruffles, teachers in many states have allocated extensive class time to test drills at the expense of standards-based curricula, and states with legitimate and sincere aspirations to raise the standards of student learning (like Florida, South Carolina, California, and Massachusetts) have been punished by having significant numbers of schools labeled as "failures" on the basis of AYP results. The decision

---

[3] Using NAEP grades 4, 8, and 12 mathematics data as a means to illustrate the stringency of the AYP requirements in NCLB, Linn examined the rates of increases that would be required to reach 100% proficiency by 2014 in selected states. Linn notes that all of the selected states recorded increases throughout the 1990s in the percentages of students scoring at the proficient level or above in all three grades. He then says, "As measured in this metric, however, the annual increases have been quite modest, averaging a little more than 1% at grades 4 and 8, and only a half of 1% at grade 12. Based on a straight-line projection of those rates of improvement, it would take 57 years for the percentage for grade 4 to reach 100. For grade 8 it would take 61 years and for grade 12 it would take 166 years. Looked at another way, the average annual rate of gain in percent proficient or above would have to increase by factors of 4, 4.3, and 11.8 at grades 4, 8, and 12, respectively, to reach 100% by 2014. Such rapid acceleration would be nothing short of miraculous." (Linn, 2003)

[4] See, for example, the October 12, 2008 article in the New York Times, "More Schools Miss the Mark, Raising Pressure" (K. Hussey), October 13, 2008 article in the New York Times headlined "Under 'No Child' Law, Even Solid Schools Falter" (Dillon, 2008) and the ongoing controversy on school "grades" in New York City as chronicled in the Education Week blog, Eduwonkette. And, specific to Florida, the July 8, 2008 article in the The Gradebook blog at TampaBay.com, entitled "School Grades Up, AYP Down."

by many states to make "proficiency" mean something achievable in this context—and thus not at all what students really need to know and be able to do—looks like common sense in this atmosphere of finger-pointing and labeling.[5]

Throughout all of this intense focus on "accountability" testing and the results of such testing, two critical supports for real improvement in public education for all students in the United States have been undermined. The first is attention to the fundamental inequities in the opportunity for students to learn across the United States public schools; these have simply been ignored. Ironically, NCLB has confirmed and publicized these inequities even as it has ignored their implications for leaving children, particularly children in poverty, behind. There is currently no conversation or debate about reviving the Opportunity to Learn Standards of the 1990s, which, whatever their inadequacies, at least tried to engage the root causes of differential performance among U.S. school children. NCLB has confirmed the shameful differences in student performance that persist along racial and socioeconomic fault lines in U.S. public education, but there has been no serious policy debate about what to do to change that performance profile. By implication, NCLB has made diagnosis of the persistent ills of the public education system sufficient; analytical investigation and treatment of those ills is not in the purview of the legislation.

The second critical support—clear and consistent performance standards that define both "minimum" and "excellent"—has been undermined by the proliferation of competing standards, all of which are deemed acceptable, no matter how they differ state to state. No real change can occur in public education and the educational attainment of public school students in the U.S. without sustained and thoughtful attention to *common* performance standards. Currently in the U.S. we have no idea what a high school diploma signifies in terms of what every student who attains the diploma knows and is able to do. We do not have even minimal commonly accepted frameworks for mathematics and reading grade-by-grade attainment. To be sure, lots of rhetoric argues for every student to take and pass algebra (for example), but such rhetoric is unconnected to systematic understanding and practice by educators in mathematics teaching from kindergarten on. By insisting on the myth of "100% proficiency" and by allowing each state to decide on its own definition of "proficient," NCLB has effectively corrupted the meaning of the terms. In practice, "proficient" means minimally competent in virtually every state, though what "minimal" means varies state by state. (See, e.g., Peterson and Hess, 2008.)

These two fundamental supports of an effective national public education system that aims to improve the educational attainment of all students need to be the focus of national education policy going forward. Unflinching and sustained attention to differential access to adequate teaching and learning opportunities and some common benchmarks for what constitutes at least the "good enough" floor for each stage of public education—Pre-K through grade 8, and grades 9–12 culminating in

---

[5] For a thorough examination of the problems of the exceptionally uneven playing field created by each state defining its own performance standards, see the report by Cronin et al. (2007) entitled *The Proficiency Illusion*.

a high school diploma —are cornerstones for both policy and implementation on the ground. This is old news. Inequities in the public education system in the U.S. and the absence of common benchmarks for student achievement across state lines have been staples in education policy debates for 25 years.

However, we face some new challenges in the U.S. The demographics of the U.S. public school student population are changing very rapidly: recent estimates suggest that by 2015, *5 years from now*, some 55% of all students in U.S. public schools will be children of poverty and/or living in households in which English is not the dominant language.[6] We already know that these demographic characteristics pose substantial barriers to student success in our current system of education. However, as a nation we have never faced the prospect of having the *majority* of our public school students characterized by these demographic variables. The long-term implications for the pipeline of students into post-secondary education and skilled jobs and careers are sobering. If we do not direct our resources into acting on what test results tell us about the unequal playing field that constitutes U.S. public education, then we face a future where insufficient numbers of young people entering the U.S. economy are prepared to maintain and grow the enterprises, public and private, that have assured U.S. citizens their very high standard of living.

4.2 Part II: What Would Be Better?

> It was impossible to get a conversation going, everybody was talking too much.
> –Yogi Berra

Some revision of No Child Left Behind appears to be inevitable. Presently, however, the voices of both state and national examiners of the effects of the legislation have focused on the impossibilities of the AYP calculations, the burden of expense imposed on states by the annual testing requirements, and the mixed messages delivered by the states' standardized tests against state standards as compared to NCLB AYP standards.[7] Robert Linn concludes a 2005 analysis of these mixed messages with this statement:

> If the goal for 2013–2014 remains unchanged, essentially all schools will fail to meet the unrealistic goal of 100% proficient or above, and No Child Left Behind will have turned into No School Succeeding. (Linn, 2005a, p. 14)

It is clear from all of this clamor that AYP requirements will be revisited and the calculation of the legislation's requirements somehow rationalized. Early indications of the direction intended by the new administration's Secretary of Education,

---

[6] See *Quality Counts 2009: Portrait of a Population* and *America's Perfect Storm* (Kirsch et al., 2007) for a detailed account of demographic change in the United States over the next two decades.

[7] In his conclusions Linn notes, "The goals established under NCLB are already unrealistic for many schools that started with low performance in 2002 and will become increasingly so, not only for those schools but for all schools as the increases in AYP targets occur" (Linn, 2005b).

Arne Duncan, suggest that the Department will attempt to link teacher evaluation
systems in the states with student test results and other indicators (like high school
graduation rates), and will pay increased attention to the disparities across state
boundaries in the rigor of state standards and tests.

If we are to make progress toward a uniform standard of educational achievement for all students in the U.S. public education system, thinking systemically
and systematically about what really affects the education outcomes for children
is essential. We have focused enormous attention on testing over the past 8 years,
but the result of all of that effort has been lots of data and little real information.
Results across states are not comparable, and we have come no closer to agreement on even minimum requirements for learning at each grade level, or even at
benchmark grade levels (like 4th, 8th, and 12th grades). We also have not assisted
teachers or those who prepare teachers in focusing their efforts on effective pedagogical content knowledge in the critical foundations of the domains. Yet without
some common ground in these areas—what test results really mean, what content
and skills must be mastered, how teachers can best use the time available to them to
assist students to these levels—we cannot change the status quo.

For the past 8 years a recurrent and justified complaint from the states has been
that the gap between the exigency of the NCLB requirements and the resources
available to assist states in both better testing and reforms based on the results of
the testing has made real progress impossible. That gap is no longer a fact. The
U.S. Department of Education in 2009 has at its disposal a record amount of money
(some $100 billion) to spend as a result of its share of the economic stimulus pack-
age (The American Recovery and Reinvestment Act of 2009 [Recovery Act]).[8] Four
"assurances" that the Department asserts "... make a critical contribution to student
results[9]" are the guiding principles for states' use of the stimulus funding:

- Making progress toward rigorous college- and career-ready standards and high-
quality assessments that are valid and reliable for all students, including English
language learners and students with disabilities
- Establishing pre-K-to-college and career data systems that track progress and
foster continuous improvement
- Making improvement in teacher effectiveness and in equitable distribution of
qualified teachers for all students, particularly students who are most in need
- Providing intensive support and effective interventions for the lowest-performing
schools

All four of these principles assume some common agreements that are not currently visible about knowledge and skills for both teachers and students. Indeed, at
present, no common basis exists on which a conversation could take place about

[8] See www.ed.gov/policy/gen/leg/recovery/index.html for an overview of the Department of
Education Recovery Act stimulus funding.
[9] www.ed.gov/policy/gen/leg/recovery/index.html, ARRA.pdf, slide5, notes

performance standards for all students, and the content and skills basis for those standards at each developmental level. Each constituent group has its own agenda and its own fix on some part of the challenge. Teachers, who are the only constituent group with direct effects on student learning, are at the mercy of whatever state policy governs their geographical location. Decisions about what are called "performance standards" have been made on the basis of political expediency in most states. And while many sets of state standards articulate sound and desirable scopes of content and skill mastery, the alignments among these standards and the accountability tests used by a given state are often perfunctory and mechanical at best. In the past 8 years, many teachers have simply worked backward from what is tested (and how it is tested) on the annual accountability assessments to decisions about scope and sequence. Rather than selecting fundamental pillars of a domain of learning as the "must do" foci of instruction, test specifications—the product of multiple considerations about what is feasible and affordable to test, not what is necessarily most important to know—have driven instructional decisions. And teachers almost never are afforded the opportunity to really learn to use assessment as a support for their instruction.

I believe that using NAEP—with some additions and revisions—affords us an opportunity to address this urgent need relatively efficiently. Without some agreed upon starting point for discussion of what students need to know and be able to do in reading and mathematics, we will never be able to address either inequities in access to opportunities to learn or defined levels of sufficient learning at each developmental level. One way we might deploy already existing resources to create these common agreements is to think more creatively about the use of NAEP assessment materials and data. Suppose that we were to use assessment materials and results *already available* in some new ways, directing some of the bountiful Recovery Act funds to analysis and implementation of these tools in multiple arenas? A full-scale assault on states' individual testing programs and the replacement of these programs with some national test is certainly doomed. However, since we have a national test in NAEP, why not think about how it might be used as a support for reform of state tests and standards?

At present, NAEP is designed to report overall trends in student achievement in the U.S. Data are gathered using an extremely complex matrix sampling plan, which ensures that *overall* trends in each state and each demographic category reported are accurate. What NAEP is not currently designed to do is to provide information on individual student performance, or even individual school performance. However, NAEP assessment tasks are widely acknowledged to be more sophisticated and powerful in design and evidence-gathering potential than virtually any in use in standardized accountability tests in the individual states. In addition, there is a wealth of useful information on the government's NCES website, that includes some 2,000 NAEP tasks, state by state disaggregated data over multiple years, background variable information about students and schools that is linked to state performance on NAEP, and much more.

How might NAEP assessment tasks and results be used for a new purpose focused on bringing all states up to a common standard? First, some analysis of the connections among the NAEP Frameworks for mathematics and reading at 4th, 8th and 12th grade levels, and states' own standards and tests must be completed. Such an analysis could indicate the extent of the alignment between NAEP and the states' content and performance standards. Second, serious rethinking of the NAEP performance standards and benchmarks in light of their potential use as national standards and benchmarks for all states and students should be undertaken, and those performance standards revised.[10] Third, thoughtful analysis of NAEP tasks and their connections to the domains of instruction should be undertaken *by teachers working with NAEP developers*. Clearly, a cross-analysis of the 50 sets of state content standards in mathematics and reading would converge on the critical framework for this instruction at the three grade levels.

Fourth, a set of equivalent tests of NAEP tasks sufficient for valid and reliable individual student reporting at 4th, 8th, and 12th grade levels in mathematics and literacy (reading and writing) should be assembled and used for all U.S. public school students to establish a baseline for achievement across all U.S. public school students. And fifth, the implications of NAEP tasks and performance levels for teacher preparation should be explored and applied by all teacher preparation institutions so that new practitioners have a concrete sense of the progression in student knowledge and skills that is expected across the K-12 continuum.

All of these steps are possible, and certainly steps one through three could be completed by 2011, the deadline for use of the non-renewable Recovery Act funding. And the cost of national benchmark testing for every student in 4th, 8th, and 12th grades would be much less than the cost of developing new state tests for every grade. More importantly, the value of using NAEP differently is in its power to establish connections across grade levels, across standards and performance benchmarks, across critical pieces of content domains. To put it differently, using NAEP as the foundation for comparable information about student learning in this fashion makes it possible to place assessment at the center of *learning*, its rightful home from which it is currently exiled.

Numerous obstacles must be recognized and then removed for the systematic use of NAEP results to serve as the basis for comparison not just of overall state by state performance levels, but of individual student achievement These obstacles are not immovable, and the promise of such an approach beyond formal interstate comparisons is very great. That such an existing wealth of assessment tools could serve as the foundation for an effort to integrate assessment—not just testing—with teaching needs to be at least seriously considered as we move forward to improve NCLB.

---

[10] For some insight into the evolution of the current "Basic/Proficient/Advanced" NAEP performance categories, and the reasons they cannot be used as currently designed for any national reporting of student-level results, see Bracey (2008) and Pellegrino et al. (1999).

4.3 Part III: Practical Solutions

In theory there is no difference between theory and practice. In practice there is.
–Yogi Berra

To demonstrate one specific positive consequence of implementing NAEP-based national benchmark testing, we need to think first about instruction, not testing. The most far-reaching and fundamental changes to the status of student achievement cannot be imposed by improving current assessment practices alone. If we do not inextricably ally assessment with instruction—as in what happens daily in each classroom—we will continue to enforce the separation of "tests" from instruction, and teachers will continue to see the tests as an external judge and jury. As Daniel Koretz pointed out in a recent conversation with an *Education Week* reporter, no one is paying much attention to the locus of instruction, the classroom. He said, "There is nobody involved in this system who has an incentive to look for good instruction anymore—all the incentives are lined up in one direction: Increase scores on the summative tests at any costs. We need to create a system in which somebody... has incentives to make sure we're not just gaming the system." (Cech, 2008, October 1. Testing Expert Sees 'Illusion of Progress' Under NCLB. *Education Week.* Retrieved September 19, 2009 from http://www.edweek.org/ew/articles/2008/10/01/06tests.h28.htm.?qs+Scott+Cech+October+2008.)

Exploration and investigation of explicit connections between assessment and instruction, which are critical to effective teaching and, thus, student learning have been peculiarly absent in the past 8 years. Instead, there has been an effort to make formal testing the most important influence in educational practice. The use of a single standardized test score as the driver not just of instructional practice and curriculum, but also the driver of judgments about teachers', educational leaders', and schools' effectiveness has weakened considerations of what actually happens, day to day, in schools. Every day, teachers plan and preside over instruction. Effective teachers do this with constant awareness of what is happening as a result of the instruction—they observe students and their responses and learning, they create opportunities for more demonstrations and practice. This is assessment.[11] Formal testing is one of many assessment modalities, and the annual standardized testing of students en masse is the assessment modality most removed from instruction.

Replacing the current culture of *testing* with a culture of *assessment* could create a fundamental shift in the ways educators approach the work of teaching and learning. There is no doubt that summative testing is here to stay. However, far more significant to the real work of education, which happens *in the classroom*, is the much larger set of activities that constitute learning and socialization. Assessment is a constant companion and support to effective instruction. Putting the principles of good assessment at the center of our preparation of new teachers, as well as the

---

[11] For a thoughtful discussion of the power of such formative assessment see, for example, Black and Wiliam (1998).

ongoing professional development of practicing teachers (and principals) could radically alter not only instructional practice, but also the attitudes and beliefs about
student learning that practitioners develop and deploy.[12] Currently, however, our
teacher preparation institutions and programs, domain-specific practitioner organizations (like National Council of Teachers of Mathematics and National Council
of Teachers of English), teacher organizations, and policy organizations do not
even agree about a vocabulary for discussing essential performance standards for
students, and the content and skills on which those performance standards rest.

Broadening the use of NAEP, so that the domain framework and attendant assessment tasks become common ground for all teachers in all states (connected to each
state's standards in explicit crosswalks), could create a basis for a national conversation and collaboration about the intersection of teaching, learning, and assessment.
Analysis of the progressive knowledge and learning connections in mathematics and
literacy from grades K-4, 4–8, and 8–12, as they would be assessed in the benchmark NAEP-based assessments, could lead to real engagement with some critical
teaching and learning issues. These include debates about learning progressions,
establishment of domain-specific content and skill frameworks, and—not least—
ongoing development of practitioners' knowledge about and practice of assessment
in the classroom. (Note, in this connection, the existing database of some 2,000
NAEP assessment tasks is a treasure trove from an instructional perspective.) These
conversations, were this common ground created, could be led by the national teachers' organizations, the accrediting bodies for teacher preparation institutions, and
organizations like the CCSSO[13] and the National Conference of State Legislators
that provide large-scale forums for education policy debate.

Specific performance benchmarks for all children across the U.S. can begin to
organize fruitful conversations about content and curriculum, and about the kinds
of pedagogical content knowledge that leads to students' success in meeting these
benchmarks. These periodic checks at grades 4, 8, and 12, on progress in student
learning not only can yield empirical evidence of the size of the gaps, if any, between
a state's own standards and accountability tests and proficiency levels, but also differential achievement in cohorts of students in different schools and districts within
a state. Empirical evidence that allows for comparison across all students in the public education system against a common set of performance standards prepares the
way for addressing inequities in educational opportunities for learning as well.

---

[12] For a sensible and thoughtful reflection on the primacy of teachers' judgments and assessments
in bolstering student achievement, see Barton, 1999, particularly pages 31–32. A fundamental shift
in the preparation of new teachers and the ongoing professional development of veteran teachers
would be a focus on defining the purpose for every teaching occasion in terms of what the desired
learning would actually look like—that is, what measurable and/or observable evidence of learning
is the goal? Once that is established, the "what shall I do" of the lesson becomes a process of
designing instruction, practice, and assessment to reach that goal.

[13] The CCSSO has already done extensive work in this area. See, for example, a new report
at www.ccsso.org/content/pdfs/Transforming Education - CCSSO discussion document.pdf. In
addition, the CCSSO has been at work on a common core standards project for some time; see
www.ccsso.org/federal_programs/13286.cfm

The kind of focused attention to common performance standards and the content and skills they embody is most important, however, because it would create an entry point for thoughtful consideration of teachers' practice. Purposeful shifts in teachers' practices—their uses of time, connections among parts of domains and across domains, implementation of teaching and learning strategies that have proven effective in other places with cohorts of students similar to theirs—is the real target of interest. Without analytical understanding and discussion of what goes on *in the classroom* we can look forward to few meaningful changes in student achievement. Well-designed and focused assessment tasks—as Lauren Resnick pointed out years ago—can serve as the axis around which fundamental changes in instruction can revolve. Indeed, on a national level, almost no other catalyst is as powerful as this one could be.

4.4 Part IV: Creating a Roadmap with a Destination

If you don't know where you are going, you might wind up someplace else.
                                                                    –Yogi Berra

The response of schools and teachers to the mandates of NCLB is instructive, and even promising. Linking accountability test results with both funding and public scrutiny is clearly a powerful motivator. What is missing at present is assessment that is worth teaching to, that allows for meaningful comparisons across the U.S., and that is connected with instruction in fundamental ways. Using NAEP content frameworks, tasks, and data differently offers the possibility of tests worth teaching to, and at least as important, the deployment of already existing public resources to assist in moving practitioners to a culture of assessment.

The ultimate achievement in the creation of an assessment culture among educators, what we might term "evidence-focused teaching," is very similar in its principles to the methodology for test design and development Russell Almond writes about in Chapter 6, this book. In this "evidence-centered design" methodology, we ask first what it is we want to measure—or, to put it another way, what it is we want to be able to say about someone's knowledge, skills, or abilities—and then articulate what the credible and sufficient evidence of such a claim about the person would be. Asking first what we want to be able to say about a person's learning, and only after we have satisfactorily articulated that, asking what we would regard as credible and sufficient evidence for saying that, is what turns most instructional planning on its head.

Thinking about assessment in this way reveals how little we can say about a student's learning status if we depend solely on standardized test results. Not only is the test itself a very limited sample of any learner's knowledge, it is a self-contained universe: we can talk about test scores in terms of the test and in terms of other test takers, but the world of instruction and the range of our aspirations for learning dwarfs the content of any standardized test.

Making the most of the time with learners is the province of the teacher, and it is s/he who is in the best position to gather, engender, and evaluate evidence. We have done very little to maximize the possibilities and promise of this naturally occurring phenomenon. But I believe that a systematic approach to focusing teacher preparation and professional development on a culture of assessment would yield enormous benefits for student learning—and, not incidentally, this would be evident in standardized test results.

However, this great shift cannot even be begun if we do not have some clear common understanding and agreement about what learning we are aiming to foster, and how the various stages of that learning are connected. Using not just NAEP assessment tasks, but the NAEP content domain and skills frameworks (however revised) and the performance standards (also revised), allows for a much more nuanced view of student learning. Creating a national assessment at three critical points in a student's schooling acknowledges a fact of human learning that annual standardized tests do not: learning is not linear and its effects resist efforts to discipline them into organized bits. Learning takes place in ill-structured fits and starts over a time continuum much less tidy than a school year.

Common benchmarks and content domain frameworks allow the professional *selection* of instructional strategies that have a much larger and more nuanced target than answering a sufficient number of this year's annual accountability test multiple choice questions correctly. If the most important goal in the NCLB legislation became a state's demonstration of real progress against the national benchmarks at 4th, 8th and 12th grade levels for all students, what schools might accomplish, and the ways they might go about accomplishing that could radically change. Not only could teachers plan and use data *across* grade levels, they could also begin to see the implications of mathematics and reading domain frameworks through all the content they teach.

Making assessment the axis of effective teaching, and preparing new teachers to think of assessment in this fashion, is fundamental to real change in student learning. Having a central critical focus—all of this is necessary, but not necessarily sufficient—would, at the very least, make it possible to begin to talk about evidence-centered teaching. It is a very unusual teacher who plans her assessment *before* s/he plans instruction. Indeed, most formal classroom assessment is an afterthought, and most teachers are ill-prepared to think systematically about assessment design and evaluation of assessment results. If, however, the first question teachers asked of themselves when planning instruction were "What will be the observable differences in what Jonathan, Rashid, Elena, or Sung can do after I teach *x*" instead of "What shall I do (usually meaning activities, assignments, content) tomorrow, this week, in this unit to teach *x*?" the clarity about the focus of each session with children would be greatly enhanced. This is so because knowing what you are looking for increases the chances of finding it.

In the case of teaching and learning, framing with some specificity what the observable evidence of students' learning in a particular topic or subject area should be generates the activities that will lead to that evidence. Having a clear sense of what learning looks like, what progress for a particular learner would be, can lead the teacher directly to those activities, assignments, and exercises that would yield that kind of evidence. And knowing the ultimate goal—what *must* students know and be able to do by a certain grade level—makes it possible to focus attention and time effectively. No one who has seen the four-inch binders of state content and skill standards given to teachers at every level would deny that such focus and selection in instruction is important.

Most teachers, particularly beginning teachers, begin in instructional design by deciding what they will "do" in a particular period of instruction. This is also the place much assessment design begins. Designing the task first, and figuring out later—if at all—what its purpose might have been or what evidence it may have yielded about the student's learning is an almost universal practice among teachers (and, truth be told, professional test makers). Changing the order of steps in instructional design, so that designing the actual activities that will take place during the lesson or sequence of lessons comes last is the single most powerful change that can be made to transform teaching. Control over what to do in class comes from analysis of why you are doing it and what you want to be able to say about its results.

What will we *do* during class? What kinds of activities should I get ready for tomorrow? How can I engage the students in this topic? What would be fun to read? How can I keep them occupied and engaged? What does the curriculum say comes next? These are the usual drivers of instructional planning for teachers.

If, however, teachers first figure out the purpose of each activity, and the learning goals each will further, and only then decide what to *do,* all of these questions become much less burdensome to answer. What activities the lesson should include, what the teacher should provide by way of instruction and resources, and—most importantly—what students should do and produce, is indicated by the teacher's analysis of what evidence she needs to support the claims she wishes to make after the instructional period is over.

The activities done in the classroom, the homework, the assignments—all of these produce evidence about student learning if they are carefully designed. And evidence of learning is exactly what the teacher wants to observe, encourage, and gather. If evidence of increased vocabulary is needed to support the claim to be made about a particular student or group of students, then clearly some activities, assignments, and resources devoted to developing vocabulary—and observation of how each part of the planned learning is progressing—are at the heart of the teacher's work with these children.

Assessing the status of a learner's vocabulary at the beginning of the period of instruction is stage one in the evidence-gathering process. Designing learning opportunities that will move him/her forward toward the desired claim becomes a shaping influence on the lesson design for the instructional period. And essential to the claim about the learner's vocabulary at the end of the instructional period is the teacher's provision of opportunities to *see* evidence of each learner's progress as a learner.

Imagine the effect if such an analytical planning process were oriented by common understanding of the critically important indicators of sufficient progress at selected developmental levels! Currently, most teachers experience their marching orders regarding curriculum as "everything not forbidden is compulsory." The only real guideline right now is the state accountability test, most often a single occasion, largely multiple-choice assessment that delivers a numerical judgment of the teacher's and school's effectiveness. We need to do better than this.

The implications of national content and performance standards that define the absolutely necessary content and both minimally acceptable and excellent performance would support not only effective instruction in the classroom, it would also profoundly alter the way teachers are prepared for the profession. While the current confused state of teacher preparation is the subject for a different paper, imagine the galvanizing effect of known and agreed-upon benchmarks for mathematics and reading at 4th, 8th, and 12th grade levels on what beginning teachers need to know and be able to do.

4.5 Conclusion

The Future Ain't What It Used to Be

–Yogi Berra

The challenges that will face the public education enterprise in the U.S. in the next two decades are formidable. In the spring of 2009, the cohort of 18-year-olds in the U.S. population peaked, and the number of young people in the U.S. population steadily declines for the foreseeable future.[14] In addition, however, the patterns of population growth are changing, and they will fundamentally alter the tasks of teaching and learning. An increasing number of public school children will come from families whose first language is not English, many of whom face the challenge of marginal incomes or outright poverty.[15]

The difficulties we face now, in 2010, with high school graduation rates stagnant since the 1970s (Barton, 2005), persistent achievement gaps among subgroups in the population, and mediocre showings in international student assessments, pale in comparison to those about to envelop our education enterprise. We will not fulfill the promise of free public education for all of our children, which is the promise of possibility and prosperity for anyone who is willing to work at learning in the U.S., if we continue to do what we have always done.

An analog for the inevitable disappointments that will attend continuing to practice testing as if it were more than a diagnostic tool—as if it were, indeed, itself an end and not a means—is the fate of technology in U.S. schools. In a decade in which the advances in technology have transformed the world's economy, the ways people create, access, and synthesize information, and, experts speculate, even cognitive processes themselves, instructional practice in U.S. schools has remained virtually unchanged from 50 years ago. A teacher from the 1950s would not find herself

[14] *American's Perfect Storm, pp. 19–20.*

[15] See *America's Perfect Storm* for a detailed analysis of the interaction among changes in the economy, demographic trends, and the persistent divergence in skill distribution among groups in the U.S. population.

uncomfortable with the instructional tools in use in most classrooms today, even though we have spent untold dollars on computers and technology-based instructional software. The stunning absence of the effects of advances in technology on the actual daily work of teachers illustrates the power of habit and culture, of course. But it also illustrates the absence of any sustained practice of evidence or inquiry as the basis for educating children. Technology has failed to profoundly alter educational practice because we have not asked the right questions. And those questions center on the exploration of what it is we want to aim for first, before we fall in love with the projectile we have for its own sake. Shifting from a culture of testing to a culture of assessment could profoundly change both the methods and the effects of instruction (just as technology promised to do, and has done, outside the world of "school"). It will not happen without profound shifts in emphasis and policy, however.

Aiming at learning demands that we first pay serious attention to what the critical learning accomplishments are, and what they look like as they unfold, before we decide how to accomplish or measure them. This is very hard work, and we have not yet done it. Until we do, we will not succeed in altering the outcomes for children.

The implications of creating a national set of benchmarks and performance standards are also profound for those who prepare teachers to enter the profession. Not only would there be some consistency in what beginning teachers need to know and be able to do in the domains of mathematics and reading, especially for K-8 teachers, there would also be the hope of shifting the culture of teacher preparation to a more evidence-centered approach to teaching and learning. This would mean that university faculty would need to alter their practices and, in many cases, bolster their own learning. Indeed, establishing common goals for all students regardless of where they live in the U.S., has a better chance of putting us on the road to understanding of the learning process than any other single change we could make.

References

Barton, P. (1999). *Too much testing of the wrong kind; too little of the right kind in K-12 education.* Princeton, NJ: Policy Information Center, Educational Testing Service.

Barton, P. (2005). *One third of a nation: Rising dropout rates and declining opportunities.* Princeton, NJ: Policy Information Center, Educational Testing Service.

Black, P., & Wiliam, D. (1998). Inside the black box: Raising standards through classroom assessment. *Phi Delta Kappan, 80*(2), 139–148.

Bracey, G. W. (2008). Cut scores, NAEP achievement levels and their discontents: the attempts of political bodies to bludgeon public schools with arbitrary performance standards. *School Administrator, 65*(6), 48–56.

Cech, S. J. (2008, October 1). Testing expert sees "Illusions of Progress" under NCLB. *Education Week., 28*(6), p.8.

Cronin, J., Dahlin, M., Adkins, D., & Kingsbury, G. G. (2007). *The proficiency illusion.* Washington, DC: Thomas B. Fordham Institute.

Dillon, S. (2008, October 13). Under 'No Child' law, even solid schools falter. *New York Times.*

http://blogs.edweek.org/edweek/eduwonkette(n.d.).

http://www.ed.gov/policy/gen/leg/recovery/index.html. (n.d.)

http://www.ccsso.org/content/pdfs/Transforming Education. (n.d.)

http://www.ccsso.org/federal_programs/13286.cfm

Hussey, K. (2008, October 12). More schools miss the mark, raising pressure. *New York Times.*

Kirsch, I., Braun, H., Yamamoto, K., & Sum, A. (2007). *America's perfect storm: Three forces changing our nation's future.* Princeton, NJ: Policy Information Center, Educational Testing Service.

Lewis, M. (2003). *Moneyball: The art of winning an unfair game.* New York: W. W. Norton.

Linn, R. (1995). *Assessment-based reform: Challenges to educational measurement.* Princeton, NJ: Educational Testing Service.

Linn, R. (2000). Assessments and accountability. *Educational Researcher, 29,* 4–16.

Linn, R. (2003). Accountability: Responsibility and reasonable expectations. *Educational Researcher, 32,* 3–12.

Linn, R. L. (2005a). *Adjusting for differences in tests.* Washington, DC: National Academy of Sciences.

Linn, R. (2005b). Conflicting demands of No Child Left Behind and state systems: Mixed messages about school performance. *Education Policy Analysis Archives, 13*(33). Retrieved July 7, 2010 from http://epaa.asu.edu/epaa/v13n33/.

Pellegrino, J., Jones, L., & Mitchell, K. (1999). *Grading the nation's report card: Evaluating NAEP and transforming the assessment of educational progress.* Washington, DC: National Academy Press.

Peterson, P. E., & Hess, F. M. (2008). Few states set world-class standards. *Education Next, 8*(3).

Porter, A. (1994). *The uses and misuses of opportunity to learn standards.* Brookings Institution conference, Beyond Goals 2000: The Future of National Standards in American Education, Washington DC.

Resnick, L., & Resnick, D. (1992). Assessing the thinking curriculum: New tools for educational reform. In B. R. Gifford & M. C. O'Connor (Eds.), *Changing assessments: Alternative views of aptitude, achievement and instruction* (pp. 37–75). Boston, MA: Kluwer Academic Publishers.

Shepard, L., Glaser, R., Linn, R., & Bohrnstedt, G. (1993). *Setting performance standards for student achievement: A report of the National Academy of Education Panel of the evaluation of the NAEPtrial State Assessment: An evaluation of the 1992 achievement levels.* Stanford, CA: Stanford University, National Academy of Education.

Solochek, J. S. (2008, July 8). School grades up, AYP down. *The Gradebook @ TampaBay.com*

Chapter 5
Sharpening the Aim: Making Strides to Create an Assessment Culture in Schools

Lynn Wicker

Abstract This chapter is in response to Mari Pearlman's chapter, Aiming at Learning: Assessment as the Critical Link. Viewing assessment as a critical link to learning is an assertion strongly supported through my experiences in the field. There must be a significant shift in thinking and practices of teachers, as well as school leaders, to strengthen this link. The suggestion that National Assessment Tasks from NAEP be used to develop a focal point using national benchmarks rather than just state level standards is also supported. The creation of a culture of assessment in any classroom and school is indeed a challenging venture, but one that must be engaged in routinely and with precision. The evidence focused teaching approach is advocated in which teachers use real-time, multiple assessments of their students and plan targeted interventions that address students' learning gaps.

Keywords Assessment culture · Evidenced focused teaching · Standards and assessments

5.1 Part I: Current State: My Perspective

The idea of aiming at learning and viewing assessment as the critical link to learning resounded clearly with me as an educational leader. I've had an interest in assessment for quite a long time, having focused my doctoral research, over 10 years ago, on authentic performance-based assessments and the impact of targeted professional development on teachers' assessment practices. Pearlman's paper raises new and interesting questions about assessment and learning.

L. Wicker (✉)
Florida State University Schools, Inc., Tallahassee, FL, USA
e-mail: lwicker@admin.fsu.edu

Pearlman states, ". . . the imposition of unrealistic goals through Adequate Yearly Progress, the culture of punishment of schools and teachers that such target shooting creates, and the persistent refusal to recognize the disparity of expectations, standards, and test rigor across different states have led to perverse results that have weakened the links between assessment and learning." (Pearlman, Chapter 4). In my experience as a school administrator since 1994, I have witnessed firsthand the dramatic shift to a focus on testing and accountability and the simultaneous weakening of links between assessment and learning. Principals and teachers have been inundated with mounds and mounds of student achievement data from testing, but are often unsure of what to do with it all. We've all been immersed in professional development on how to review and understand the data, how to analyze the data and even how to identify and use instructional interventions with our students who are struggling. However, I have not yet witnessed a strong shift to the practice and culture of evidence-focused teaching which Pearlman advocates. She says,

> Changing the order of steps in instructional design, so that designing the actual activities that will take place during the lesson or sequence of lessons comes last is the single most powerful change that can be made to transform teaching. Control over what to do in class comes from analysis of why you are doing it and what you want to be able to say about its results (Pearlman, Section 4.4).

Making this type of shift in the thinking and practices of teachers is, in part, the work of everyone in a school or district collectively, but also it is critical that the leadership in schools and districts have a deep understanding of the need for this change in the order of thinking and working. A deep understanding involves school leaders possessing a working knowledge of both instructional strategies and student progress monitoring to help guide teachers in making this shift in professional practice. Strong instructional leadership coupled with what Pearlman describes as ongoing professional development of practicing teachers (and principals), would most certainly begin to transform instructional practice as well as what teachers believe and know about student learning.

Pearlman's historical recounting of testing practices in public education in the United States is evidence of the almost experimental approach to addressing the question, "What is the point of testing children using standardized testing tools?" Teachers and school administrators have experienced decades of changes in approaches to testing. Practitioners have been trained in the Continuous Improvement Model, School Reform models, Effective Schools Research and countless other approaches to the use of testing, transforming schools and student achievement outcomes. Pearlman suggests that "throughout all of this intense focus on accountability testing and the results of such testing, two critical foundations of real improvement in public education for all students in the United States have been undermined" (Pearlman, Section 4.1). The existence of fundamental inequities for students in opportunities to learn continues to be a barrier for real improvement in public education. Real improvement is also thwarted by a lack of clear and consistent performance standards that define both "minimum" and "excellent". It is laudable that individual states have developed performance standards with their own definitions of proficiency, but without some degree of standardization across states, it is impossible to make comparative statements about percentages of students across the country attaining proficiency in math and reading when the standards and even the measures are inconsistent. Once again, intense confusion is created for teachers and school administrators who are trying to work to achieve national proficiency expectations for student achievement. If the United States is serious about increasing the level of academic proficiency of students and reaching the No Child Left Behind targets by 2014, then having national standards and performance expectations should be part of the plan.

5.2 Part II: What Would Be Better? Aim Higher Using National Assessment of Educational Progress (NAEP) Assessment Tasks

Which of the following two options would better serve our educational needs: To remain confused, disillusioned and focused on the mathematical impossibilities of reaching No Child Left Behind targets by 2014, or to actually begin conversations about Pearlman's suggestion that we use National Assessment Tasks from NAEP to develop a focus for educators? This focus would link what students are learning with national benchmarks and give teachers immediate and ongoing information about how their students are doing, throughout the school year.

To bring the question closer to home: Has Florida gone far enough with its current focus on State content and assessment standards? The stage has been set in Florida for employing a systematic approach that utilizes Sunshine State Standards and the Florida Comprehensive Assessment Tests (FCAT). However, I would still like to explore the use of the NAEP Assessment Tasks and the move towards an evidence-centered approach to instructional practice. I am in total agreement with Pearlman "That such an existing wealth of assessment tools could serve as the foundation for an effort to integrate assessment—not just testing—with teaching needs to be at least seriously considered as we move forward to improve NCLB" (Pearlman, Section 4.2).

5.3 Part III: A Culture of Assessment

Pearlman asserts that, " If we do not inextricably ally assessment with instruction—as in what happens daily in each classroom—we will continue to enforce the separation of tests from instruction, and teachers will continue to see the tests as an external judge and jury" (Pearlman, Section 4.3). As instruction occurs in classrooms each day, teachers make informal judgments about what their students know and what remains to be learned. This activity is always running in the background—perhaps not obvious to the casual onlooker.

Assessments should never be an afterthought or an "add on" to any type of instructional work. Including serious thinking about appropriate assessments during the beginning stages of instructional planning is a powerful way to increase the effectiveness of teachers as they wonder about the success and impact of their teaching. Teachers have a much better sense of the impact of their instruction if they first consider appropriate assessments in the planning stage. The creation of a culture of assessment in any classroom and school are indeed challenging ventures, but ones that must be engaged in routinely and with precision.

So what does a school that has a culture of assessment look like? Culture, in general, includes a broad swath of behaviors, beliefs, values, and symbols that a group accepts, usually without thinking about them. Using this definition, what we'd expect to see in a school with a culture of assessment would be behaviors that include teachers planning lessons with the end in mind of what they want students to be able to know and do, as well as determining the methods to use that would provide evidence that such learning has taken place. Teachers would routinely use multiple forms of assessments throughout the school year, capitalizing on the value of formative feedback that will, in turn, inform their teaching, interventions, and future assessments. Observing these consistent assessment behaviors could indicate that teachers believe in and value the effective use of assessments to inform their instruction. Assessment artifacts and work samples that have new significance to teachers become symbols of the culture of assessment. The cycle continues with a sense of automaticity that this culture embodies. Cultures are never born overnight, and a culture of assessment is certainly no different.

5.4 Part IV: Evidence Focused Teaching

Two of the most important questions that educators can ask are, What knowledge, skills and abilities do we want students to have, and how will we know that they have them? These questions are fundamental in the teaching/learning process as we seek to provide evidence to support claims that learning has taken place.

Classroom teachers who have engaged in meaningful professional development on the use of assessments as well as how to analyze, interpret and use data, are ahead of the curve in being able to provide evidence that student learning has taken place. Teachers should certainly be using multiple assessment measures to plan for targeted interventions. Helping teachers connect what they learn from student achievement data and informal assessments to appropriate interventions is paramount to creating this culture of assessment.

The evidence focused teaching approach that Pearlman describes in her chapter is another way of saying that teachers should be using real-time, multiple assessments of their students and then planning targeted interventions that address students' learning gaps. This takes a lot of effort and expertise to accomplish, but should be viewed as non-negotiable in the instructional process.

Pearlman believes, "that a systematic approach to focusing teacher preparation and professional development on a culture of assessment would yield enormous benefits for student learning" (Section 4.4). It is encouraging to note that the teacher preparation programs in the College of Education at Florida State University are all engaged in meaningful assessment practices for their teacher education candidates. Their wide array of assessment focused experiences, as well as an overall assessment system culture, is creating dynamic shifts in the teaching practices of novice teachers.

The faculty in teacher preparation courses and programs at FSU assess critical tasks of the candidates, in which they look at multiple sources of evidence that demonstrate subject matter competence as well as pedagogical competence. The Florida Department of Education's Teacher Education program approval process requires that all programs focus on an assessment system that is comprehensive and continuous over the course of the teacher candidate's program. This focus on assessment is providing rich data to drive the continuous improvement of the teacher education programs as well as to document an impact on student learning.

5.5 Conclusion

The evidence is in: change is here to stay. Changes in demographics, student learning needs, and evolving assessment technologies available to teachers are forces to be noted. Important decisions must be made every day in schools and classrooms about which assessments to use and what should be done with what is learned from those assessments. Advocating for creating cultures of assessment in schools is a positive first step to connect assessments back to instruction.

We have a long way to go in classrooms, schools and school districts towards attaining a vibrant culture of assessment. Embracing the value of professional development for teachers in the use of assessments, as well as nurturing a culture of assessment in both schools and in pre-service teacher education programs are great places to begin the journey. Powerful learning emanates from powerful planning paired with appropriate assessments.

Chapter 6
Using Evidence Centered Design to Think About Assessments

Russell G. Almond

Abstract Evidence-centered assessment design (ECD) provides a simple principle as the basis of assessment design: assessment tasks should be designed to provide evidence of the claims which the assessment designers wish to make about the examinees. This paper looks at the Bayesian model of evidence which underlies much of the ECD philosophy. It then goes on to explore how the ECD principle can help assessment designers think about three important issues in the future of assessment: (1) How can we organize evidence about student performance gathered from diverse sources across multiple time points? (2) How should we balance information gathered about multiple aspects of proficiency? (3) How should we collect evidence from complex tasks? The chapter illustrates these ideas with some examples of advanced assessments that have used ECD.

Keywords Evidence-centered assessment design · Decision analysis · Constructed response · Diagnostic assessment

6.1 A Language for Talking About New Kinds of Assessments

In early 1997, Bob Mislevy, Linda Steinberg, and I began a series of meetings about what we would later come to call *Evidence-Centered Assessment Design* (ECD; Mislevy, Steinberg, & Almond, 2003). Our goal was to create a language that would encompass both high-stakes selection/placement assessments currently in use and new emerging types of assessments, such as simulation-based assessments and portfolio assessments. To that end, we invented terms for aspects of assessment design that were often glossed over because of hidden assumptions about purpose, format, and delivery environment. In some cases, we deliberately avoided established terms

R.G. Almond (✉)
Research and Development, Educational Testing Service, Princeton, NJ, USA
e-mail: ralmond@ets.org; almond@acm.org

V.J. Shute, B.J. Becker (eds.), *Innovative Assessment for the 21st Century*,
DOI 10.1007/978-1-4419-6530-1_6, © Springer Science+Business Media, LLC 2010

in order to encourage assessment designers to think more broadly about assessment. For example, we avoided the common term *item* in favor of new terms *task* and *observable*, because these could encompass traditional multiple-choice tests as well as item sets, simulation tasks, and portfolio assessments.

This chapter uses the language of ECD (Section 6.3) to explore some of the issues that will arise in developing new kinds of assessments. In particular, it looks at three issues that have arisen in recent assessment design projects: integrating assessment results from diverse sources and across time (Section 6.4), designing assessment which taps multiple aspects of proficiency (Section 6.5), and working with complex constructed response tasks (Section 6.6). Section 6.2 looks at the mathematical treatment of evidence, which lies at the heart of much of assessment design. Readers looking for more information and discussion about ECD than is presented here are invited to visit the ECD Wiki (http://ecd.ralmond.net/ecdwiki/ECD/ECD/). In particular, http://ecd.ralmond.net/ecdwiki/ECD/Exercises/ offers a set of discussion problems.

6.2 The Mathematics of Evidence

Although we tried to make ECD neutral to the model used for scoring the assessment, ECD works most naturally when we think about evidential reasoning in a Bayesian way (Schum, 1994). The key idea is that our state of information about an unknown proposition or claim can be represented by a probability distribution. When additional evidence about that claim is received, then the state of information can be updated using Bayes theorem. Section 6.2.1 reviews this idea in more detail. Section 6.2.2 expands the Bayesian model of evidence to define the *weight of evidence*—the evidentiary value of a given piece of evidence. Section 6.2.3 describes *influence diagrams*—a tool for evaluating how evidence is used in making decisions.

6.2.1 Bayesian Model of Evidence

In ECD, the purpose of an assessment is defined, in part, through the *claims* we wish to make about an examinee on the basis of the outcomes. A claim is a statement about an examinee whose truth we wish to establish, for example: "Anne Alias has sufficient mathematical skills to take the Algebra I course."

In order for a claim to be useful, it must pass the *clarity test* (Howard & Matheson, 1981b). The purpose of the clarity test is to avoid problems caused by ambiguity in the wording of definitions for variables. Unfortunately, "sufficient mathematical skills to take the Algebra I course" does not pass the clarity test. The usual way to address that problem is to consider a hierarchical breakdown of the skill. For example, we could start by breaking Mathematics down into the five content strands defined in the National Assessment of Educational Progress (NAEP). Then, for each of the strands, we would need to be specific about what concepts and procedures the student would need to have mastered. Rarely is it practical to resolve all ambiguity in the claims, but enough ambiguity needs to be resolved so that the design team can work without misdirected effort or communication problems among team members.

Let C be a claim, and let $P(C)$ be the probability that the claim holds for a randomly chosen student from the target population for the assessment. This is known as the *prior* probability for the claim. Often this can be derived from population statistics for the target population, or a sufficiently close proxy (e.g., last year's examinees).

Let e represent some piece of evidence related to this claim, and let $P(e|C)$ represent the probability of observing that evidence when the claim holds and $P(e|\overline{C})$ represent the probability of observing that evidence when the claim does not hold. These two probabilities are sometimes called the *likelihood* of the evidence. Given the prior and the likelihood, we can update our beliefs about the claim holding for the student using Bayes' theorem:

$$P(C|e) = \frac{P(e|C)P(C)}{P(e|C)P(C) + P(e|\overline{C})P(\overline{C})}. \tag{1}$$

The updated probability, $P(e|C)$ is called the *posterior* probability.

The distinction between *data* and *evidence* becomes clearer in this mathematical framework. Data become evidence when they are linked to a claim or hypothesis through the likelihood. Data provide good evidence when the difference between $P(e|C)$ and $P(e|\overline{C})$ is large. The weight of evidence quantifies that difference.

6.2.2 Weight of Evidence

Good (1950, 1985) defines the *weight of evidence* that e provides for C as

$$W(C:e) = \log \frac{P(e|C)}{P(e|\overline{C})}. \tag{2}$$

Thus, the kinds of task that provide good evidence are ones in which the probability of a good outcome given that the claims hold is high, and the probability of a good outcome given that the claims do not hold is low. Applying Bayes theorem (just the numerator of Equation (1) is needed as the denominator cancels out) to both the numerator and denominator of Equation (2) produces an alternative definition of the weight of evidence:

$$W(C:e) = \log \frac{P(C|e)}{P(\overline{C}|e)} - \log \frac{P(C)}{P(\overline{C})}. \tag{3}$$

In this second definition, the weight of evidence is the difference between the posterior log odds that the claim holds and the prior log odds. Thus, good evidence is evidence that produces a big change in the probability distributions.

Now consider an observable outcome from a task, E, which we have not yet observed. Assume it could take on one of the values $e_1, \ldots, e_k$. Good and Card (1971) define the *expected weight of evidence* that E provides for C as

$$EWOE(C : E) = \sum_{e \in E} W(C : e)P(e \,|\, C). \qquad (4)$$

This is just the expected value of the weight of evidence, where for technical reasons the expectation is taken over the conditional distribution when the claim holds.

Madigan and Almond (1995) propose using the expected weight of evidence for selecting "tests" in the context of medical diagnosis. Shute, Hansen, and Almond (2008) use this method for task selection in an Assessment *for* Learning system called ACED (Adaptive Content for Evidence-based Diagnosis), which provided informative feedback after failed attempts at problem solving. In its adaptive mode, ACED always presented the task that had the highest expected weight of evidence for overall proficiency. Interestingly, students using ACED with both adaptive task selection and elaborated feedback showed significant gains pre-test to post-test, while students in other groups did not. Although this may have been related to the size of the sample, it also may be that tasks that have high expected weights of evidence are in the student's zone of proximal development (Vygotsky, 1978) and hence have high value for both learning and assessment.

6.2.3 Influence Diagrams

Another measure related both conceptually and mathematically to the expected weight of evidence is the *Value of Information* (Matheson, 1990). The easiest way to describe this measure it through a graphical notation for decision problems called *influence diagrams* (Howard & Matheson, 1981a). Influence diagrams are an extension of Bayesian networks (used to represent evidence in educational contexts by Mislevy, 1994; Almond & Mislevy, 1999; Mislevy et al., 2003, and in other places), adding to the Bayesian network special nodes to represent decisions and the value of outcomes.

Figure 6.1 shows a typical influence diagram. The diagram contains three types of nodes representing different kinds of variables:

- *Chance nodes (Circles).* These represent variables that cannot be directly controlled by the decision maker. The arrows pointing into these nodes represent factors that influence their values. To complete the influence diagram, we must specify the probability distribution for the chance variable given its parents (nodes pointing to it) in the graph. In the example (Fig. 6.1), the distribution of the SKILL AT END OF COURSE is conditional on SKILL AT TESTING TIME and the chosen SKILL INTERVENTION. The distribution of TEST RESULT is conditioned on both SKILL AT TESTING TIME and SELECTED TEST. The distribution of SKILL AT TESTING TIME is unconditional (no parents in the graph).

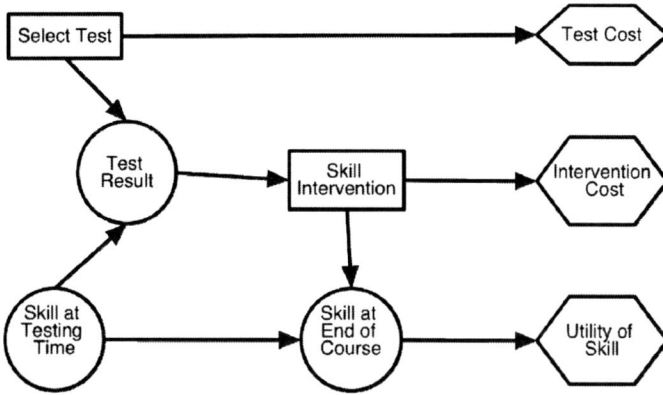

Fig. 6.1 Influence diagram for calculating value of information for a placement test

- *Decision nodes (Rectangles).* These represent variables that can be directly controlled by the decision maker. The arrows pointing into these nodes represent values that are known to the decision maker at the time the decision is made. In the example graph, the TEST RESULT is known when the SKILL INTERVENTION decision is made, but no information (other than general population information) is known when the SELECT TEST decision is made.
- *Utility nodes (Hexagons).* These represent the (un)desirability of the outcomes. The node UTILITY OF SKILL represents the relative value of possible skill states the student could wind up in. This would of necessity include both the desirability of learning the skill for its own sake and the future ability to learn additional skills that it unlocks. The INTERVENTION COST and TEST COST represent the different costs for different instructional and testing options. Note that these costs include both financial costs and the opportunity cost of taking the student away from other instruction.

While decision nodes are conceptually simple, utilities hide a subtle complexity. In particular, it is often difficult to get the costs and rewards into the same units so one can be traded for the other. For instance, what costs (whether in terms of money or class time) are we willing to incur, in order to get a student from the basic to the proficient level in one skill? Further, are we willing to potentially put other students at risk by inappropriately giving them remedial instruction? Adding to the complexity is the fact that in most public education contexts, the decision maker is a community; the members of that community may place different relative values on different outcomes. In many cases, however, the outcome is clear for a broad range of utility functions and exact utilities are not needed.

Influence diagrams offer a way to approach the question of whether the evidence is worth gathering, or more specifically: "How much should an educator be willing to pay for a diagnostic assessment administered at Time 1?" Obviously, the educator wants to get enough value out of the subsequent educational decisions to offset the costs (both monetary and lost instruction time) of the diagnostic testing. The added value from the test is known as the value of information (Matheson, 1990).

As a baseline, consider a simplified model without the diagnostic test (Fig. 6.2). Here the educator has no basis for making the instructional decisions other than the population information inherent in the probability tables underlying the influence diagram. Therefore, the optimal intervention will be the same for all students, producing a one-size-fits-all policy. If the chosen policy works reasonably well for a reasonable number of students, then this option might be sufficient. If the diagnostic test is to add value to the system, it must be able to beat this straw model.

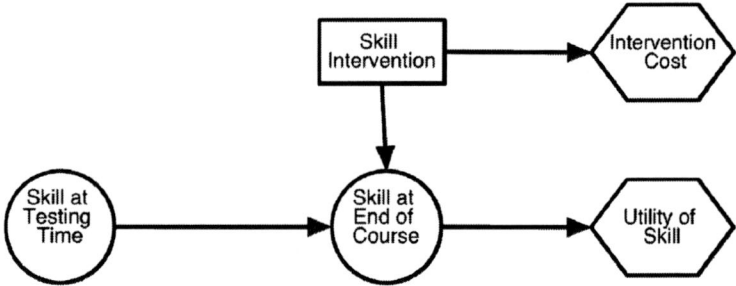

Fig. 6.2 Simplified model without placement test

Now consider the perfect information model shown in Fig. 6.3. Here we assume that the students' exact knowledge states are magically determined and uploaded into the educator's computer. The educator should then be able to make the optimal decision for each student. This should have a higher expected utility than the no information model (although the cost of implementing a conditional decision might be higher).

The difference between the expected utility from the model in Fig. 6.3 and the model in Fig. 6.2 is the value of perfect information. This is an upper bound on what the educator should pay for the diagnostic test. The test may not be necessary. For example, consider a teacher deciding between two sets of educational material. It may be that only one of the two sets of material will help students meet the teacher's

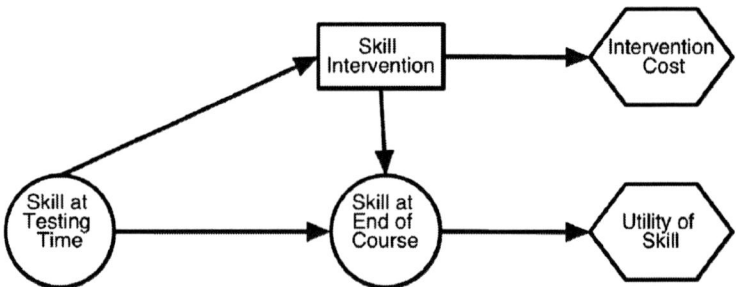

Fig. 6.3 Perfect information (initial skill state known)

goal. Or it could be that both sets of material have roughly equivalent effects in moving students towards the goal, in which case the teacher would make the decision on the basis of cost or other considerations. Additional information about the student proficiency would not be useful in either case. The problem here is that the decision space is impoverished (the teacher does not have a broad enough selection of options) and no assessment, now matter how good, will make a difference.

The difference between the expected utility from the no information model (Fig. 6.2) and the diagnostic testing model (Fig. 6.1) is the value of information. This is what the educator should be willing to pay for a particular diagnostic test. The influence diagram describes a possible interpretation for the assessment. The value of information provides a quantitative measure of the validity of that interpretation. Tests are useful to educators and should be adopted by them to the extent that they help them make instructional decisions and improve their educational outcomes. Unless the information provided by the assessment is aligned with the decision that an educator must make, then building more reliable assessments does not add value for the educator.

6.3 The Evidence-Centered Design (ECD) Models

As Evidence-Centered Assessment Design is described in a number of other publications, this section will offer only a brief review. Mislevy et al. (2003) provide a complete exposition of the theory and Mislevy, Steinberg, Almond, and Lukas (2006) provide an accessible introduction. This section provides only a brief review.

In ECD, the completed design for an assessment program is called the *Conceptual Assessment Framework* (CAF). It is a collection of design objects called "models." A complete CAF requires at least one of all of the types of models shown in Fig. 6.4 (and usually contains many task and evidence models and sometimes more than one model of the other types). Figure 6.4 also captures the most important relationships among the models.

Briefly, the most important functions of the six models are as follows:

- *Student Proficiency Model.*[1] The most important job of this model is to define a number of proficiency variables, S, and to provide an initial (population) distribution over the possible proficiency profiles, $P(S)$. This provides the prior for Bayes theorem. Reportable scores are statistics of this distribution. The claims are very important to the proficiency model because they help define the proficiency variables.
- *Evidence Model.* This model describes how the work products obtained from students attempting tasks (as described in the task models) are used to update the distribution over the possible proficiency profiles. This is usually broken up into

---

[1] This model has been called the *Student Model, Proficiency Model* and *Competency Model* in various ECD publications.

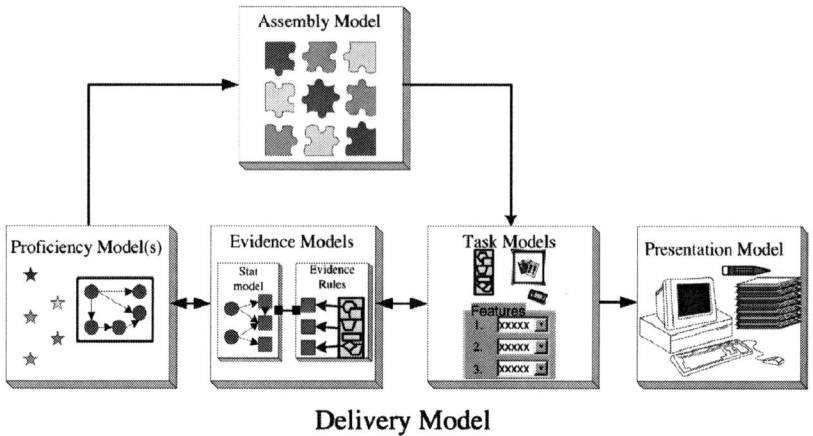

Delivery Model

Fig. 6.4 ECD conceptual assessment framework (CAF)

two parts: (a) the *rules of evidence*, which provide a scoring rubric for how to set the *observable outcome variables*, **E**, from a student work product, and (b) the statistical model, which provides the likelihood for Bayes theorem, $P(\mathbf{E}|\mathbf{S})$.

- *Task Model*. This model describes a situation under which valid evidence can be gathered. The task model variables represent manipulable aspects of that situation. These can either be directly manipulated by the task authors (e.g., picking numbers for a math problem) or indirectly manipulated by choosing stimulus material (e.g., picking a reading passage which then determines the semantic density of the text). Mislevy, Steinberg, and Almond (2002) describe many ways that task model variables can affect the evidentiary properties of the assessment.

- *Assembly Model*. This model controls how many tasks of what kinds are needed to constitute a valid form of the assessment. This could be instructions for assembling forms, similar to traditional test specifications, or in the case of adaptive tests, rules for pool construction, selecting tasks from the pool, and terminating the assessment. This model is sometimes omitted in treatments of ECD but it plays an important role in determining the effective meaning of the proficiency variables. For example, consider a variable labeled UNDERSTANDS GRAPHS AND TABLES. If one form of the assessment provided a student with only graph tasks and no table tasks, the effective meaning of the variable would be different than the meaning its name implies. A rule specifying the minimum of each task type could fix that problem.

- *Presentation Model*. This model describes how various tasks will be displayed to the examinee. It has proven to be very useful for international assessment where computer versions of the test are given in some locations and paper and pencil in others (depending on computer and power availability, and security concerns). Increasingly, test designers are interested in the possibility of task presentation on handheld devices (PDAs and smart phones). However, they need to consider when an alternative form of presentation changes the nature of the task (e.g., trying to scroll an extended text passage on a mobile phone).

- *Delivery Model.* This is a catchall for important design constraints that are not captured in other parts of the system. For example, ID requirements for the examinees. If the person who sits for the exam is not the same as the one for whom the score is reported, this is a serious challenge to the basic evidentiary argument.

The ECD models were very much designed with the idea of using the Bayesian paradigm to represent evidence (although ECD can be stretched to encompass some commonly used scoring models, such as counting the number of correct items). Almond and Mislevy (1999) describe a simple Bayesian model for scoring. When Student i sits for the assessment, a copy of the student proficiency model is made for that student. This is represented as a probability distribution $P(\mathbf{S}_i)$, where $\mathbf{S}_i$ is the proficiency profile for Student i. Now suppose, we observe evidence $\mathbf{E}_{ij}$ from Student i interacting with Task j. The evidence model for Task j, provides us with $P(\mathbf{E}_{ij} | \mathbf{S}_i)$, and applying Bayes theorem yields $P(\mathbf{S}_i | \mathbf{E}_{ij})$. The posterior expresses our current state of knowledge about the student's proficiency. This process is repeated (using the posterior in the previous step as the prior in the next step) until the evidence from all of the tasks in the assessment that were presented to the student is absorbed. Then the resulting posterior model is used to generate scores.

6.4 Integrating Evidence from Diverse Sources

One of the more useful features of the ECD framework is its ability to handle evidence from diverse sources. Section 6.4.1 describes an ECD-based framework for accumulating evidence from different learning objects. Section 6.4.2 extends that framework to situations where evidence accumulates over longer periods of time.

6.4.1 ECD as an Evidence Integration Framework

The rise of computing has brought with it a host of new computerized educational content. One of the earlier efforts in providing a common framework for sharing results from these learning objects was the Sharable Content Object Reference Model (SCORM) sponsored by the U.S. Department of Defense's Advanced Distributed Learning initiative.[2] In the vision outlined in the SCORM specifications

---

[2] The IMS Global Consortium's Common Cartridge Alliance specification is similar in nature and is based, in part, on earlier versions of SCORM. All of the remarks in this section apply to SCORM, Common Cartridge Alliance and similar interoperability efforts.

(ADL, 2009), there exists a universe of Sharable Content Objects (SCOs). A typical SCO might consist of a video lecture follow by some multiple-choice questions. Or it might be a complex simulation. A Learning Management System (LMS) selects and launches an appropriate SCO. The student completes (or not) whatever activities are contained in the SCO and then the SCO reports the results back to the LMS, which archives and maintains them.

SCORM and other similar specifications overlook a critical issue: the results coming back from the SCO are data and not evidence! Unless those data are tied to some claims of interest, there is little that the LMS can do other than simply record the results generated by the SCO.

ECD provides a framework for turning the data coming from SCOs into evidence. A course designer can encode the complex of knowledge, skills and abilities targeted by the course as a proficiency model. The LMS can store student specific versions of this proficiency model for every student taking the course.

Each SCO that the course designer wants to use requires an evidence model. The evidence model tells how to interpret the results of that SCO for the purposes of updating this proficiency model (a different choice of proficiency model would also require a different evidence model). The rules of evidence describe which results from the SCO are used as evidence and describe any transformation that needs to be done to those results (e.g., rescaling, averaging, or establishing a cut score for "success"). The statistical part of the model describes how the observables, the outputs of the rules of evidence, relate to the proficiency variables. As results come back from SCOs, the LMS runs the evidence rules to calculate the observable outcomes. It then applies Bayes theorem to update the probability distribution over proficiency profiles in light of the new evidence (Almond & Mislevy, 1999).

This schema has two potential difficulties. The first is that the ECD framework assumes that a student's proficiency remains unchanged over the course of the assessment, while we expect that the student's proficiency will improve over the course of instruction. Section 6.4.2 talks about extending the ECD framework to include changes over time. The second is how to get the probabilities (or other parameters) that are needed to complete the evidence models.

One possibility is to use Bayesian logic on the parameters of the system. The course designer would fill out a structured questionnaire for each SCO added to the system. This questionnaire would help the designer define the observable for the SCO and describe how they are related to the proficiency variables. It would also ask questions about the strengths of those relationships which would be used to produce prior distributions for the parameters of the ECD models. These prior parameters could be used to immediately score the student interactions with the system, producing results that are no worse than an arbitrarily weighted number right system (both are based on expert assigned weights). As sufficient data (outcomes from students using collections of SCOs) become available, Bayesian inference can be used to replace the prior distributions for parameters with posterior distributions. This should improve the quality of inferences that come from the system (the amount of improvement will depend on how much information the data provide about the parameters).

6.4.2 ECD Over Time

ECD as laid out in Mislevy et al. (2003) assumes that the student's proficiency stays roughly the same throughout the period of the assessment. However, there are many applications for which this assumption does not hold. We would be disappointed if a student's proficiency did not improve in the course of a semester.

Almond (2007) presents a framework for taking measurements at a multiple time slices. The basic idea is to consider the assessment as part of a formative assessment and instruction cycle. At each time point, the instructor assesses the student's (or students') current proficiency and then makes a decision about what to do in the next instructional period. This is essentially a repeat of the decision problem in Fig. 6.1 many times.

Stringing these together produces Fig. 6.5. Here $S_1, \cdots, S_T$ are the proficiency variables at each time point; $E_1, \cdots, E_T$ are the observable outcome variables (evidence) from each time point; and $A_1, \cdots, A_T$ are the instructional activities or actions selected by the educator at each time point. There are two relationships we must define. The first is $P(E_t | S_t)$, but this is just an evidence model! The second is $P(S_{t+1} | S_t, A_t)$; this is called the *proficiency growth model*.

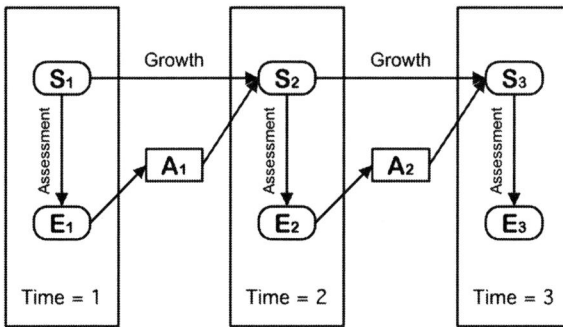

Fig. 6.5 Instruction and assessment as a Markov decision process

Under a few additional assumptions (in particular, we must assume that the utility or reward can also be factored into a reward for each time slice), Fig. 6.5 is a partially observed Markov decision process (POMDP; Boutilier, Dean, & Hanks, 1999). It is partially observed because we only see E_t and not S_t. The good news is that POMDPs are a popular research topic in computer science and many efficient algorithms for solving them have been developed. In particular, POMDP models support the following operations:

- *Filtering*—Using past observations to improve our estimate of the student's current skill.
- *Forecasting*—Using past observations to predict the student's future skill (under some educational policy).
- *Planning*—Selecting a series of activities to maximize the chance of reaching a goal learning state.

The proficiency growth model is an extension of the original ECD framework. If we assume that there is no choice of action, and that the change is roughly linear for all students, the model of Fig. 6.5 can be reexpressed using hierarchical linear models, in the manner of Singer and Willett (2003). The *mover–stayer* model (Glück & Spiel, 2007; Meiser, Stern, & Langeheine, 1998) is a more complex extension of this idea in which there are two latent classes associated with each time step: *movers* whose skill increases, and *stayers* whose skill stays about the same. In other words, there are two latent classes which have different slopes associated with the growth classes. Almond (2007) proposes a more complex version of this model which includes the effects of prerequisites on instruction.

Although the POMDP framework is simple and flexible, many challenging problems remain. A key issue is that there must be some kind of vertical scaling of the evidence models, and a lack of constraints on the model to enforce the vertical scaling can cause identifiability issues (Almond, in press). Still, considering assessment as part of a dynamic system for improving students is critical for the kinds of formative uses of assessment that are described in Black and Wiliam (1998).

6.5 Assessments of Multiple Aspects of Proficiency

One critical area of tension between cognitive scientists and psychometricians is how many variables to include the proficiency model. Cognitive scientists are fond of breaking down the domain into small proficiencies and skills, while the experience of psychometricians has been that subscores, particularly in assessments of cognitive skills, are highly correlated. The test construction procedures for many time-limited assessments increase this high correlation, as the time limit means that items that do not have high correlation with the main target dimension are eliminated to make the reliability of the overall score higher. This procedure potentially eliminates tasks that have good diagnostic value: separating students who have SKILL 1 but not SKILL 2 from students who have SKILL 2 but not SKILL 1. Furthermore, the subscores are often based on only a few items giving them lower reliability. This has caused many psychometricians to discourage the use of diagnostic assessment, particularly when that term is used merely to describe subscores based on test content specifications (Sinharay & Haberman, 2008).

ECD has a long history of embracing multivariate proficiency models (Mislevy et al., 2003). The earliest versions of ECD assumed multivariate proficiency models, but later practitioners noticed that many aspects of the theory could be simplified when the purpose of the assessment was to give a single score. One of the goals of ECD is to provide test designers with techniques and language that enable them to work through the design trade-offs that come with multiple proficiency variables. Section 6.5.1 discusses how the evidence propagation works when there are multiple proficiency variables. Section 6.5.2 shows a few examples of multivariate proficiency models, and Section 6.5.3 discusses how evidence models need to change in response to the multiple aspects of proficiency. Finally, Section 6.5.4 describes some field tests with an Assessment *for* Learning system that uses a multidimensional proficiency model.

6.5.1 Direct and Indirect Evidence

Consider the model in Fig. 6.6. In this simple model there are two skills which are correlated (the direction of the edge represents statistical conditioning and is chosen arbitrarily). There are also three observable outcome variables from three different tasks. Task 1 (OBS 1) is a simple task tapping only SKILL 1 and Task 2 (OBS 2) taps only SKILL 2. Task 3 (OBS 3) is an integrated task that requires both skills.

Fig. 6.6 An illustration of direct and indirect evidence. Proficiency variables are labeled with *circles* and observable outcome variables with *triangles*

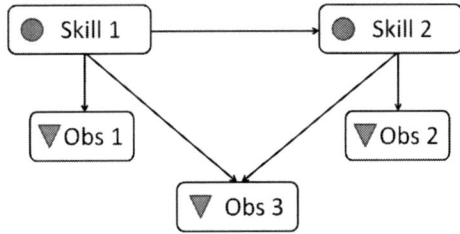

Consider the evidence from observing OBS 1. This provides direct evidence for SKILL 1, and because SKILL 1 and SKILL 2 are correlated this provides indirect evidence for SKILL 2. Similarly, OBS 2 provides direct evidence for SKILL 2 and indirect evidence for SKILL 1.

Wainer et al. (2001) develop the mathematics behind this intuition. The degree to which a given inference is based on direct or indirect evidence is based on two factors: the correlation between the skills and the standard error of measurement of the observables providing direct evidence for the target skill. If the standard error is high, and the correlation is high, then the indirect evidence will dominate the direct evidence and the scores for the target skill will be shrunk towards the overall mean performance. If the standard error is low and the correlation is low, then the direct evidence will dominate and there will be little shrinkage.

What happens with the integrated task is a little more complicated. Suppose that the task is conjunctive in nature, so that both skills are required for a good outcome. If the student has a poor outcome on the task, we know that there is deficiency in one of the two skills but not which one. Often both integrated and simple tasks are needed in the assessment to be able to fully distinguish all of the possible proficiency profiles. Sometimes, one of the two skills will be difficult to observe directly. In that case, having some simple tasks that tap just the other skill is important, so that the remaining skill can be addressed by subtraction.

6.5.2 Proficiency Model Revisited

As soon as there is more than one proficiency variable, the question arises of how to structure the relationships among them. There is a tendency for subject matter experts to want to provide hierarchical breakdowns on the knowledge, skills and abilities important in the domain. Figure 6.7 shows a proficiency model based on a hierarchical breakdown; the proficiency model for the ACED system (Shute et al., 2008). The design team deliberately chose to base their proficiency model on the hierarchical breakdown to make adaptive task selection easier.

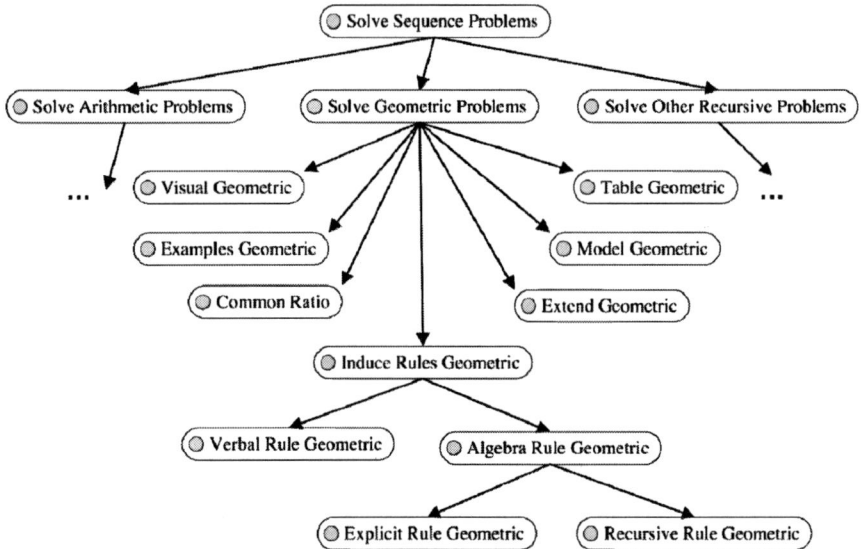

Fig. 6.7 Part of the proficiency model for ACED. Change visual to pictorial and table geometric to Table Representation

In the previous section, it was the correlation structure among the proficiency variables that determined the relationships between direct and indirect evidence. This argues that a good proficiency model should do a good job of capturing the correlations. There is a close relationship between the inverse correlation matrix and the graphical models sometimes used to represent multidimensional distributions (Whittaker, 1990). In particular, if the proficiency variables have a multivariate normal distribution, a zero in the inverse correlation matrix indicates the variables in that row and column are independent. Almond (2010) suggests using the correlation matrixes that come out of factor analysis and structural equation modeling to produce graphical structures for the proficiency model.

Proficiency models need not be hierarchical. Consider two possible proficiency models for a hypothetical language examination (Mislevy, Almond, & Steinberg, 2002). Figure 6.8 is a minimalist model that expresses the idea that the language is required to provide subscores based on the four modalities—READING, WRITING,

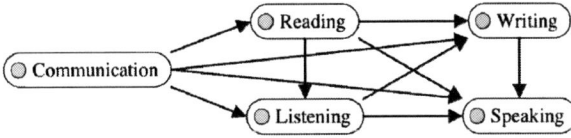

Fig. 6.8 A language proficiency model based on the four modalities

SPEAKING, AND LISTENING—as well as an overall score—COMMUNICATION. This graph is densely connected both because the various modal skills are highly correlated and because the assessment design calls for integrated tasks which induce correlation in the knowledge about the proficiencies (even when the proficiencies themselves are uncorrelated in the population). Figure 6.9 is a more elaborate model in which the correlation among the modal skills is explained by various variables representing concepts from the theory of communicative competence (see Mislevy et al., 2002, for a more complete description of how ECD plays out in language assessment). Note that Sociolinguistic competence is not directly related to the four modal skills. If this variable is to be reported as part of the model, then the assessment should contain tasks that will provide direct evidence of this competence.

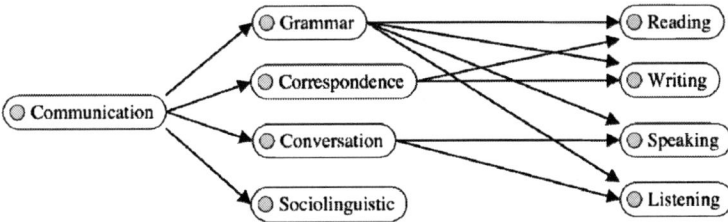

Fig. 6.9 A language proficiency model based on communicative competence theory

6.5.3 Evidence Model Revisited

Moving from one to many proficiency variables has a big impact on the evidence model. When there is only a single proficiency, the evidence is only concerned with the strength of the relationship between the observable and the proficiency variable. When there are multiple proficiency variables, an additional question arises: "Which of the proficiency variables are relevant for the observable and how are they related?"

If we restrict our attention to tasks which yield a single binary observable outcome variable, then we can use the Q-matrix (Fischer, 1973; Tatsuoka, 1984) to represent the relationship between the observable and the proficiency variables (Section 6.6 discusses the case with more complex tasks). The proficiency variables are often called *attributes* in the literature on cognitive diagnostic models, especially in the rule space (Tatsuoka, 1990) and attribute hierarchy modeling (Leighton, Gierl, & Hunka, 2004) paradigms; however, the term "attribute" in their usage corresponds more closely to the level of a proficiency variable in the ECD usage.

The Q-matrix is a simple incidence matrix in which the columns represent proficiency variables or levels of proficiency variables and the rows represent tasks (items). The cell q_{jk} is given the value of 1 when Skill k is relevant for Task k. Table 6.1 shows the Q-matrix for an experimental Reading test. The proficiencies are $S_1, \ldots, S_4$ and the strings beginning with "VB" are identifiers for the items. Evidence models correspond to unique rows of the Q-matrix; here the 1st and 3rd item (row) share the same evidence model. Gierl, Leighton, and Hunka (2007) point out a number of interesting features of the assessment that can be computed by looking at the Q-matrix. In particular, it is straightforward to see how many tasks address each proficiency by summing the columns.

Table 6.1 A Q-matrix for an experimental reading test

Evidence model	Task name	S_1	S_2	S_3	S_4
EM8	VB533037	1	0	0	0
EM2	VB533038	0	0	1	0
EM8	VB533039	1	0	0	0
EM4	VB533041	0	1	0	0
EM3-PC4	VB533431	0	0	1	1

Almond (2010) recommends augmenting the Q-matrix to provide additional information about each evidence model. Table 6.2 shows the augmented Q-matrix for the ACED Assessment *for* Learning environment (Shute et al., 2008). First note that in the main body of the table, instead of marking the cells with 0 or 1 the cells are marked with $+$ or $++$ to indicate which proficiency variables are more important. These can be used to set priors for discrimination parameters. Second, an additional column is added to indicate the expected difficulty of the task.

The third column marked "Anchor" takes care of a technical issue that arises when calibrating the model (Almond, Mislevy, & Yan, 2007). To identify the zero point in the scale we need to either (a) declare the mean of the pretest population to be zero, or (b) select a set of items which will have an average difficulty of zero. This needs to be done for each proficiency variable. The anchor column identifies the anchor set to which the task belongs.

The fourth column selects a *design pattern* (i.e., a parametric form for the probability of the proficiency variable given the observables) for the evidence model (Almond et al., 2001). Common choices are: *compensatory*— more of one skill compensates for less of another, *conjunctive*—all skills needed to perform well, *disjunctive*—only one skill needed to perform well, and *inhibitor*—minimum level of one skill needed, once the threshold is met, the other skill controls performance. Each of these choices of design pattern maps to a different parameterization for the evidence model. This allows a mixture of different kinds of tasks to be included on the same assessment.

Table 6.2 The augmented Q-matrix for ACED (excerpts)

Task Model	Common ratio	Example Geo	Extend Geo	Model Geo	Table Geo	Verbal Rule Geo	Visual Geo	Difficulty	Anchor	Design pattern	Task ID
CommonRatioTM	+							Easy	Ratio	Comp.	tCR1a
CommonRatioTM	+							Easy	Ratio	Comp.	tCR1b
CommonRatioTM	+							Med.	Ratio	Comp.	tCR2a
CommonRatioTM	+							Med.	Ratio	Comp.	tCR2b
CommonRatioTM	+							Hard	Ratio	Comp.	tCR3a
CommonRatioTM	+							Hard	Ratio	Comp.	tCR3b
ExampleGeoTM		+						Easy	Example	Comp.	tExampleGeo1a
ExampleGeoTM		+						Med.	Example	Comp.	tExampleGeo2a
ExampleGeoTM		+						Hard	Example	Comp.	tExampleGeo3a
ExtendGeoTM			+					Easy	Extend	Comp.	tExtendGeo1a
ModelExtTabGeoTM			+	++	+			Easy	Model	Comp.	tModExtTabGeo1a
TableExtendGeoTM			+		++			Easy	Table	Comp.	tTabExtGeo1a
VerbExtModGeoTM			+	+		++		Med.	Verbal	Comp.	tVerbExtModGeo2a
VerbModGeoTM				+		++		Hard	Verbal	Comp.	tVerbModGeo3a
VisExtGeoTM			+				++	Easy	Visual	Comp.	tVisExtGeo1a
VisExtTabModVerbGeoTM			+	+	+	+	++	Med.	Visual	Comp.	tVisExtTabModVerbGeo2a
VisExtVerbModGeoTM			+	+		+	++	Med.	Visual	Comp.	tVisExtVerbModGeo2a

6.5.4 The ACED Experience

One assessment that brought all of these elements together was ACED (Shute et al., 2008). ACED is an Assessment *for* Learning system designed to cover Algebraic sequences. Tasks can be selected adaptively (using the weight of evidence algorithm) and when students answer a question incorrectly, they can be given informative feedback including a worked solution to the problem. (The administrator can turn adaptive selection and feedback on and off.) A small sample field trial ($n = 268$) was conducted using only the geometric sequences portion of the model and tasks. Figure 6.7 shows the geometric sequences portion of the ACED proficiency model, and Table 6.2 shows a portion of the Q-matrix (there were a total of 63 geometric series problems).

Figure 6.10 shows the proficiency levels for a "class" (25 students randomly selected from the ACED evaluation study). The percentages in each bar are calculated by taking the posterior probability of being at each proficiency level for each student in the class and averaging them (Almond, Shute, Underwood, & Zapata-Rivera, 2009). In the sample, the COMMON RATIO and EXTEND SEQUENCE proficiencies are clearly better developed. This makes sense in the context of the study, as geometric sequences were not a normal part of the curriculum for the school from which the students were drawn; however, finding a common ratio and extending a sequence was part of the general curriculum.

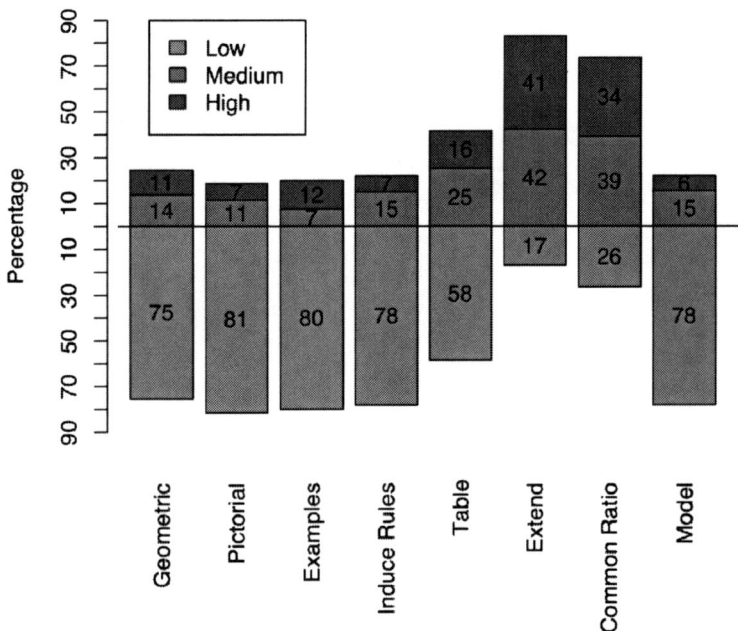

Fig. 6.10 Expected percentages of students at three proficiency levels for ACED "class"

Diagnostic assessments tend to run into one of two problems (Sinharay & Haberman, 2008): either the reliability of the subscores is low or the use of indirect evidence to stabilize the subscores shrinks them back to the overall score so much that they are indistinguishable from the overall score (GEOMETRIC). Table 6.3 looks at the reliability of the subscores associated with each node in the proficiency model. The Bayesian model used to score ACED has a similar effect to the Wainer et al. (2001) augmentation procedure in using indirect evidence to increase the precision of the subscores. Note also that the overall reliability is very close to the reliability of a simple number right score with the same items: reliability comes from good overall test design and not from fancy psychometrics.

Table 6.3 Reliability for ACED scores by proficiency variable

Proficiency variable	Reliability
Solve geometric problems	0.88
Pictorial geometric	0.82
Examples geometric	0.92
Common ratio	0.90
Extend geometric sequence	0.86
Induce rules geometric	0.78
Verbal rule	0.67
Algebra rule	0.76
Explicit rule	0.62
Recursive rule	0.76
Model geometric sequence	0.80
Table representation	0.82
Number right score	0.88

So do the ACED subscores provide additional value? It depends on the purpose of the assessment. If the purpose is merely to assess the students' overall level, then a single score may suffice. If the purpose is to assess how the students are doing on inducing rules, then the subscores provide the best possible information for that question. (See Weaver & Junker, 2004, for more discussion of this issue.) As discussed before, the real key is making sure that the scores provide information that is actionable by teachers. If the teachers can use the subscore information to make better decisions, then it is worth providing. If the teachers can't use the information, what is the point of providing it?

The ACED field trial provides an interesting perspective on this issue. The students using ACED were given a pretest and posttest on geometric sequences. The students who used ACED with both adaptive item selection and elaborated feedback showed significant gains between pretest and posttest; the students in the other conditions of the study did not (Shute et al., 2008). Moreover, the learning during the assessment does not seem to have affected the reliability or validity of the overall score. In fact the correlation between the overall GEOMETRIC score from ACED and the posttest was slightly higher for the students in the adaptive condition with elaborated feedback. The sample sizes are too small for a definitive conclusion, but this seems to be an example of an assessment really promoting learning.

6.6 Evidence from Complex Tasks

Perhaps the most important role for ECD in the future of assessment is in helping designers think about the role of complex tasks in assessments. These are tasks
that could yield multiple observable outcome variables. For example, a complex
stimulus (e.g., a reading passage or a video) followed by multiple related items,
complex constructed responses (e.g., essay, diagrams or tables); multi-step problems, problems calling for both an answer and an explanation, complex simulations
(e.g., Behrens, Mislevy, Bauer, Williamson, & Levy, 2004; Gitomer, Steinberg,
& Mislevy, 1995), and assessments embedded within other activities (e.g., games
Shute, Ventura, Bauer, & Zapata-Rivera, 2009) all have the potential for producing
multiple observable outcomes. But do multiple observables really produce better
evidence?

There are two general kinds of questions that the assessment designer must
answer: (1) how should the observable variables be defined? (Section 6.6.1) and (2)
how do the observable variables relate to the proficiency variables? (Section 6.6.2)
These are the key questions answered by the evidence model. Exploring these questions before spending a long time on the task model is important in guiding the work
of test development. After all, why spend time developing a new type of task if it is
not providing the needed evidence, or if more efficient alternatives are available?

6.6.1 Observables and Rubrics

Although Bayesian networks and other statistical methodologies offer the hope
of modeling complex dependency patterns among observable outcome variables
(Almond, Mulder, Hemat & Yan, 2009), the critical insight is that the more independent the observables are, the more information the task will yield. This insight
is not new to ECD, and it has often gotten compiled into common design patterns
for designing complex tasks. Consequently, it is worth decomposing some of the
common design patterns for complex tasks.

- *Multiple discrete items following a complex stimulus.* The canonical example of this item type is the reading passage, although computer technology
  allows for a large number of other kinds of stimulus material. Test developers have gotten good at selecting items that tap different parts of the text: e.g.,
  main idea, and vocabulary in context. The problem here is a "topic familiarity"
  effect, which is well modeled with the testlet model (Wainer, Bradlow, & Wang,
  2007). Identifiability issues arise when topic familiarity and one of the target
  proficiencies are correlated.
- *Complex Instructions.* If a group of items share the same set of complex instructions, then there may be dependence among the observed outcomes because a
  student who did not understand the outcomes is likely to have gotten everything
  wrong. Here, something that looks like the testlet model, but using the inhibitor

design pattern seems appropriate (Almond et al., 2009). The problem is that this set of items yields little evidence when the instructions are not understood.

- *Trait Scoring.* Classical trait scoring, where raters are asked to rate the same performance on multiple traits (Spandel & Stiggins, 1990), is another method that generates multiple dependent observables. One problem is that even though the traits may be defined in a way that seems independent, they are dependent either because the underlying skills are acquired in a dependent fashion or because the constraints of the task make them so. Consider the traits of fluent text production and critical thinking in writing. These are highly correlated in many studies (Gansle, VanDerHeyden, Noell, Resetar, & Williams, 2006). This could be because the skills are learned at the same time, or it could be because students who can produce text fluently have more time to concentrate on the critical thinking piece of the task.
- *Correct Answer and Coherent Explanation.* This design pattern occurs frequently in mathematics assessments, where explanation is one the process skills in the National Council of Teachers of Mathematics standards (NCTM, 1989). The problem here is that explanation ability for a given procedure is usually acquired only after the skill is at least partially learned, and tends to only show up for people on the higher end of the scale.
- *Correct Answer and Efficiency.* This design pattern is commonly used in simulation-based assessments. HyDRIVE (Gitomer et al., 1995), NetPASS (Behrens et al., 2004), and IMMEX (Stevens & Thadani, 2007) all use this pattern.
- *Correct Answer and Novelty.* This design pattern is appropriate when the goal is to measure creative problem solving. Shute et al. (2009) propose this model for problem solving in the context of computer games, but it seems appropriate for many situations in which it is possible to (a) clearly test whether or not a solution is correct, and (b) produce some kind of similarity measure between solutions.

Thinking about both product observables and process observables can help the design team extract more information from complex tasks. *Product observables* are pieces of evidence that can be gathered by evaluating the final output of the student's work. Examples include correctness of the solution, completeness of the solution and consistency of the solution. *Process observables* are pieces of evidence that can be gathered by evaluating a transcript of the students attempt to solve the problem. Examples include number of attempts, revisions (number and extent), unnecessary actions, and sparing use of time or resource consuming activities. Because more and more assessments are being administered via computer, these process observables are becoming easier to capture and more research is needed in understanding their relationships to the proficiency variables.

Part and parcel of defining observables is defining the *rules of evidence*—the rubrics that will be used to distinguish between the various levels. Whether humans or computers will score the task, lack of ambiguity in the rules helps reduce construct irrelevant variance due to inconsistent application of the scoring rules.

Building a good library of examples of student work annotated with the corresponding levels of the observables variables is necessary for both human and computer scoring. In the case of human scoring, these examples are used to train the human raters and can be used to check the human raters' performances. Computer scoring generally uses one of two methods: algorithmic methods or machine learning methods. In algorithmic scoring, the rubric becomes the specification for computer software, and the labeled examples provide a valuable resource for testing that software. In the case of machine learning algorithms, some kind of classification model is fit to the annotated data to try and reproduce the annotations. The annotated corpus of examples is necessary for both building and testing these algorithms.

One final note, the levels of the outcome variable should map to different levels of proficiency. That is, for a well designed observable, going from one level of performance to another implies that at least one of the proficiency variables has changed. All too often rubrics are created by defining a correct solution, defining a null solution and assigning partial credit by interpolating between the two. However, unless those interpolated points correspond to qualitative changes in the skills required to produce the resulting work product, it is hard to see how the evidence from the partial credit should be applied.

6.6.2 Many-to-Many Mappings

When there are many proficiency variables and many observables in the task, defining the statistical part of the evidence model becomes a matter of defining a many-to-many mapping. Although the Q-matrix could be extended to include a different row for each observable outcome variable, this would not necessarily capture the patterns of dependency among the variables. Bayesian networks are useful because the graphical notation allows the modelers to specify complex patterns of dependencies (Almond, DiBello, Moulder, & Zapata-Rivera, 2007; Almond et al., 2009).

In the case where there is only a single proficiency variable, it is rarely worth maintaining multiple observables. When there are multiple observables from the same task in the statistical part of the model, the pattern of dependence among them must be modeled (or assumed to be negligible). It is often better to use some kind of mechanical rule to combine the observables into a single observable and then apply a partial credit model to the result, as this reduces the number of parameters that must be elicited or estimated. If there is more than one proficiency variable in the model, each observable variable should draw on a unique combination of proficiency variables.

Observable outcome variables are also used for providing feedback to the examinee. Often the lower level observable variables are used for feedback and then combined for summary scoring. For example ETS's Criterion ^{SM} online essay scoring service (Attali & Burstein, 2006) defines a number of observables corresponding to individual issues in grammar, usage, mechanics and style (e.g., missing comma, spelling error, or passive voice). These are used to form the individual feedback messages and then combined into counts for the various error types before going into the overall model for the essay score.

6.7 Evidence and Argument

Assessment in the twenty-first Century will be different in ways that we, standing at the beginning of the new century, cannot begin to imagine. Older heuristic approaches to assessment design, which often rely on assumptions compiled into the heuristics, will unexpectedly fail when the assumptions are violated. What we need is a set of first principles from which we can reason about assessment design. ECD provides a very clear principle: think about how the observations supply evidence for the claims we wish to make about the students.

As a final illustration of that principle in action, consider the problem of extracting evidence from collaborative work, work that students do in small teams. If we think about a proficiency model that spans several students, and each student's proficiency as a separate variable in that model, then we are back to the multiple proficiency case explored in Fig. 6.6 and the same methods should apply. However, as before, we will need some samples of individual work to help us sort out the contributions of the individual team members.

The value of information calculations (Section 6.2) teach an important lesson. Unless the evidence from an assessment is well aligned with the purposes for which it will be used, the assessment will have little value for its end users. For assessments to support learning, assessment designers must work closely with instructional specialists, making sure that the claims of the assessment inform the instructional decisions.

The most interesting potential for ECD is its ability to integrate information from diverse sources (Section 6.4). Potentially, any activity done by a student is evidence about that student's proficiencies (although some activities will provide better or clearer evidence). All that educators need to do is to build an evidence model for the activity to describe how the outcomes relate to the targeted proficiencies.

This leads to the idea of *ubiquitous assessment*: assessment that happens all the time and is seamlessly embedded in the students other work. Tanimoto (2001) describes some of the issues that arise in what he calls *unobtrusive assessment*. The increased availability of computer technology makes it easy to capture the results of routine student work. It could be that twenty-first century assessment will be so well integrated in the students' day-to-day work that the students never notice it.

Acknowledgments Evidence-centered assessment design was originally a three-way collaboration between myself, Bob Mislevy and Linda Steinberg. Although this work represents my perspective on ECD, much of my perspective has become sufficiently mixed with ideas that originated with Bob or Linda. Similarly, my perspective has been expanded by discussions with too many colleagues to mention. Malcolm Bauer, Dan Eigner, Yoon-Jeon Kim, and Thomas Quinlan made numerous suggestions that helped improve the clarity of this chapter.

Any opinions expressed in this chapter are those of the author and not necessarily of Educational Testing Service.

References

Advanced Distributed Learning (ADL). (2009). *SCORM 2004 4th Edition Version 1.1 Overview*. Retrieved September 06, 2009, from http://www.adlnet.gov/Technologies/scorm/SCORMS Documents/2004%204th%20Edition/Overview.aspx.

Almond, R. G. (2007). Cognitive modeling to represent growth (learning) using Markov decision processes. *Technology, Instruction, Cognition and Learning (TICL)*, 5, 313–324. Retrieved from http://www.oldcitypublishing.com/TICL/TICL.html

Almond, R. G. (in press). *Estimating parameters of periodic assessment models*. To appear in Educational Testing Service Research Report series, Princeton, NJ.

Almond, R. G., DiBello, L., Jenkins, F., Mislevy, R. J., Senturk, D., Steinberg, L. S., et al. (2001). Models for conditional probability tables in educational assessment. In T. Jaakkola & T. Richardson (Eds.), *Artificial intelligence and statistics 2001 (*pp. 137–143). San Francisco: Morgan Kaufmann.

Almond, R. G., DiBello, L. V., Moulder, B., & Zapata-Rivera, J.-D. (2007). Modeling diagnostic assessment with Bayesian networks. *Journal of Educational Measurement*, 44(4), 341–359.

Almond, R. G., & Mislevy, R. J. (1999). Graphical models and computerized adaptive testing. *Applied Psychological Measurement*, 23, 223–238.

Almond, R. G., Mislevy, R. J., & Yan, D. (2007). *Using anchor sets to identify scale and location of latent variables*. Paper presented at Annual meeting of the National Council on Measurement in Education (NCME), Chicago.

Almond, R. G., Mulder, J., Hemat, L. A., & Yan, D. (2009). Bayesian Network models for local dependence among observable outcome variables. *Journal of Educational and Behavioral Statstics, 34*(4), 491–521.

Almond, R. G., Shute, V. J., Underwood, J. S., & Zapata-Rivera, J. -D. (2009). Bayesian networks: A teacher's view. *International Journal of Approximate Reasoning, 50*, 450–460 (Doi: 10.1016/j.ijar.2008.04.011).

Almond, R. G. (2010). 'I can name that Bayesian network in two matrixes'. *International Journal of Approximate Reasoning, 51*, 167–178.

Attali, Y., & Burstein, J. (2006). Automated essay scoring with e-rater V. 2.0. *The Journal of Technology, Learning, and Assessment, 4*(3), 13–18. Retrieved from http://escholorship.bc.edu/jtla/vol4/3/

Behrens, J. T., Mislevy, R. J., Bauer, M., Williamson, D. M., & Levy, R. (2004). Introduction to evidence centered design and lessons learned from its application in a global E-Learning program. *International Journal of Measurement, 4*, 295–301.

Black, P., & Wiliam, D. (1998). Inside the black box: Raising standards through classroom assessment. *Phi Delta Kappan, 80*(2), 139–147. Retrieved from http://ditc.missouri.edu/docs/blackBox.pdf.

Boutilier, C., Dean, T., & Hanks, S. (1999). Decision-theoretic planning: Structural assumptions and computational leverage. *Journal of Artificial Intelligence Research, 11*, 1–94. Retrieved from citeseer.ist.psu.edu/boutilier99decisiontheoretic.html.

Fischer, G. H. (1973). The linear logistic test model as an instrument in educational research. *Acta Psychologica, 37*, 359–374.

Gansle, K. A., VanDerHeyden, A. M., Noell, G. H., Resetar, J. L., & Williams, K. L. (2006). The technical adequacy of curriculum-based and rating-based measures of written expression for elementary school students. *School Psychology Review, 35*(3), 435–450.

Gierl, M. J., Leighton, J. P., & Hunka, S. M. (2007). Using the attribute hierarchy method to make diagnostic inferences about examinees' cognitive skills. In J. P. Leighton & M. J. Gierl (Eds.), *Cognitive diagnostic assessment: Theories and applications* (pp. 242–274). Cambridge, UK: Cambridge University Press.

Gitomer, D. H., Steinberg, L. S., & Mislevy, R. J. (1995). Diagnostic assessment of troubleshooting skill in an intelligent tutoring system. In P. D. Nichols, S. F. Chipman, & R. L. Brennen (Eds.), *Cognitively diagnostic assessment* (pp. 73–101). Mahwah, NJ: Lawrence Erlbaum Associates.

Glück, J., & Spiel, C. (2007). Studying development via item response models: A wide range of potential uses. In M. von Davier & C. H. Carstense (Eds.), *Multivariate and mixture distribution rasch models: Extensions and applications* (pp. 281–292). New York: Springer.

Good, I. J. (1950). *Probability and the weighing of evidence*. London: Charles Griffin.

Good, I. J. (1985). Weight of evidence: A brief survey. In J. Bernardo, M. DeGroot, D. Lindley, & A. Smith (Eds.), *Bayesian statistics 2* (pp. 249–269). Amsterdam: North Holland.

Good, I. J., & Card, W. (1971). The diagnostic process with special reference to errors. *Methods of Information in Medicine, 10,* 176–188.

Howard, R. A., & Matheson, J. E. (1981a). *Principles and applications of decision analysis*. Menlo Park, CA: Strategic Decisions Group.

Howard, R. A., & Matheson, J. E. (1981b). Influence diagrams. In R. A. Howard & J. E. Matheson (Eds.), *Principles and applications of decision analysis*. Menlo Park, CA: Strategic Decisions Group.

Leighton, J. P., Gierl, M. J., & Hunka, S. M. (2004). The attribute hierarchy model: An approach for integrating cognitive theory with assessment practice. *Journal of Educational Measurement, 41,* 205–236.

Madigan, D., & Almond, R. G. (1995). Test selection strategies for belief networks. In D. Fisher & H. J. Lenz (Eds.), *Learning from data: AI and statistics V* (pp. 89–98). New York: Springer.

Matheson, J. E. (1990). Using influence diagrams to value information and control. In R. M. Oliver & J. Q. Smith (Eds.), *Influence diagrams, belief nets and decision analysis* (pp. 25–48). Chichester: Wiley.

Meiser, T., Stern, E., & Langeheine, R. (1998). Latent change in discrete data: Unidimensional, multidimensiona, and mixutre distribution Rasch models for the analysis of repeated observations. *Methods of Psychological Research Online, 3*(2). Retrieved from http://www.mpr-online.de//issue5/art6/article.html.

Mislevy, R. J. (1994). Evidence and inference in educational assessment. *Psychometrika, 12,* 341–369.

Mislevy, R. J., Almond, R. G., & Steinberg, L. S. (2002). Design and analysis in a task-based language assessment. *Language Testing, 19*(4), 477–496.

Mislevy, R. J., Steinberg, L. S., & Almond, R. G. (2002). On the roles of task model variables in assessment design. In S. Irvine & P. Kyllonen (Eds.), *Generating items for cognitive tests: Theory and practice* (pp. 97–128). Mahwah, NJ: Erlbaum.

Mislevy, R. J., Steinberg, L. S., & Almond, R. G. (2003). On the structure of educational assessment (with discussion). *Measurement: Interdisciplinary Research and Perspective, 1*(1), 3–62.

Mislevy, R. J., Steinberg, L. S., Almond, R. G., & Lukas, J. F. (2006). Concepts, terminology and basic models of evidence-centered design. In D. M. Williamson, R. J. Mislevy, & I. I. Bejar (Eds.), *Automated scoring of complex tasks in computer-based testing* (pp. 15–47). Mahwah, NJ: Lawrence Erlbaum Associates.

National Council of Teachers of Mathematics (NCTM). (1989). Curriculum and performance standards for school mathematics. Author.

Schum, D. A. (1994). *The evidential foundations of probabilistic reasoning*. New York: Wiley.

Shute, V. J., Hansen, E. G., & Almond, R. G. (2008). You can't fatten a hog by weighing it – or can you? Evaluating an assessment for learning system called ACED. *International Journal of Artificial Intelligence in Education, 18*(4), 289–316. Retrieved from http://www.ijaied.org/iaied/ijaied/abstract/Vol_18/Shute08.html.

Shute, V. J., Ventura, M., Bauer, M. I., & Zapata-Rivera, D. (2009). Melding the power of serious games and embedded assessment to monitor and foster learning: Flow and grow. In U. Ritterfeld, M. J. Cody, & P. Vorderer (Eds.), *The social science of serious games: Theories and applications* (pp. 295–321). Philadelphia, PA: Routledge/LEA.

Singer, J. D., & Willett, J. B. (2003). *Applied longitudinal data analysis: Modeling change and event occurrence*. New York: Oxford University Press. (ISBN: 0195152964.)

Sinharay, S., & Haberman, S. J. (2008). How much can we reliably know about what examinees know? *Measurement: Interdisciplinary Research and Perspectives, 6,* 46–49.

Spandel, V., & Stiggins, R. L. (1990). *Creating writers: Linking assessment and writing instruction.* New York: Longman.

Stevens, R. H., & Thadani, V. (2007). Quantifying student's scientific problem solving efficiency and effectiveness. *Technology, Instruction, Cognition, and Learning, 5*(4), 325–338.

Tanimoto, S. L. (2001). Distributed transcripts for online learning: Design issues. *Journal of Interactive Media in Education, 2001*(2). Retrieved 2009-09-26 from http://www-jime.open.ac.uk/2001/2/.

Tatsuoka, K. K. (1984). *Analysis of errors in fraction addition and subtraction problems* (NIE Final report NIE-G-81-002). University of Illinois, Computer-based Education Research, Urbana, IL.

Tatsuoka, K. K. (1990). Toward an integration of item response theory and cognitive error diagnosis. In N. Frederiksen, R. Glaser, A. Lesgold, & M. G. Shafto (Eds.), *Diagnostic monitoring of skill and knowledge acquisition* (pp. 453–488). Mahwah, NJ: Lawrence Erlbaum Associates.

Vygotsky, L. (1978). *Mind in society: The development of higher mental processes.* Cambridge, MA: Harvard University Press.

Wainer, H., Bradlow, E. T., & Wang, X. (2007). *Testlet response theory and its applicaitons.* New York: Cambridge University Press.

Wainer, H., Veva, J. L., Camacho, F., Reeve, B. B., III, Rosa, K., Nelson, L., et al. (2001). Augmented scores—"Borrowing strength" to compute scores based on a small number of items. In D. Thissen & H. Wainer (Eds.), *Test scoring* (pp. 343–388). Mahwah, NJ: Lawrence Erlbaum Associates.

Weaver, R., & Junker, B. W. (2004). *Model specification for cognitive assessment of proportional reasoning* (Department of Statistics Technical Report No. 777). Carnegie Mellon University: Pittsburgh, PA. Retrieved December 11, 2008, from http://www.stat.cmu.edu/cmu-stats/tr/tr777/tr777.pdf.

Whittaker, J. (1990). *Graphical models in applied multivariate statistics.* Chichester: Wiley.

Chapter 7
Thinking About Assessments in a Transitional Time

Kris Ellington and Vincent Verges

Abstract Russell Almond supports the use of ECD for designing innovative assessments with diverse sources and types of evidence. From the perspective of a large state such as Florida that uses standards-based assessments to make high-stakes decisions, the ECD approach holds promise, but also poses challenges. In this response to Russell Almond's support of ECD, the authors focus on three key questions as they relate to this approach. The first question regards gathering coherent evidence across multiple time points, which can be challenging due to the need for professional development and timely reporting, among other considerations. The second question focuses on how to balance information gathered from multiple aspects of proficiency. Florida's experience and future plans with assessments of writing and the use of technology frame this discussion. Lastly, the question of collecting evidence from complex tasks involves even more challenges than are cited by Almond. Practical experience shows that the cost of including complex tasks, the challenges of student proficiency, and the logistics of field testing are major considerations when these tasks are used in large-scale assessments.

Keywords Evidence-centered design · FCAT · Assessment · Testing · Standards · Learning · Accountability · Technology

In this response to Almond's paper, we have highlighted some ideas that are relevant to our work in Florida on large-scale summative assessments as well as potential future work in formative assessments. Our insights come from backgrounds as secondary mathematics teachers, curriculum leaders (Ellington as a district curriculum coordinator and Verges as a school assistant principal), and years spent working with a variety of education and assessment professionals on Florida's K-12 summative assessments in reading, writing, science, and mathematics. Florida's model for item and test design, test assembly, administration, scoring, and reporting (available

K. Ellington (✉)
Accountability, Research, and Measurement, Florida Department of Education, Tallahassee, FL, USA
e-mail: kris.ellington@fldoe.org

in *The FCAT Handbook*—http://fcat.fldoe.org/handbk/fcathandbook.asp) has been crafted and refined over the years with guidance from several groups: stakeholders (including legislators), state agency assessment staff, Commissioners of Education, State Board of Education members, as well as national assessment company specialists. Many of the elements of evidence-centered design (ECD) can be found in Florida's model for the Florida Comprehensive Assessment Test (FCAT), but under different labels and different formats.

We have focused this paper around aspects of Almond's paper on which we feel qualified to respond based upon our professional experience and knowledge. Our response will be structured around the three important issues in the future of assessment, as identified by Almond, followed by some final thoughts.

7.1 How Can We Organize Evidence About Student Performance Gathered from Diverse Sources Across Multiple Time Points?

Almond contends that evidence about any student performance should first be framed around what one wants to be able to say about the students. He logically refers to score reports as a good starting point for organizing this evidence. Florida expends considerable time, money, and effort to build score reports for student performance on statewide assessments that provide the most meaning and accessibility for a variety of stakeholders. This effort takes place precisely because the state is very interested in not only communicating what the scores can be used for, but also how the scores should not be used. Organizing such evidence takes on a new level of complexity when one considers evidence from a variety of sources over multiple points in time.

First, consider the aspect of evidence across multiple time points. As more states, including Florida, investigate formative assessments, addressing this issue becomes more critical. We have seen some challenges to this movement based on our own experiences. Assessment at different "time slices," as Almond refers to them, makes great sense logically, but this method is only valid if a plan for targeted instruction exists that is based on the assessment outcomes. This plan requires considerable resources, including professional development for teachers, to develop and take to scale. Another challenge is that stakeholders may not embrace the utility of assessments across multiple time points. Some teachers, parents, students, and even some legislators see periodic assessments as an interruption to teaching and learning, taking away from instructional time. Most assessment and curriculum professionals would argue that well-considered measures, organized logically, and with clear indications of instruction that is needed based on the results, make more efficient use of classroom time, and thus are worth the time and effort. Given that summative assessments such as Florida's are used as indicators for progress as required by No Child Left Behind, it makes great sense to not rely on just one measure taken each year. All too often, however, these scores are reported at the end of the school year when teachers cannot make direct use of the results to benefit that year's students. The students do not have sufficient individual information for a diagnosis of specific needs, and teachers must wait an entire year to determine if changes in instructional programs based on a prior year's results are indeed effective.

As for gathering evidence from diverse sources, we are fortunate to live in the age of rapidly-expanding capabilities of technology to gather and classify data over a period of time. Computer adaptive testing allows us to more accurately classify and diagnose student performance in a shorter period of time. Technology gives us the ability to collect a multitude of data in both large districts and small districts. However, we continue to face two outstanding challenges to meaningful data collection on a broader scale. One is that instructional programs lack coherence across school districts and states. This makes it difficult to gather meaningful bodies of evidence to make more informed local, state or national observations, or decisions related to student learning. The other challenge is related to technology. Much the same way we lack coherence in instructional programs, we also lack compatibility in hardware, software, and information management. This incompatibility also hinders our ability to optimize how we gather and analyze evidence from diverse sources. Perhaps as we begin to move toward a national collaborative for content standards, collecting evidence from diverse sources will become less of a challenge.

7.2 How Should We Balance Information Gathered About Multiple Aspects of Proficiency?

In his treatment of this topic, Almond immediately strikes at the heart of the issue of examining multiple aspects of proficiency. He addresses the challenge of selecting tasks that measure the desired domain most accurately, and providing enough tasks to measure all desired traits within reasonable time limits. Florida has recently struggled with this in trying to create a large scale writing assessment that serves several purposes. The ideal assessment would provide us with sufficient observations of writing to make student-level judgments of writing proficiency while also providing enough information to make programmatic decisions, and this test would also ideally allow us to equate results from year to year. One of the ways Florida had hoped to achieve this cross-year linking was through the use of multiple-choice items to measure student proficiency in focus, organization, support, and proper conventions in writing. Student results showed some correlation between performance on the actual writing tasks and performance on the multiple-choice portion of the test, but this correlation was not sufficiently strong to make student-level decisions (one of which was a pass/fail decision for high-school graduation). The effort to create such a writing assessment is still ongoing in Florida, and solutions currently being considered reflect many of the concepts Almond addresses related to gathering information on multiple aspects of proficiency. Taking several samples of student writing at multiple points in the year is one example. Also, use of analytic scoring, or trait scoring, would provide multiple discrete observations on each sample (Cohen, 1994). Florida is also considering the use of automated essay scoring. Many argue that this is more consistent than the use of human scorers in evaluating the quality of student writing. Mark Shermis treats this topic more thoroughly in Chapter 10 (this volume).

Students will increasingly be using technology for assessments beyond just writing. This will give us the ability to use innovative item types and tasks to gather information about multiple aspects of proficiency. Challenges to the use of technology and innovative assessments are costs associated with hardware, software, infrastructure, and the assessments themselves. Even though initial costs may be high, the savings over the long term will be great. However, a significant concern is the current inequity in schools' and students' access to technology.

In addition to the long term cost-benefits of the use of technology, we anticipate improvement in the quality of information gathered as well as a significant reduction in time to report results. We are hopeful that these benefits will provide sufficient impetus to reduce or eliminate inequities in technology access. Gohl, Gohl, and Wolf (2009) cite the above challenges and benefits, among others, but also call on policymakers to formulate coherent policies at the local, state, and federal levels that encourage aligned standards and assessments that rely on technology. They also offer ideas on a variety of funding streams to address inequities in technology access, such as the Achievement Through Technology and Innovation (ATTAIN) Act and E-Rate.

7.3 How Should We Collect Evidence from Complex Tasks?

Florida's assessment content advisory committees have, from the inception of criterion-referenced, standards-based state assessments in 1998, been proponents for the inclusion of complex tasks in FCAT to the greatest extent possible. Many of these educators, like us, have both personally experienced and witnessed in others the impact of such tasks on our schools. Conversations among teachers changed to include a focus on the nature of student work as we learned about constructed-response tasks and examined student responses. The result was more clarity and agreement about the expected level of performance of students and instruction focused on problem solving and other high-order thinking skills. Florida's improving performance on such external measures as the National Assessment of Educational Progress (NAEP) may be, in part, a result of this focus.

Almond points out some of the challenges with these complex tasks. We have encountered several other challenges with the use of complex tasks in large-scale, summative assessments such as FCAT.

(a) *Cost*. The monetary cost of developing and scoring these types of tasks is considerably greater than that of selected-response items (e.g., multiple choice, gridded response). There is also a time cost: these items take longer to score and delay the reporting of assessment results. As technology innovations in automated scoring and user interfaces continue to occur, both of these costs may become less of a deterrent to the use of complex tasks.

(b) *Student proficiency.* We have experienced two challenges related to students' ability to respond to complex tasks. First, this type of test item is likely to function differently among population subgroups. Differential item functioning (DIF) criteria are much more likely to be violated during field testing for short- and extended-response test items than for multiple-choice items. Second, when improved instruction in the thinking and communication skills required by these tasks lags behind the use of complex tasks in assessment, performance on these tasks may be so poor that some are not usable and others provide only limited information to the scoring model. In Florida, this has been a particular challenge in science.

(c) *Field testing.* For complex tasks that take students more time to complete, such as a writing essay, field testing must be done during a different period of time than the operational testing. These longer field-test tasks, if included in the spring testing timeframe, could negatively impact performance on the scored items due to students' test fatigue. A different challenge occurs with context-dependent item sets, where a complex stimulus is followed by discrete but related items. More items must be field tested with the stimulus than are needed because some will not meet statistical criteria for use in the operational test. To ensure that the block of field-test items is not too long, the set of items has to be distributed across test forms. Each item is then field tested in a different context from the one in which it might eventually be used, creating less reliable field-test statistics.

While more words have been used here to describe the challenges as opposed to benefits of these complex tasks, we wholeheartedly believe that the challenges do not outweigh the value they bring to teaching and learning.

7.4 Final Thoughts

Almond supports the use of ECD for design of forward-looking assessments with diverse sources and types of evidence. The ECD approach seems capable of modeling many parts of an innovative assessment system, including diverse measures given over time and support of policy considerations. Much has been learned in the years since large-scale, standards-based tests were launched in Florida, including an understanding of the role they play in teacher and school accountability. The impact of policy related to high-stakes assessments must be recognized and deliberately included in the design of new systems for measuring student proficiency.

As we write this paper, the nation appears to be moving towards a common core of content standards and the potential of a national test of these standards. Additionally, interest and emphasis on formative, classroom-level assessments has increased. It is a pivotal time for the assessment community to examine and develop new approaches to the design of assessments with a focus not only on that which is easy to measure but what is important to measure. We believe that Almond has captured some of the needs and challenges in his paper.

In considering the ECD framework from our perspective as practitioners, it called to our minds the recently popularized understanding of expertise. Gladwell (2008), in his book *Outliers: The Story of Success*, cites such researchers as K. Anders Ericsson (a faculty member in the Center for Expert Performance Research at Florida State University) regarding the development of expertise (Ericsson, Krampe, & Tesch-Römer, 1993). This research tells us that expertise is a result of many hours, some studies say 10,000, of deliberate practice. According to our calculations, that is about 5 work years, which we have met and exceeded in our work on large-scale assessment in Florida. However, by and large, we have focused our practice on Florida's system and have become comfortable with the associated vocabulary. ECD, a different model using different terminology, would require a similar commitment to understand and implement but is clearly worthy of this effort!

References

Cohen, A. (1994). *Assessing language ability in the classroom*. Boston: Heinle & Heinle.
Ericsson, K. A., Krampe, R. Th., & Tesch-Römer, C. (1993). The role of deliberate practice in the acquisition of expert performance. *Psychological Review, 100*, 363–406.
Gladwell, M. (2008). *Outliers: The story of success*. New York: Little, Brown and Company.
Gohl, E. M., Gohl, D., & Wolf, M. A. (2009). Assessments and technology: A powerful combination for improving teaching and learning. In L. M. Pinkus(Ed.), *Meaningful measurement: The role of assessments in improving high school education in the twenty-first century*. Washington, DC: Alliance for Excellent Education.

Chapter 8
Participatory Assessment of 21st Century Proficiencies

Daniel T. Hickey, Michelle A. Honeyford, Katie A. Clinton,
and Jenna McWilliams

Abstract The explosion of new social network technologies has highlighted the awkward relationship between new "Twenty-first century" media practices and existing educational systems. Traditional content standards, achievement tests, and accountability pressures threaten nascent efforts to foster equitable, transparent, and credible participation in these practices. The current push to design external tests and standards to assess these new practices may actually exacerbate this problem, due to the fundamentally social nature of these proficiencies. Large-scale standardization and testing of aggregated achievement of these proficiencies should be done cautiously and in isolation from classroom-based efforts to foster worthwhile participation. Likewise, within classrooms, more interpretive efforts are first needed to define social contexts that foster worthwhile social participation in these practices before individual proficiency is assessed. To foster both participation and proficiency while also meeting existing and future accountability goals, a design-based participatory assessment framework with multiple levels of increasingly formal outcomes is introduced.

Keywords Formative assessment · Social media · Twenty-first century skills

New media technologies are resulting in new communities based on new forms of communication, learning, and self-expression (Ito et al., 2008; Shirky, 2008). Many of these communities are organized around creative expressions, including traditional expressions (e.g., *AllPoetry*) and newly popularized forms of traditional expressions (e.g., fan fiction at *FictionAlley* and music remixes at *ccMixter*).[1] These communities exemplify "affinity spaces" (Gee, 2004) that feature low barriers to entry, support for creating and sharing, informal mentoring of newcomers, and a strong sense of social connection. Media scholar Henry Jenkins and his colleagues

D.T. Hickey (✉)
Learning Sciences Program, Indiana University, Bloomington, IN, USA
e-mail: dthickey@indiana.edu

[1] For convenience and space considerations, references will be omitted throughout for resources that can be readily identified and located via popular search engines.

V.J. Shute, B.J. Becker (eds.), *Innovative Assessment for the 21st Century*,
DOI 10.1007/978-1-4419-6530-1_8, © Springer Science+Business Media, LLC 2010

at Project New Media Literacies explored this phenomenon in their consideration of "participatory cultures," where "not every member must contribute, but all must believe they are free to contribute when ready and believe that what they contribute will be appropriately valued" (2006, p. 7). Such practices are already a primary creative outlet for many youth (Drotner, 2007; Goldman, Booker, & McDermott, 2007). While these practices are not yet pervasive enough to merit proponents' hype or critics' hysteria, many youth who would not otherwise be developing these new media proficiencies are now doing so in these digital networks and developing traditional proficiencies in the process.

These cultural changes have led to tremendous interest in these new proficiencies and many efforts to define them. Jenkins and colleagues (2006) identified eleven new proficiencies needed to participate in these new communities: *play, performance, simulation, appropriation, multitasking, distributed cognition, collective intelligence, judgment, transmedia navigation, networking,* and *negotiation.* While such labels and notions have long been used to characterize proficiency, it is the manner in which they are being taken up in new digital media networks in ways that make them essential in the workplaces, classrooms, and cultures of the future that is fostering this explosion of interest. For example, in the widely cited *Framework for Twenty-First Century Learning* (Partnership for 21st Century Skills, 2007a) recognition of these and related newer proficiencies has led advocates to reframe and extend four categories of more conventional skills and themes.[2] Such proficiencies are even more pronounced in the *National Educational Technology Standards* (ISTE, 2007), which include six categories of student standards that are largely defined by new media and technology.[3] If these proficiencies are defining how knowledge is communicated and who is empowered to do so (Lisbon Council, 2007; Partners in Educational Transformation, 2008; Partnership for Twenty-First Century Skills, 2005), they should be central to education. If schools are to address them, it is important to consider how they are characterized (defining what they are), assessed in classrooms (indicating whether they have been learned), and tested (estimating who is capable). This chapter reviews current trends in these regards, and introduces an alternative strategy that might help accomplish widely held goals for these proficiencies.

---

[2] Thus the category *Learning and Innovation Skills* includes *communication and collaboration* along with *critical thinking and problem solving* while *Life and Career* skills includes *flexibility and adaptability* along with *productivity and accountability.* Many of the more specific practices that this paper is concerned with are most directly relevant to the skills included in the category of *Information, Media, and Technology Skills.* A fourth category consists of *Core Subjects and Twenty-First Century Themes.*

[3] These include *Creativity and innovation, Communication and collaboration, Research and information fluency, Critical thinking, Problem solving and decision making, Digital citizenship,* and *Technology operations and concepts.*

8.1 New Media the Technology Proficiencies and Schools

Recent studies reveal the tremendous levels of "hanging out, messing around, and geeking out" in friendship-driven and interest-driven social networks (Ito, 2008). This has highlighted the awkward relationship between these communities and schools. Concerns over privacy, pornography, piracy, and plagiarism ("the four Ps") obscure the level and quality of creative activity occurring in these networks.

The numerous online fan fiction communities offer an instructive example. In these communities, young people are deeply engaged in reading, writing, posting, commenting, editing, and evaluating their own and others' works in ways quite similar to the types of creative and critical engagement encouraged in formal literature and creative writing courses (Black, 2008). A key notion in these communities is that of the "canon"—the set of facts, characters, realities, and worlds developed by the original author or authors of a book, television show, or film. In the highly critical fan fiction communities that develop around a canonical text, creative works may deviate from the canon, but only if it is clear that the writer has done so intentionally and only if the deviation offers what the community agrees is a useful or important addition to the body of fan-produced materials building on the original text.[4] Active participants in fan fiction communities will surely develop a deeper and more useful understanding of genre, fiction, and literary criticism than will a student who attends a lecture and reads a textbook about these notions. Nonetheless, few teachers accept fan fiction for class assignments. Teachers question the cultural relevance of the original text and are unable to ascertain originality. While fan fiction sites are even more resolute about plagiarism, the communities are self-policing and highly organized around specific texts and sub-genres. Even a single confirmed instance may trigger a permanent ban. But the notion of "plagiarism" is approached in a more authentic way that accounts for the highly subjective way that most practicing writers appropriate source ideas and materials for new expressions.

8.1.1 Why Bother?

If these new proficiencies are easy to learn outside of schools, why should schools bother? Equity, a primary function of schools, is one answer. Jenkins (2006) pointed out that access alone is not enough—participatory cultures involve particular mindsets and skillsets that define valued action. Learning these "dispositions for doing" requires first-hand experiences in the actual social and cultural practices circumscribing their use. The widening *participation gap* in new media is a concern,

---

[4] A cardinal sin in fan fiction communities is writing what's called a "Gary Stu" or "Mary Sue" story, one in which the hero is a thinly disguised version of the writer. Nonetheless, newcomers who post such expressions are quickly recognized and likely to be given encouragement and immediately useful guidance for developing a more original work.

because proficiency with new media practices has become so important in many of the most important aspects of economic, civic, and political life. Put differently, this gap blocks opportunities for learning "the new embodiments of 'being literate' in contemporary culture" (Steinkuehler, Black, & Clinton, 2005).

A second set of concerns identified by Jenkins and colleagues (2006) is the *ethics challenge,* including issues of fair use, copyright, and slander, in addition to traditional questions of plagiarism. These new informal networks lack the mentoring, professional standards, and constrained access of traditional media and media mentoring programs (e.g., school newspapers; see James, 2008). Additionally, the very nature of online discourse presents new ethical concerns. As summarized by boyd (2008), new media discourse is relatively *persistent, searchable, replicable,* and generally *addressed to invisible audiences.* These features foster *transactive* interactions (where media is customized for one's personal enjoyment) and *shared control* (where content and expertise are co-created; see Xenos & Foot, 2008). This complex interactivity precludes the traditional institutional controls over ethical media use.

A third set of concerns is *transparency.* Media literacy programs have traditionally focused on transparency in terms of critical reading and thinking. Metzger and Flanagin (2008) describe how socially networked media raise new criteria for evaluating the credibility of information. There is clearly a bigger role for schools than telling students they cannot trust Wikipedia (e.g., Laucius, 2009). Schools are a vital place for young people to learn to judge credibility, recognize commercial messages, and understand the differences between centrally coordinated media efforts and broader public movements.

8.2 Efforts to Bridge the Void Between New Proficiencies and Schools

These and other concerns have prompted a range of responses. One type of response seems to characterize these new proficiencies as *participatory practices.* These "practice-oriented" responses emphasize the social and cultural contexts in which these proficiencies are emerging and are mostly carried out with the support of private philanthropies or as individual scholarship. The second type of response characterizes these new proficiencies as individual skills. These are more focused on standardizing and measuring them and are generally supported by government agencies and businesses. There are certainly overlaps and exceptions; some communities seem to be responding in both ways (such as the educational technology and educational gaming communities). But the difference seems distinct enough to consider and search for points of tension and potential synergy.

8.2.1 Practice-Oriented Responses to New Media and Technology

In recent years practice-oriented responses to new media and technology have attracted significant support from private philanthropies. Among the most notable sources of support is the MacArthur Foundation's *Digital Media and Learning Initiative*. These efforts have also received significant support from the Pew Charitable Trusts' *Internet and American Life* initiatives, the Hewlett Foundation, and others. In addition to these more formal efforts, the national and local initiatives of pioneers in New Literacy Studies, new media studies, and those engaged in new approaches to writing have also pushed the field to consider how to address the gap between in- and out-of-school learning.

8.2.1.1 New Literacy Studies

One strand of practice-oriented responses is rooted in what came to be called the New Literacy Studies (Barton, 1994; Gee, 1996; Heath, 1983; Scribner & Cole, 1981; Street, 1984). The New Literacy Studies (NLS) conceptualizes literacy as a social practice. Representative of this approach, Gee's theory of Discourse (as opposed to the more narrow conversational "discourse") describes how reading and writing are always "part and parcel of, and inextricable from, specific social, cultural, institutional, and political practices" (1999, p. 356). Here, learning to read and write is about learning what "counts" as meaningful to a dominant group, and this requires having experiences in the particular form of that group's life. Gee defines being literate as having control of what he calls secondary Discourses. Where primary Discourses are ways of using language learned in one's home and community, secondary Discourses are associated with "secondary institutions," such as schools. By defining literacy as control of secondary Discourses, Gee (1989, p. 542) suggests that "when one is learning to read and to write, one is actually learning ways of reading and writing that connect up with the values, purposes, and worldviews of the secondary Discourse wherein the learning is occurring (and, consequentially, which exist in relation to the learner's primary Discourse—for better or worse)."

Anticipating the broader set of issues we now face, Gee and colleagues argued previously that "literacy pedagogy has traditionally meant teaching and learning to read and write in page-bound, official, standard forms of the national language... [but] now must account for the burgeoning variety of text forms associated with information and multi-media technologies" (The New London Group, 1996, p. 11). Reciprocally, Leu, O'Bryne, Zawilinski, McVerry, and Everett-Cacopardo (2009, p. 265) contend that "looking past the technological aspects of the Internet to analyze the underling social practices... helps the research community to see the Internet not as a technology but rather as a context in which to read, write, and communicate." A representative survey of research and educational applications reflecting this perspective is included in the *Handbook of Research on New Literacies* (Coiro, Knobel, Lankshear, & Leu, 2008; see also Alvermann, 2002; Lievrouw & Livingstone, 2006). As interdisciplinary research contributes to our understanding of the Internet, theories about specific new literacies (e.g., text messaging, Lam, 2006; multimodal storytelling, Hull & Nelson, 2005; social networking, boyd & Ellison, 2007) are contributing to the larger theory of New Literacies in this "open-source approach to theory development" (Leu et al., 2009,

p. 265). This diversity of practice and corresponding focus on more local theories challenges traditional assumptions about content standards, measurement, generalizability, and formal theorizing that frame the more measurement-oriented responses.

8.2.1.2 New Media Studies

Scholars and educators in media and communication have been at the forefront of responses to new media and technology. Their stance is playfully illustrated by the "lolcat" phenomenon (pictures of cats with overlay text in "kitty pidgin," or "lolspeak"). Media scholars point out that this phenomenon spread so rapidly because anyone could visit ICanHasCheezburger.com to create new meanings (i.e., a new lolcat) that would quickly reach a broad and receptive audience (Jenkins, 2006). New lolspeak texts emerged (e.g., lolcat bible), and newcomers could readily participate in developing and establishing community norms (e.g., by joining the wiki discussion board at lolcatbible). Additionally, these communities offer multiple avenues for new users to learn the ways of lolspeak, including a "lolspeak guide" and "how to make lolz" tutorial. As with videogaming, the relevance of this example for schools is most apparent after looking beyond the content of the meaning being made to focus on the ease with which they are made and shared (Shirky, 2008).

The research literature and practitioner journals, education blogs, and other outlets reveal substantial efforts to develop and study classroom curricula that embrace ideas of participatory culture as defined by media scholars. One notable example is the Teachers' Strategy Guide (TSG) developed by Jenkins' Project New Media Literacies with the support of the MacArthur Foundation. The guide, called *Reading in a Participatory Culture*, explores the implications of participatory culture for teaching a classic text (Melville's *Moby-Dick*) in the high school English classroom. This chapter will return to this example, which has been central to our collaboration to define new assessment strategies. Another notable initiative is the socialmedia-classroom.com community which builds on the ideas of Rheingold (2007) and shares ideas and materials for teaching a variety of new media technologies.

8.2.1.3 New Approaches to Writing

The prominence of writing in these new practices has prompted Brandt (2005, 2009) and others to argue that we are in a second stage of mass literacy. New media has made writing the basis for a mass literate experience, and educational institutions should respond to this shift. The National Council of Teachers of English has been particularly responsive. The NCTE report *Writing in the Twenty-First Century* (Yancey, 2009) points out that new media means "composers become composers not through direct and formal instruction alone (if at all), but rather through what we might call an extracurricular social co-apprenticeship" (p. 5). Thus, "our impulse to write is now digitized and expanded—or put differently, newly technologized, socialized, and networked" (2009, p. 5).

Examining the consequences of this shift, the NCTE report explored the recent "pranking" of the Advanced Placement writing exam. A Facebook group (eventually numbering 25,000) encouraged test takers to write and then cross out the phrase "THIS IS SPARTA" in their essay responses. For the NCTE, this seemingly innocuous example illustrates how students increasingly understand (a) the power of networking, (b) how messages circulate and how to control them, (c) the new audiences for twenty-first century compositions, and (d) how to "play" the testing game. Thus, students "refused to write to a teacher-as-examiner exclusively; they wrote as well to live teachers who might be amused..., they wanted not a testing reader, but a human one" (p. 6). The report draws on the example to ask: How can we build on all this knowledge? We worry that many responses to new media fail to do so, and that any new standardized measures of new proficiencies will be utterly compromised by more nefarious networked pranking once an expensive new test starts being used to make important judgments.

The National Writing Project's *Teaching the New Writing* (Herrington, Hodgson, & Moran, 2009) examines how writing teachers across the nation are responding to new technologies. For example, in *Teaching Writing Using Blogs, Wikis, and other Digital Tools*, Beach, Anson, Breuch, and Swiss (2008) show how digital tools can transform schools to engage students in "meaningful multimodal literacy practices." Hull and Nelson (2005) illustrated the potential for multimodal literacy in their ongoing work with *Digital Underground Storytelling for Youth*, an urban after-school/summer program. They argued that multimodality increases the "multiplex ways by which people can make meaning in the world" and affords "a democratizing force" by incorporating the "views and values of more people than ever before" (p. 226). In Chicago, *The Digital Youth Network* shows the promise of a hybrid digital literacy program that brings in- and out-of-school learning closer together by developing students' new media literacies in an after-school learning environment so students can utilize them in school.

8.2.1.4 Challenges for Practice-Oriented Responses

Reflecting the purpose of this chapter, we believe that accountability presents the greatest challenge to practice-oriented educational responses to new media and technology. Particularly in the U.S., we expect that schools will continue to be held strictly accountable to scores on externally-developed standardized tests. These concerns are exacerbated by continuing demands for "scientifically-based" evidence using such tests (e.g., Shavelson & Towne, 2002) where individual students are randomly assigned to experimental and comparison conditions (e.g., Towne & Hilton, 2004). Given the rewards and punishment associated with test performance, teachers and schools have good reason to employ individualized computer-based test preparation programs that essentially train students to recognize numerous isolated associations. As long as a handful of those learned associations are recognized on a targeted test, statistically significant gains can be obtained in as little as 5–10 hours of individualized training (e.g., Ysseldyke & Tardrew, 2007). From the perspective of the practice-oriented responses, this new knowledge has almost no educational value beyond raising scores on targeted tests. We assume that increased use of these practices under the *No Child Left Behind* Act is largely responsible for corresponding declines on unrelated non-targeted tests and other non-tested outcomes (Ghezzi, 2006; Winerip, 2005). However, publishers of test prep programs (who are increasingly also publishers of school tests *and* targeted tests) have been very successful using this evidence to market their products to schools and school systems. This was particularly the case for the supplemental educational services mandated for persistently underperforming schools under NCLB. In many schools, teachers are unable to use the computer labs for participation in increasingly important new media and technology practices relevant to their content areas because they are (at least in our experience) booked prepping students for and administering high-stakes tests.

Our initial review of practice-oriented new media curricula did not reveal any evidence of increased achievement on external tests. While test-based accountability is clearly in transition, we assume that schools and students in all western countries will always encounter externally-developed, high-stakes tests. We further assume that broad adoption of innovative practices will continue to require convincing evidence of impact on externally-developed achievement tests. As described next, the second category of responses to new media and technology *may* result in a solution to this problem.

8.2.2 Measurement-Oriented Responses to New Media and Technology

The second category of responses to new media and technology, measurement-oriented responses, is attracting substantial sponsorship from business interests and governments. In general, these responses aim to foster new proficiencies by changing educational standards and tests and then using these changes to drive classroom assessment and teaching.

8.2.2.1 Changing Standards and Tests

The pressures described in the introduction have led to calls for sweeping changes in educational standards and tests of those standards. For example, The Partnership for Twenty-First Century Skills has developed a comprehensive framework that includes "learning and innovation skills" along with more specific media and technology skills and "core subjects and Twenty-First century themes." Likewise, the International Society for Technology in Education (ISTE) has identified National Educational Technology Standards for both students and teachers (NETS-S and NETS-T); their *NETS Online Technology Assessment* is now starting to be widely used.[5] Many states are also investing substantial resources and funding into revamping their standards and assessments in this direction.

The rationale behind these responses is that new standards and tests will drive schools to transform themselves. The Partnership for Twenty-First Century Skills asserts that "the movement to embrace and foster widespread adoption of Twenty-First Century skills hinges on identifying ways to assess students' adoption and acquisition of this knowledge" (2005, p. 5). Likewise, the Education Sector recently released a report called *Measuring Skills in the Twenty-First Century.* The report is part of their initiative to "[b]uild on the strengths of the current school accountability systems, more fully and effectively measure the depth and breadth of student's educational experiences, and encourage educators, parents, policy makers, and the larger public to pursue educational equity and excellence for all students" (Silva, 2008, p. iii). Other similarly inspired efforts that are described elsewhere include the *College and Work Readiness Assessment* (Council for Aid to Education), the *Rainbow Project* (the College Board), the *Self-Directed Learning Inventory* (Metiri), and *iSkills* (Educational Testing Service).

The technology industry has strongly supported these efforts. The Partnership for Educational Transformation, formed by Cisco, Intel, and Microsoft in 2009, is aiming to revamp international standards and tests, including the *Program for International Student Assessment* (PISA) run by the Organization for Economic Cooperation and Development, and the *Trends in International Mathematics and Science Study* (TIMSS) run by the International Association of the Evaluation of Educational Achievement. Technology also plays a central role in these new tests. Web-based administration coupled with computer-adaptive testing has slashed testing and scoring time and is making possible groundbreaking new test formats (Quellmalz & Pellegrino, 2009), while the evidence-centered design (ECD) approach pioneered by Mislevy and colleagues (e.g., Mislevy, Steinberg, & Almond, 2003) allows tests to incorporate sophisticated multi-dimensional models of student reasoning. Assessment innovators are starting to combine networked testing, ECD models, and virtual reality technology to assess Twenty-First century skills in immersive virtual environments (e.g., Shute, Ventura, Bauer, & Zapata-Rivera, 2009).

Among government-led testing efforts, the UK's Qualifications and Curriculum Authority has been particularly ambitious, including their *Key Stage 3 ICT Literacy Assessment, A-Level Examination of the Moving Image,* the web-based *Certificate of Digital Creativity,* the *eVIVA* portfolio assessment, and an annotation system. The U.S. government has been slower to respond, but the Obama administration has

---

[5] Another set of standards developed by the Metiri Group addresses the concern that "policymakers and educators have not yet clearly defined what it means to be 'educated' in a Digital Age." Their *enGauge Twenty-First Century* initiative catalogues four sets of skills (*digital age literacy, inventive thinking, effective communication,* and *productivity*); these skills underlie their *Dimensions21 Framework* that schools can use to audit their "readiness to implement Twenty-First Century Learning" and asses their students' "engagement and self-directed life-long learning."

stated that "their vision for a Twenty-First century education begins with demanding more reforms and accountability, coupled with the resources needed to carry out that reform" (White House, 2009). Their *Education Agenda* asserts that "teachers should not be forced to spend the academic year preparing students to fill in bubbles on standardized tests." Instead, the administration aims to "improve the assessments used to track student progress to measure readiness for college and the workplace and improve learning in a timely, individualized manner." These and other indications point to a significant U.S. response in terms of federal policy and state-led testing efforts in the coming years.

8.2.2.2 New Curriculum and Classroom Assessments

Of course, the driving force behind the measurement-driven responses is the assumption that the new standards and tests will drive educational reform. The Partnership for Twenty-First Century Skills (2007b) argues that schools should (1) create necessary standards, (2) develop, implement, evaluate, and improve assessments, (3) align formative and summative assessments to curriculum and instruction, and (4) develop a professional development strategy. Drawing on research that became well established in the 1990s, their white paper points to curricular strategies such as problem-based learning, cooperative learning, and the use of real world contexts that might be used in these new curricula. Notably, the Partnership recognizes the important role that formative classroom assessments play in helping teachers align their curricula with summative external tests: "Such assessments make it possible to diagnose learning gaps and address them before they lead to more fundamental misunderstandings of knowledge or misapplication of skills" (p. 4). Similarly, one of the five working groups in the Partnership for Educational Transformation was called *Classroom Learning Environments and Formative Evaluation* and aimed to "review classroom-based ICT-enabled learning environments that emphasize interactive, formative assessments and provide opportunities for students to reach important criteria at their own rates and derive implications for summative assessment and for classroom practices aligned with assessment reform" (2008, p. 15).

8.3 So, What Is the Problem?

To many observers, it must seem that these two strands of education-related responses to new media and technology and the combined efforts of educational researchers, philanthropies, government, and industry within them are all poised to help new media literacies and Twenty-First century proficiencies in schools and more broadly. Our concern is that the fundamental tensions between these approaches will thwart their shared goals. In short, we worry that the constraints of high-stakes external measures will still result in overly narrow definitions of these new proficiencies and that these tests in turn will lead to overly narrow classroom instruction and assessment. More specifically, we take issue with the idea of *starting* with external tests and then aligning classroom instruction and assessment to those tests.

Our concerns stem partly from our embrace of the participatory views of learning underlying most of the practice-oriented responses. These views of learning are rooted in situative theories of cognition that treat communal social activity as primary representations of knowledge and treat the thoughts and behavior of individuals as secondary representations of that knowledge (e.g., Greeno, 1998). As illustrated by the various practice-oriented responses summarized above, these participatory/situative views suggest that the most worthwhile responses to new media should *start* with a more social characterization of these proficiencies as distributed communal practices. Put differently, we agree that efforts to foster these new proficiencies should not start by measuring them. Quite to the contrary, we believe that large-scale efforts to standardize and measure these proficiencies on high-stakes tests should be *isolated* from efforts to interpret and promote them in the social and cultural contexts in which they might be more formally taught (e.g., classrooms and schools). The argument that we are building in this chapter is that doing so should (a) allow more individual students to become more "proficient" by the standards of those very tests, (b) strengthen the accuracy and value of the evidence gathered with the various tests of new proficiencies now being proposed, and (c) reduce the need for costly and potentially problematic new formats for these tests.

While our approach is rooted in established theories of cognition and learning, our argument is pragmatic. We are not engaging in the debate over whether individuals "possess" new media and technology skills that they take with them from task to task or whether individuals are capable of learning components of these skills in isolation (e.g., Anderson, Reder, & Simon, 1996). Instead, we argue that framing new proficiencies *primarily* as specific skills that can be measured in isolation from their contexts of use necessarily overlooks the most important aspects needed to foster them in schools (Greeno, 1997). Thus, we contend that these new proficiencies should primarily be framed as social practices, which are best understood by interpreting the ways they are used and learned in the social networks in which they emerge (or might emerge). We further contend that these proficiencies should be framed secondarily as individual conceptual understanding, as might be understood by assessing whether individuals can solve similar problems that require those proficiencies. We then argue that only once the proficiencies have been interpreted in their social context and then assessed as individual understanding should they be measured in the aggregate on any conceivable standardized external test.

In short, we believe that the next generation of achievement tests should be used "at a distance" to track and evaluate the success of curricula and policies in fostering broad attainment of these new proficiencies. Our argument is grounded in two primary aspects of validity theory.

8.3.1 Evidential Validity

As detailed by Messick, 1994 and summarized in Hickey, Wolfe, and Kindfield (2000), the validity of evidence has traditionally concerned *content*, *substance*, *structure, generalizability,* and relationship with *external* measures. The participatory/situative views of learning underlying the practice-oriented responses as well as our approach assume that any proficiencies are closely bound to the sociocultural contexts in which they emerged and are continually evolving. This is exacerbated when such practices are (a) inherently social, such as new media literacies, and (b) measured in a sufficiently general context to reliably estimate achievement independent of any particular learning and performance context. This means that successful participants in new media and technology practices may appear "illiterate" on narrow literacy assessments while high-scoring test-takers may not be able to participate successfully in a broader range of literacy and new media communities.

Theoretically, we embrace the doubts of situativity theorists (e.g., Greeno & Gresalfi, 2008) about the validity of scores from *any* individual assessment of knowledge. But we choose to pragmatically sequester that concern, because we also agree that policy makers and program evaluators need measures that are aligned to common standards (and largely independent of particular curricular approaches) in order to provide valid evidence for documenting the impact of policies, tracking long-term improvement, conducting studies that generalize beyond the sample, etc. For better or worse, our efforts aim to bridge the tenuous void between these two positions.

Many participants in the measurement-oriented responses to new media present their challenge as a more complex version of the validity challenges facing all measurement efforts (see Hobbs & Frost, 2003). One of ten methodological challenges outlined by the Partnership for Educational Transformation's 2009 report is "the need to distinguish individual contributions and skills on tasks that are done collaboratively" (p. 14). Recapitulating prior testing debates, measurement-oriented responses assume that this problem can be addressed using more open-ended assessment formats and by relaxing some of the psychometric models that presume a large pool of unrelated items whose relative difficulty and ease of guessing can be precisely estimated. This assumption is reflected in the methodological needs outlined by the Partnership. These include the need to (a) detail the wider range of skills that can only be assessed with new technologies, (b) design complex tasks so that failure on one task component does not cascade through the remaining components, (c) determine the extent to which new items should be equivalent to legacy paper and pencil tests, and (d) develop new theories and models of scoring students' processes and strategies (2009, p. 14).

The preceding paragraph reflects recognition of the constraints of traditional test formats. We applaud and encourage these and other efforts to explore alternatives. Nonetheless, we worry that the methodological, technological, economic, and political constraints inherent in large-scale high-stakes testing will result in test scores that are far less convincing evidence of proficiency than current achievement tests. This would be a repeat of the demoralizing demise of assessment reforms in the 1990s. In that case, promised improvements in instruction and student learning never materialized and arguably helped set the stage for the excesses (and absurdities) of the *No Child Left Behind* Act of 2001(see Kirst & Mazzeo, 1996 and Baker, 2003). Among the many other obstacles facing the measurement-oriented responses, we worry about the dynamic social contexts of these new proficiencies, in light of the time required to develop new large-scale tests and item formats. In 1995, an authentic "Twenty-first century" solo/collaborative assessment might have involved a multi-media development project; by 2005, it might have involved building a hypothetical website. Right now, many would argue it would need to include building a wiki; in the near future, it seems that some form of social networking would be necessary to maintain authenticity. While some classroom teachers *might* be able to adapt their instruction and classroom assessments to local and/or new social media practices, standardized tests by their very nature are less able to accommodate these changes. Returning to the *THIS IS SPARTA* prank, we further worry that the measurement-oriented responses are failing to anticipate new digital social networks that will compromise these new tests in ways that are impossible to anticipate. For example, as *TurnItIn.com* began helping educators respond to paper-selling websites, new socially networked alternatives began emerging to thwart that response (Hutton, 2006).[6] Massive item pools and computer-based testing are now thwarting many previously effective cheating strategies (such as hiring individuals to memorize items or sending correct answers to individuals in later time zones). But these solutions depend on the very assumptions that the newer tests aim to relax. A small pool of complex multi-part items will be an inviting target for networked cheaters and unscrupulous businesses. But we are even more worried about a type of "cheating" that is seldom labeled as such by most observers.

8.3.2 Consequential Validity

In considerations of validity, less attention has been directed to the consequences that the design, use, or interpretation of a particular assessment have for learners (e.g., Messick, 1994; Shepard, 2000). This is typically referred to as "consequential validity" (though Frederiksen & Collins, 1989, introduced the term "systemic validity" which more closely resembles how we think about the consequences of assessment and testing practices). As highlighted in the National Research Council report *Knowing What Students Know* (Pellegrino, Chudowsky, & Glaser, 2001) and explicitly represented in all of the measurement-oriented responses, the content and format of tests drive the content and format of instruction. We are concerned about the consequences for learning, teaching, and policy when these new proficiencies are included in external tests, particularly when significant consequences are attached to the performance of individuals, classrooms, schools, states, or countries.

Our concern with the measurement-driven responses is quite simply that they will favor curricula that directly expose students to specific associations that might appear on targeted tests. We expect that this trend will be exacerbated by (a) continued policies favoring the use of externally-developed tests in randomized

---

[6] One new plagiarism strategy being circulated apparently exploits a functionality of TurnItIn to succeed (Lancaster & Clarke, 2008).

experimental designs, (b) continued consolidation in the publishing/testing industry, and (c) the push to integrate curriculum, test prep, and testing into instructional management systems.[7] We think that these trends will further remove these new proficiencies from actual new media and technology practices. If so, these responses will not address concerns over equitable, transparent, and credible participation in new media and technology practices. They may exacerbate the concerns.

8.4 A Proposed Participatory Alternative

The views of cognition and learning that drive our concerns with the evidential and consequential validity of the measurement-oriented responses also underlie our proposed alternative. We argue that pushing very hard on situative views of assessment and testing yields coherent ways of refining school-based participation that can indirectly but consistently raise scores on externally-developed achievement measures. We further argue that doing so enhances the evidential validity of those scores and the consequential validity of those measurement practices.

Assessment and measurement specialists have been relatively slow to acknowledge situative views of knowing and learning. As exemplified by the enduring debate over different assessment formats (e.g., Pellegrino et al., 2001), the fundamental tension in educational assessment has concerned *which* individual model of cognition is most relevant (i.e. "behavioral/associationist" vs. "cognitive/rationalist"). As a caveat, this chapter is not intended as a defense of situative assumptions about knowing and learning that are detailed elsewhere by others. Rather, this chapter aims to show how a design-based model of refinement that emerged from those assumptions can sidestep these more philosophical debates between competing individually-oriented approaches and between individual vs. social approaches. Instead, our alternative offers a model of iterative refinement that ultimately leads to tractable empirical comparisons using external tests.

8.4.1 Situative and Sociocultural Considerations of Assessment and Testing

The Spencer Foundation's *Idea of Testing* project brought together scholars with a range of perspectives that were not widely represented in educational assessment and testing. A report drafted in 2002 (Moss, Pullin, Gee, & Haertel, 2005) outlined

---

[7] We are particularly concerned with Twenty-First century versions of popular programs such as the widely used *SuccessMaker* and other similar programs that have expanded under NCLB. At the time of this writing, nearly any Google search including the phrase "Twenty-First Century Skills" yielded an adlink for the *Expert 21* curriculum just released by Scholastic Inc. An animated banner on the program's website vigorously directs visitors to detailed information about obtaining funds for the curriculum under nine different federal grant programs. While we have yet to examine the program in detail, it strongly features both traditional achievement tests and new Twenty-First century assessments and seems quite consistent with the other measurement-oriented responses.

the goals of this effort and a new book (Moss, Pullin, Gee, Haertel, & Young, 2008) included insightful considerations of the implications of situative theory for assessment. By highlighting the role of context, these considerations argued that (1) all assessments and tests are part of a broader "activity systems," (2) that these systems are defined by interactions between learners and their environment, and (3) that this environment is defined by the range of the tools employed, such as language, computers, and other learners. If this is true, then a coherent interpretation of evidence or consequences must *start* with broader social systems. In their consideration, Greeno and Gresalfi (2008, p. 187) argued that "from a situative perspective assessments that purport to measure students' knowledge in simple quantitative terms, without taking the assessment activity into account, simply do not make sense... The frame of reference for an assessment of someone's knowing is the activity system in which the person participates in generating information that is used in evaluating what he or she knows."

By elevating the importance of the context in which any activity occurs over the cognitive activity that a particular score is presumed to represent, situative perspectives argue that we never really "know," in the positivistic sense, what students really "know." When we say that our approach pushes hard on situative perspectives, we mean that we extend this argument to all formal assessments of learning. Rather than treating tests as positivistic evidence of individual knowledge, we view the act of taking an external test as participation in a peculiar (if not bizarre) form of discourse (Hickey & Zuiker, 2005).

While we embrace these assumptions in our approach, we make a pragmatic compromise that reflects the realities of organized educational contexts. We acknowledge that formal assessments and external tests support discourse that serves specific useful functions that are inevitable in any compulsory educational context. However, rather than using the secondary representations of knowledge in external standards and tests to drive classroom practices, we instead shape the enactment and design of classroom practices in ways that we are confident will improve students' participation in a broad range of discourse practices, including external tests.

In reference to the notion of participatory culture that is the larger context and inspiration for this work, *participatory assessment* is the alternative response to new media that we outline and exemplify in the remainder of this chapter. This work has been funded by the MacArthur Foundation's Twenty-First *Century Assessment Project for Situated and Sociocultural Approaches to Learning*, an effort directed by James Gee (see Gee, 2007) as part of the Digital Media and Learning (DML) program. The Twenty-First Century Assessment initiative has pushed the development of new assessment approaches, including some of the ECD work by Mislevy and Shute referenced earlier, some of the participants in the Partnership for Educational Transformation, and the work of the assessment theorist Delandshere (e.g., 2002). Our contribution to this larger effort is a collaboration between an assessment design team at Indiana University (the first and second authors) and the developers of the Teachers' Strategy Guide (TSG) at Project New Media Literacies at Massachusetts Institute of Technology (the third and fourth authors).

8.4.2 An Initial Application of Participatory Assessment to the Teachers' Strategy Guide

The Teachers' Strategy Guide adopted the practices of participatory culture and new media to engage secondary language arts classrooms in worthwhile conversation with a classic text (Melville's *Moby-Dick*). It consisted of four units—*Motives for Reading, Appropriation and Remixing, Negotiating Cultural Spaces,* and *Continuities and Silences.* Reflecting the assumptions about participatory culture outlined by Jenkins et al. (2006), the TSG assumed that reading and writing—and literacy more broadly—comprise a variety of critical and creative practices. These include "old" practices (e.g., genre study, creative and persuasive writing, literary analysis) and "new" practices (e.g., remixing, fan fiction, and blogging). Reflecting a fundamental shift in what it means to be "literate," the TSG treated both old and new literacy practices as social practices that can be fostered by communal engagement mediated by new digital technologies. For example, the *Appropriation and Remixing* unit explored things like the difference between creative expression and plagiarism, the new media practices of *remixing* and *transmedia navigation,* and the importance of traditional notions like *genre* and *audience* in making meaningful creative expressions. It did so with a range of innovative activities using *Moby-Dick,* the Mixed Magic Theatre's contemporary remix *Moby-Dick: Then and Now* (via online videos of the staged production and interviews with the director and actors), and other remixes of the much-appropriated classic text, including the music video *Ahab* (from nerdcore pioneer MC Lars).

Our collaboration was initiated as the four units of the TSG were taking shape. We spent roughly six months making revisions to the draft units to embed or add the various assessments described below. We then worked intensively with Becky Rupert, an experienced English Language Arts teacher at Aurora Alternative High School in Bloomington, Indiana. Aurora serves students who, for a range of reasons, have not experienced success in conventional high school settings. The two teams collaborated closely, refining our principles and theories as Becky incorporated various TSG activities and units across three trimesters.

8.4.3 Key Aspects and Assumptions of Participatory Assessment

8.4.3.1 Multiple Levels of Assessment

Central to our approach is the alignment of learning across three or more assessment levels. This aspect of the approach emerged in prior studies of inquiry-oriented multimedia science software (e.g., Hickey, Kindfield, Horwitz, & Christie, 2003; Hickey & Zuiker, 2005; Taasobshirazi, Anderson, Zuiker, & Hickey, 2006) and 3-D immersive educational multi-user videogames (Barab et al., 2007a, 2007b; Hickey, Ingram-Goble, & Jameson, 2009). Each of these projects aimed to enhance inquiry-based learning while obtaining broadly convincing evidence of that learning. They did so by aligning learning across three assessment levels. At the first level were informal "discursive" formative assessments that fostered participation in worthwhile communal discourse around the inquiry-learning activities. These were aligned to a second level consisting of conventional classroom performance assessments designed to tap students' individual understanding. At the third level, conventional external achievement measures were used to measure the broader consequences of these refinements on aggregated student achievement. Put most succinctly, this approach (1) aligns communal discourse to (2) maximize individual understanding in order to (3) indirectly increase aggregated achievement. After multiple cycles of refinement, the sort of statistically and pedagogically significant achievement gains on external measures that have eluded inquiry-oriented curricula were obtained.

As summarized in Table 8.1, our approach actually distinguishes between five different assessment levels.[8] Each level defines a specific point along a continuum of increased "distance" from the enactment of specific activities in specific classrooms. Consistent with the levels used in the summative evaluation by Ruiz-Primo, Shavelson, Hamilton, and Klein (2002); we label these levels *immediate, close, proximal, distal,* and *remote.* But our situative assumptions and focus on formative functions lead us to characterize those levels and their interaction quite differently.

8.4.3.2 A Focus on Assessment Orientation and Timescale

Our assessment levels are *oriented* towards different educational activity systems. Each level is oriented towards an increased scope of learning, assessment, and feedback. At the immediate level, *event-oriented* assessments concern the enactment of a curricular activity in a particular classroom context. These assessments acknowledge that every enactment of a given curricular activity is different and situated in the particular classroom context. As will be elaborated below, our immediate-level assessments consist of informal "event reflections" that are embedded in the actual activity. They promote reflection on the way that domain knowledge is being taken up in the discourse during that activity.[9]

---

[8] The nature of the actual levels has evolved substantially over the various projects and are continuing to evolve in the current project. The important point here is that the levels are discrete points along a continuum that ranges from informal interpretation of contextualized communal participation at the immediate level to highly formalized measurement of decontextualized aggregated achievement at the remote level; semi-formal assessment of individual understanding falls somewhere between those extremes.

[9] Contrary to prevailing views of assessment that focus primarily on individuals, our participatory approach treats the informal interpretation of discourse in the enactment of activities as "assessment." Thus, the insights about educational discourse that these immediate-level assessments generate are "evidence." Likewise, the process by which that evidence shapes that same discourse is considered "feedback." Rather than distinguishing this informal reflection from "assessment," our situative theory and participatory approach characterizes all assessments and tests as elements in specific forms of educational discourse. Therefore, the use of increasingly abstract (i.e., decreasingly contextualized) representations of domain knowledge in those assessments and tests foster increasingly abstract and decontexualized discourses. Across levels, this discourse is meaningful for discussions about educational practices that occur over increasingly lengthy periods of time and concern increasingly larger educational activity systems. This is the essence of what we mean by "pushing hard" on situative views of assessment.

Table 8.1 Five levels of assessment and their varied formative functions for different audiences

Level	Orientation and type	Timescale	Assessment practice	Formative function for students	Formative function for teachers	Formative function for designers and researchers	Formative function for policy makers
Immediate	Event-Oriented *Reflections*	Immediate	Informal reflection on the enactment of specific curricular activities	Shape participation in curricular activities	Refine discourse around the enactment of the curricular activities	Refine features of the curricular activities and teacher guidelines	(none)
Close	Activity-Oriented *Reflections*	Days	Informal reflection on the implementation and design of specific curricular activities	Shape participation in worthwhile discourse	Refine enactment of curricular activities and reflections	Refine features of the reflection rubric, specific design principles	(none)
Proximal	Artifact-oriented *Rubrics*	Weeks	Rubrics for analyzing artifacts for evidence of understanding of targeted formalisms	Shape understanding of specific concepts	Remediation for individual students and topics	Evaluate entire curriculum and general design principles	(none)
Distal	Standards-oriented *Assessments*	Months	Student performance on constructed or selected performance assessments (essay items, web-based activities, etc.)	(none)	Impact of curriculum on related understanding	Evaluate finished curriculum and meta-design principles	Help identify worthwhile curricula and make curricular policy
Remote	Achievement-oriented *Tests*	Years	Externally-developed tests of knowledge aggregated across entire populations of students	(none)	(none)	Deliver evidence of long term achievement and behavior in controlled studies	Learn about impact of selected curricula and curricular policies

At the close level, assessment is *activity-oriented*. Close-level assessments are "activity reflections" that occur after a curricular activity is completed. While still quite informal, they promote students' reflection on the domain knowledge that was central to the goals of the curricular activity. This broadening continues out to *artifacts* in the proximal level, *standards* in the distal level, and *achievement* in the remote level. The distinction between levels builds on Lemke's (2000) notion of *timescales*. Evidence at different levels provides feedback that drives change over different time intervals. Feedback from the immediate-level event reflections changes the way classroom activities are being enacted—immediately. This is a faster feedback cycle than the one associated with close-level activity reflections, which concern the way the larger activity effectively engaged students in participating in and with the relevant idea. The feedback from the close-level activity reflections is more intended to impact (1) students' design of their own artifacts, (2) students' enactment of subsequent activities, and (3) the teacher's implementation of the activity in subsequent classes. But these activity systems are more fleeting than the ones defined by students drafting their artifacts or completing formal exams. Even slower still are the activity systems that use feedback from external achievement tests. Our approach assumes that the feedback from remote level tests is only useful (i.e., valid) for broader policy and curricular decisions that occur over a timescale of years. In this way, timescale frames the validity of different forms of assessment.

8.4.3.3 A Focus on Formative and Summative Functions

Assuming that learning is primarily social change leads us to treat assessment levels as "formative." Assessments at all levels have formative potential, but they are formative for audiences that engage in educational practice at different timescales. In this way, our approach sets aside the traditional dichotomy between formative and summative assessments, focusing instead on different assessment *functions*. We assume that all assessments have both formative and summative potential; we further assume that the nature of this potential depends on what (event vs. activity) or who (student, teacher, administrator, or policy maker) is being informed by that evidence. Hence, the evidence from distal-level, norm-referenced achievement tests that measure improvement over years has formative potential for policies and decisions that occur on that same time scale. As highlighted by the empty cells in Table 8.1, our approach assumes that this same evidence has no formative potential for students or teachers; the function of remote-level tests for them is entirely summative. This is, of course, contrary to the current push for "data-driven" teaching.[10]

---

[10] Of course, it is possible to speculate about ways that remote-level tests can be used formatively by teachers. But our approach assumes that the negative consequences for curriculum, student learning, and evidential validity far outweigh any potential benefits of doing so. We concur with assessment scholars like Popham (2006) and Shepard (2007) who argue that the formative potential of standardized achievement tests is quite limited (and often overstated).

Participatory assessment treats all participants in the education process as potential "learners." This includes students, teachers, designers, administrators, and policy makers. We strongly believe that policy makers and administrators are now failing to use achievement evidence to improve achievement and are often using it in ways that undermine learning. But we still believe that this evidence, when used differently and more carefully, has untapped potential for improving learning by informing policy makers and policies over the longer term.

8.4.3.4 Design-Based Iterative Refinements

Our approach draws from contemporary design-based research (DBR) methods (e.g., Cobb, Confrey, diSessa, Lehrer, & Schauble, 2003). Rejecting the conventional distinction between "basic" and "applied" research, DBR emphasizes the development of "intermediate-level" theory and then situates those theories alongside the pertinent contextual factors that define their relevance and shape their continued refinement. In this way, DBR focuses on the development of design principles to help refine "local" theory in the context of reform. Hence, the design principles from this collaboration are most relevant to the refinement of secondary new media language arts curricula; they would have to be refined more to be useful for other domains and even more for non-classroom contexts.

Our approach embraces Lemke's (2000) suggestion that it is useful to analyze activity across three timescales, focusing on activity at a central timescale and aligning to those across adjacent timescales. In general, our approach extends this suggestion across three iterative cycles of refinement. As elaborated in Hickey, Zuiker, Taasobshirazi, Schafer, & Michael (2006), an initial *implementation* cycle aligns the immediate level to the close level and evaluates impact on the proximal level; a second *experimentation* cycle aligns the close-level to the proximal level to impact the distal level. A final *evaluation cycle* uses the distal and remote outcomes to evaluate the long-term consequences of the curriculum.

8.4.3.5 Proficiencies as Formalisms and Boundary Objects

A situative view of learning means that knowledge is primarily represented by successful participation in domain-specific discourses. Take, for example, our students' ability to use different narrative *genres* to make new meanings for particular audiences when remixing a source text. We view this "ability" as a communal practice that is closely bound to particular narrative, media, and social contexts. Our students' ability to explain the role of genre in creative remixing on a formal classroom exam or performance assessment is seen as another context defined by its narratives, media formats, and social configurations. Likewise, students' ability to use their knowledge of genre to discriminate between more-correct and less-correct associations on an external test is yet another context with yet another set of configurations. Rather than working "back" from the abstract knowledge defined by standards and tests, our approach works forward from the communal knowledge practices. It does so by characterizing the proficiencies targeted by a particular curriculum *and* represented in externally-developed standards as "formalisms."

The notion of formalisms reframes proficiencies as "boundary objects" (Bowker & Star, 1999) that can inhabit multiple activity systems, enabling communication and collaboration across those systems. When a proficiency is characterized as a formalism or a boundary object, it "answers to different sets of audiences and pursues different sets of tasks" (Star & Griesemer, 1989, p. 388). As Moss, Girard, and Haniford (2006, p. 146) point out, "a boundary object is a particular kind of cultural tool that not only crosses boundaries of activity systems, such as a mandated assessment, but is also plastic enough to meet the local needs while maintaining a common identity across sites . . . . A mandated assessment would function as a boundary object when actors in the local context are able to cooperate in providing necessary information to outsiders while maintaining a productive level of authority and agency over their own practice."

Our framework essentially stretches this characterization of "mandated assessment" across the different activity systems represented by our five assessment levels. Relative to our *Appropriation and Remixing* activities, this included (1) discussion of *genre* in the enactment of those activities, (2) the way that *genre* was introduced and used by those activities, (3) the way students used *genre* in their creative artifacts to make them more meaningful, (4) the formal interrogation of students' understanding of the role of *genre* on an end-of-unit assessment, and (5) the inclusion of items from the language arts subtest of the graduation qualifying exam that touch on students' knowledge of *genre.*

8.4.4 Examples and Descriptions of Assessments for the Teachers' Strategy Guide

Across our collaboration, we continually refined both the assessments for the TSG and the design principles behind them. Our collaboration is continuing as we design new activities that can be used with other texts and take better advantage of existing and emerging digital social networks. The following examples reflect some of our more recent insights, and some have been revised since our work with the TSG to reflect those insights and better illustrate the approach.

8.4.4.1 Immediate-Level Event Reflections

Immediate-level assessments concern the way activities get enacted in particular classrooms with particular students. The actual "assessments" consist of *event reflections*. These are embedded prompts intended to immediately shape the discourse that defines those enactments. Once we had reviewed the draft activities in the TSG to better clarify the formalisms they were targeting, we then revised the text of those activities to prompt worthwhile reflection on those formalisms. Thus, an immediate-level event reflection for an *Appropriation and Remixing* activity that involves *genre* (e.g., viewing MC Lars' music video *Ahab*) would simply ask students to reflect on the way genre is being used in that activity: *How is* genre *being used to create new meaning in this remix?*

Obviously, immediate-level assessment is extremely informal. Some will find it too informal to qualify as "assessment." However, four design features make these seemingly commonplace prompts a key element of a systematic approach. First, they are carefully phrased to focus on the activity, rather than individual understanding of the targeted formalism (i.e., not *Who can tell us what genre means?*). This extends the research literature on classroom discourse and the stipulation against "known answer" questions (e.g., Erickson, 1996) into the realm of assessment. We assume that a premature focus on individual understanding is summative and undermines the formative function of the nascent communal discourse that invites struggling learners to enlist targeted formalisms. Second, the reflective prompts are introduced in sets that scaffold increasingly sophisticated communal discourse within the enactment. As shown in Table 8.2 (second column), the prompts start out with the more routine *conceptual* engagement concerning the concepts underlying the formalism. Building on the ideas of Gresalfi, Barab, Siyahhan, and Christensen (2009), subsequent prompts move the discourse to the more challenging *consequential* engagement (concerning the consequences of the formalism for practice) and *critical* engagement (concerning better or alternative perspectives or practices).

Across our collaboration, we worked with Becky and her students to help use the event reflections to ensure that every student had an opportunity to enlist the formalism in informal discourse during the activity. Each activity typically had several modes of discourse, including online discussions, small group work, and class discussions. Together, we discussed a broader notion of participation at this level that every student should at least be actively listening to more articulate classmates who are themselves struggling to make meaning of challenging new ideas. Immediate-level assessment is designed to draw in and scaffold the participation of students who otherwise may not enter the conversation directly. Part of our inspiration comes from the way that the "lurking" by most newcomers in social networks crucially prepares them to engage more meaningfully once they feel ready (e.g., Gray, 2004). Immediate-level assessments increase the opportunities students have to participate. They do so in part by directing the focus of students' participation towards the activity rather than themselves. This represents one of our central assessment design principles: a formalism must be enlisted by a community of learners before it can be enlisted *correctly* by that same community.

The third systematic feature of our immediate-level assessments is the way the prompts are carefully worded to foster discourse around the domain-specific nuances that give the formalisms their communicative power. For example, the immediate-level conceptual reflection uses the more specific new media term *remix,* while the consequential prompt uses the more generic term *appropriation.* This is intended to foster discourse that extends the communicative potential of the formalism (e.g., knowing that all remixes are appropriations but not vice versa). The

Table 8.2 Examples of immediate, close, and proximal assessments of the way that knowledge of genre is used to make new meaning when appropriating and remixing source texts

	Assessment Level		
	Immediate-level	Close-level	Proximal-level
Degree of engagement	Event-oriented reflection	Activity-oriented reflection	Artifact-oriented reflection
Conceptual (reflecting on the formalism itself)	How is genre being used to create new meaning in this remix?	In what ways was genre used to make new meaning in remixes that were included in this activity?	How does your remix use genre to create new meaning for particular audiences?
Consequential (reflecting on the consequences of the formalism for practice)	How is the way that genre is used in this appropriation make it particularly meaningful to some of us?	How did the remixes that were selected or included in this activity impact the way genre was used to create new meaning?	In what ways did your choice of genre for your remix limit or expand the meaning you could create?
Critical (reflecting critically on the way the formalism was enlisted)	Is there a different, or better, or more creative way that this remix could be using genre?	What are some different, better, or more creative ways that genre could have been used in this activity?	Can you think of reasons why someone else might have used genre to create meaning differently than you did?

fourth feature of the event reflections is their alignment with the close-level *activity reflections* that occur at the end of the activities. The prompts prepare students to successfully engage with corresponding reflection questions at the end of the activity. Returning to our TSG example, the notion that remixing sources in different genres as a way of appealing to particular audiences is actually quite a sophisticated idea for secondary students to "understand," much less to enlist in their own creative remixes.[11] By introducing this sophisticated idea in the "no stakes" immediate-level discourse, the class is better prepared to enlist this idea in the next, slightly more formal discourse around the close-level assessment.[12]

---

[11] Reflecting our concern with working back from testable standards to classroom practices, the most closely corresponding high-school literature standard in Indiana was "Analyze characteristics of subgenres, types of writings such as satire, parody, allegory, and pastoral that are used in poetry, prose, plays, novels, short stories, essays, and other basic genres" (English Language Arts Standard 11.3.1).

[12] It would be most straightforward to label our immediate, close, and proximal level practice as "participatory assessments" and distinguish them from conventional (i.e., non-participatory) individual assessments and tests. However, it is actually the alignment across levels and the balancing of formative and summative functions within and across all of the levels of communal, individual, and aggregated activity that ultimately comprises what we mean by participatory assessment.

8.4.4.2 Close-Level Activity-Oriented Reflections

The close-level reflective questions are similar to the immediate-level questions but concern the way the activity was designed and implemented by the teacher. We assume that discussing and critiquing the design and implementation of entire activities begins abstracting the formalism from its context of use, while continuing to resist a premature focus on individual understanding. As shown in Table 8.2, close-level reflections are essentially discussion questions posed to the class by the teacher after an activity is completed. They are still quite informal, and embrace the four features described above. Much of our design work now consists of experimenting with different ways of wording and presenting questions and examining the direct impact on discourse and their indirect impact on the artifacts students create. For example, when teachers present them verbally, the discussion unfolds more quickly, and teachers can use their judgment to select where to start and how sophisticated they should get. We have also experimented with putting them on paper and asking students to write down any reflections that they have (including "I don't know" or even "I don't care") and then immediately and informally discussing their answers.[13] Near the end of our collaboration (and in our newest work), the prompts were used in online forums. As with the immediate-level questions, the formative focus on communal discourse – and the lack of a summative focus on understanding – invites more meaningful participation from even recalcitrant participants.[14]

The anthropological notion of *prolepsis* helps explain why it is so important to align assessments across increasingly formal levels. As introduced to educators by Rogoff and Gardner (1984), prolepsis refers to the way that future activities shape activity in the present. If a class of students comes to learn that they will eventually need to enlist formalisms correctly, they are more likely to attempt to enlist those formalisms initially. Hence, the initial units in a curriculum should use fairly routine prompts across levels, like the ones in Table 8.2. The very first activity should help the class of students see that engaging in discourse around the activity and event reflections directly prepared them to create more compelling and creative artifacts. The proximity of the levels makes it obvious that participating in one level will facilitate participation at the next level.

8.4.4.3 Proximal-Level Artifact-Oriented Reflections

Our proximal assessment practices straddle the boundary between communal and individual engagement and begin converging with conventional assessment

---

[13] One thing we learned early on was that when the teacher picks up the written responses and attempts to use them summatively to assess individual understanding, it was impossible to use the activity to foster the forms of discourse that we were after.

[14] On several occasions, our apparent success was signaled by conversations that started with "I don't know, but..." followed by a sufficiently sophisticated discourse around the targeted formalism.

practices. For the most part, our proximal assessments are defined by a set of reflection questions used to guide students' critical review of their artifacts, and come at the end of a larger unit of instruction. Our proximal assessments for the TSG mostly consisted of reflections for the artifacts students created during the various TSG activities (e.g., a piece of writing, remix, blog post). The reflections are used by students and teachers to assess whether the artifacts showed that students had appropriately enlisted the formalism(s) targeted by the activity.

We did not begin focusing on proximal assessments until our collaboration around the TSG was well underway. We used the opportunity to try out different formats of proximal assessments. Our efforts to apply the situative assessment design principles to artifacts and student portfolios were informed by other portfolio assessment literature. Habib and Wittek (2007) helped us appreciate the situated functions of artifacts in portfolio assessment; this, in turn, helped us appreciate the distinction that Dysthe, Engelsen, and Lima (2007) made between *working portfolios* and *presentation portfolios,* as well as Popham's (1997) warnings about "dysfunctionally detailed" rubrics. We began creating *artifact-oriented reflective assessments* that students could use to assess their own artifacts before submitting them; their responses to the questions were assessed by the teacher, for a grade. As shown in the rightmost column of Table 8.2, these reflective questions ask students to state how their artifact shows that they understand the formalism; teachers can then review these statements and use them to assign points or grades as they see fit. As with the immediate- and close-level assessments, the questions are carefully worded to summatively assess the *artifacts* that students create while being formative regarding students' understanding of the targeted formalisms. By providing these reflection questions to students as they are creating their artifacts, the assessment provides clues as to what insights the artifacts should illustrate without being overly specific. The act of reading and answering the questions while creating her artifact reciprocally helps the individual student build a more abstract cognitive representation of the formalism; the individual's written responses to the questions then provide the teacher with relatively objective evidence of that knowledge. The questions are carefully structured to avoid that natural tendency for students to demand overly specific feedback on the salient features of their artifact (i.e., "Is *this* what you want?"). By building on the scaffolding of the immediate-level and the close-level reflective prompts and focusing on a small number of formalisms (sometimes just one for brief activities), most students should have no problem creating an artifact that embodies a sophisticated use of formalisms like the one in our example. By carefully aligning the immediate- and close-level assessments and feedback, teachers and innovators can set remarkably high standards for the artifacts that students produce. This, in turn, serves to motivate participation and creates a non-punitive context within which teachers can provide additional feedback that supports additional learning. Students' responses and the artifact they refer to then provide teachers with a powerful basis for revisiting formalisms that are still not being enlisted appropriately.

8.4.4.4 Distal-Level Standards-Oriented Assessments

Distal-level assessments directly assess individual students' understanding of the targeted formalism and do so in a new and even more abstract context that is directly shaped by whatever external content standards to which the students, teacher, and curriculum are accountable. In the case of the TSG, which had originally been designed to target the eleven new media proficiencies outlined by Jenkins et al. (2006), we began developing conventional performance assessments and essay items near the end of our collaboration. An essay item for the remixing example we have been using would simply ask students to explain in their own words and using an original example how genre can be used to generate new meaning when creating remixes and appropriations for different audiences.

As explained in the first part of this paper, our overall approach aims to align practice-oriented responses to relevant content standards. In most cases this will include conventional content standards. To reiterate, our overall design research approach aims to align assessments across the immediate, close, and proximal levels in the initial implementation cycles. This is in part because the gap between most innovative curricular activities and traditional content standards is simply too great to close in a single implementation cycle. Near the close of our TSG collaboration, we began examining the relevant content standards in our state to begin thinking about the sorts of distal assessments we would use to begin evaluating the impact of the TSG on standards-oriented external tests and begin broadening the TSG activities and our new assessments accordingly. Consider, for example, that the most relevant state standard regarding our genre example is "Analyze characteristics of subgenres, types of writings such as satire, parody, allegory, and pastoral that are used in poetry, prose, plays, novels, short stories, essays, and other basic genres." Obviously this standard is still quite removed from the knowledge targeted by the activities in the *Appropriation and Remixing* unit. Reflecting what it means to work from the practices out to the standards, a subsequent revision cycle would search for ways to expand the existing practices and assessments (particularly the proximal assessments) to extend the discourse around those activities to incorporate these broader, more abstract ideas. Our assumption is that the discourse community that emerges around the core practices such as the ones described above should be well prepared to engage in such conversations. Because this discourse community was in part shaped by participation in the assessment practices described above, those same practices could then be used to readily align the curriculum to those external standards. Thus, rather than adding new activities to the *Appropriation and Remixing* unit to encompass the standard referenced above, we might instead just add an item to the proximal-level reflective rubric that raises the issue, provide formative feedback accordingly, and add a distal item to the final assessment to assess that understanding and provide additional formative feedback as necessary.

8.4.4.5 Remote-Level Achievement-Oriented Tests

As implied above, external achievement tests have a very specific formative function in our approach. This function is limited to measuring the broader impact of a particular curriculum on broader educational outcomes that are entirely independent of that curriculum. As our TSG collaboration extended over just a single year, we were able to systematically consider only the standards that our students' high school graduation test might reference and had just begun considering how those standards would have actually been manifested in the actual test. For example, we noted that the source texts that students were asked to write about in the writing sample in the just-released items all concerned classic texts and that the actual prompt was for a persuasive essay that was actually quite close to what we had been covering in the TSG.

8.4.5 Continuing and Future Efforts

Our collaboration around the original Teachers' Strategy Guide was concluded after the year of effort described above. Project New Media Literacies is in the process of formally publishing that curriculum in its current form, along with many of the assessments created in our collaboration. New versions of some of the activities in the TSG are currently being developed as part of a new project called the *Participatory Activities and Assessment Network* through which we are working with Becky and several other secondary English teachers to develop and refine more discrete participatory curricula and assessments following the approach described above. In addition to new versions of the TSG activities, we are working with the teachers to identify promising activities that will be appealing to their students *and* can potentially be aligned to accountability standards via the process previously described. We are designing a digital social network to foster the "spread" of these activities and assessments to larger numbers of teachers. Specifically, we are working with teachers to develop and integrate participatory activities and assessments into their curricula and then helping these innovative teacher-leaders share their "no-stakes" evidence from the immediate-level and close-level assessments (essentially accounts and recordings of reflective discourse) and their nascent expertise with the activity to help other teachers implement them in their own classrooms. Teachers can then compare their success on the "low-stakes" proximal assessments by inviting their students to post their own artifacts on the network. In addition to creating the network and social structures that foster this process, our research team will also develop distal-level assessments for the most popular and promising activities and begin formally assessing the impact of those activities on standards-oriented understanding.

Eventually (after perhaps two years), we hope to have enough activities that many new teachers can include them throughout the school year. We assume that doing so would lead to even more of the dramatic transformation of classroom culture that we witnessed in Becky's classroom. Furthermore, we hope to have multiple teachers at the same school doing so, leading to the kinds of broader transformations we are starting to see at Aurora High School as a consequence of Becky's success. At such a time, it will be appropriate to begin carefully documenting gains on existing standards-oriented achievement tests, as well as on the sorts of new Twenty-First century skills tests referenced above. For the reasons outlined in this chapter, we believe that such a scaled up implementation of our curriculum would show significantly larger gains on these external measures than the curricula that are now emerging from the more measurement-oriented responses or the existing curricula they aim to supplement or supplant. For the same reasons, we also believe that our students would show larger gains on external measures of traditional proficiencies as well.

8.5 Conclusion

Obviously, this alternative approach is still in its infancy and raises far more problems than it solves. Because it is so solidly rooted in newer situative and participatory views of cognition and learning that have not been widely appreciated by the assessment and measurement community, we assume that some will find it quite dense and perhaps overly complicated. Conversely, because our approach acknowledges concerns over accountability that have been ignored or dismissed by the community associated with the practice-oriented responses, we anticipate puzzlement from some over our interest in improving performance on such measures. In response, we reiterate that this approach is a resolutely pragmatic one. We contend that most efforts to foster ethical, equitable, and transparent participation in new media and technology practices will eventually be forced to confront the tensions that we have explored in this chapter. We hope that this chapter provides useful suggestions for how these two very different communities of educational practice might work together to accomplish widely held goals in this regard.

Acknowledgements This work was supported by the MacArthur Foundation's Digital Media and Learning Initiative. We thank Jim Gee, Henry Jenkins, Erin Reilly, Anna van Someren, and Hilary Kolos for their contributions to the ideas, research, and curricula described in this chapter.

References

Alvermann, D. E. (2002). *Adolescents and literacies in a digital world*. New York: Peter Lang Publishing, Inc.
Anderson, J. R., Reder, L. M., & Simon, H. A. (1996). Situated learning and education. *Educational Researcher, 25*(4), 5–11.
Baker, E. L. (2003). Multiple measures: Toward tiered systems. *Educational Measurement: Issues and Practice, 22*(2), 13–17.
Barab, S., Sadler, T., Heiselt, C., Hickey, D., & Zuiker, S. (2007b). Relating narrative, inquiry, and inscriptions: A framework for socioscientific inquiry. *Journal of Science Education and Technology, 16*, 59–82.
Barab, S., Zuiker, S., Warren, S., Hickey, D., Ingram-Goble, A., Kwon, E., et al. (2007a). Situationally embodied curriculum: Relating formalisms and contexts. *Science Education, 91*, 750–782.
Barton, D. (1994). *Literacy: An introduction to the ecology of written language*. Oxford: Blackwell.
Beach, R., Anson, C., Breuch, L., & Swiss, T. (2008). *Teaching writing using blogs, wikis, and other digital tools*. Norwood, MA: Christopher-Gordon Publishers, Inc.

Black, R. W. (2008). *Adolescents and online fan fiction*. New York: Peter Lang.

Bowker, G. C., & Star, S. L. (1999). *Sorting things out: Classification and its consequences*. Cambridge, MA: MIT Press.

boyd, d. (2008). Why teens ♥ MySpace: The role of digital publics in youth culture. In D. Buckingham (Ed.), *Youth, identity and digital media* (pp. 119–142). Cambridge, MA: MIT Press.

boyd, d, & Ellison, N. B. (2007). Social network sites: Definition, history, and scholarship. *Journal of Computer-Mediated Communication, 13*, 210–230.

Brandt, D. (2005). Writing for a living: Literacy and the knowledge economy. *Written Communication, 22*(2), 166–197.

Brandt, D. (2009). *Literacy and learning: Reflections on writing, reading, and society*. Hoboken, NJ: Jossey-Bass.

Cobb, P., Confrey, J., diSessa, A., Lehrer, R., & Schauble, L. (2003). Design experiments in educational research. *Educational Researcher, 32*(1), 9–20.

Coiro, J., Knobel, M., Lankshear, C., & Leu, D. J. (2008). *Handbook of research on new literacies*. New York: Routledge.

Delandshere, G. (2002). Assessment as inquiry. *Teachers College Record, 104*(7), 1461–1484.

Drotner, K. (2007). Leisure is hard work: Digital practices and future competencies. In D. Buckingham (Ed.), *Digital youth: Learning and identity*. Cambridge, MA: MIT Press.

Dysthe, O., Engelsen, K. S., & Lima, I. (2007). Variations in portfolio assessment in higher education: Discussion of quality issues based on a Norwegian survey across institutions and disciplines. *Assessing Writing, 12*(2), 129–148.

Erickson, F. (1996). Going for the zone: The social and cognitive ecology of teacher-student interaction in classroom conversations. In D. Hicks (Ed.), *Discourse, learning and schooling*. Hillsdale, NJ: Lawrence Erlbaum.

Frederiksen, J. R., & Collins, A. (1989). A systems approach to educational testing. *Educational Researcher, 18*(9), 27–32.

Gee, J. P. (1989). Literacy, discourse, and linguistics: What is literacy. *Journal of Education, 171*(1), 5–25.

Gee, J. P. (1996). *Social linguistics and literacies: Ideology in discourses* (2nd ed.). London: Taylor & Francis.

Gee, J. P. (1999). *An introduction to discourse analysis: Theory and method*. New York: Routledge.

Gee, J. P. (2004). *Situated language and learning: A critique of traditional schooling*. New York: Routledge.

Gee, J. P. (2007). *A 21st Century assessment project for situated and sociocultural approaches to learning*. Proposal to the John D. and Catherine T. MacArthur Foundation.

Ghezzi, P. (2006, March 3). Report: Georgia student tests are too easy. State works to revise standards for achievement. *Atlanta Journal Constitution* (A1).

Goldman, S., Booker, A., & McDermott, M. (2007). Mixing the digital, social and cultural: Learning, identity and agency in youth participation. In D. Buckingham (Ed.), *Digital youth: Learning and identity*. Cambridge, MA: MIT Press.

Gray, B. (2004). Informal learning in an online community of practice. *Journal of Distance Education, 19*(1), 20–35.

Greeno, J. G. (1997). On claims that answer the wrong questions. *Educational Researcher, 26*(1), 5.

Greeno, J. G. (1998). The situativity of knowing, learning, and research. *American Psychologist, 53*(1), 5–26.

Greeno, J. G., & Gresalfi, M. S. (2008). Opportunities to learn in practice and identity. In P. A. Moss, D. C. Pullin, J. P. Gee, E. H. Haertel, & L. J. Young (Eds.), *Assessment, equity, and opportunity to learn*, pp. 170–199. Cambridge, MA: Cambridge University Press.

Gresalfi, M., Barab, S., Siyahhan, S., & Christensen, T. (2009). Virtual worlds, conceptual understanding, and me: Designing for consequential engagement. *On the Horizon, 17*(1), 21–34.

Habib, L., & Wittek, L. (2007). The portfolio as artifact and actor. *Mind, Culture, and Activity, 14*(4), 266–282.

Heath, S. B. (1983). *Ways with words: Language, life, and work in communities and classrooms.* Cambridge, UK: Cambridge University Press.

Herrington, A., Hodgson, K., & Moran, C. (Eds.). (2009). *Teaching the New Writing: Technology, Change, and Assessment in the 21st-Century Classroom.* New York: Teachers College Press.

Hickey, D. T., Ingram-Goble, A., & Jameson, E. (2009). Designing assessments and assessing designs in virtual educational environments. *Journal of Science Education Technology, 30,* 837–861.

Hickey, D. T., Kindfield, A. C. H., Horwitz, P., & Christie, M. A. (2003). Integrating curriculum, instruction, assessment, and evaluation in a technology-supported genetics environment. *American Educational Research Journal, 40*(2), 495–538.

Hickey, D. T., Wolfe, E. W., & Kindfield, A. C. H. (2000). Assessing learning in a technology-supported genetics environment: Evidential and systemic validity issues. *Educational Assessment, 6*(3), 155–196.

Hickey, D. T., & Zuiker, S. J. (2005). Engaged participation: A sociocultural model of motivation with implications for assessment. *Educational Assessment, 10,* 277–305.

Hickey, D. T., Zuiker, S. J., Taasobshirazi, G., Schafer, N. J., & Michael, M. A. (2006). Three is the magic number: A design-based framework for balancing formative and summative functions of assessment. *Studies in Educational Evaluation, 32,* 180–201.

Hobbs, R., & Frost, R. (2003). Measuring the acquisition of media-literacy skills. *Reading Research Quarterly, 38,* 330–355.

Hull, G., & Nelson, M. E. (2005). Locating the semiotic power of multimodality. *Written Communication, 22,* 224–260.

Hutton, P. A. (2006). Understanding student cheating and what educators can do about it. *College Teaching, 54*(1), 171–176.

International Society for Technology in Education. (2007). *The ISTE National Educational Technology Standards (NETS-S) and performance indicators for students.* Eugene, OR: Author.

Ito, M. (2008). *Hanging out, messing around and geeking out: Living and learning with new media.* Cambridge, MA: MIT Press.

Ito, M., Bittanti, M., boyd, d, Herr-Stephenson, B., Lange, P. G., & Robinson, L. (2008). *Living and learning with new media: Summary of findings from the digital youth project.* The John D. and Catherine T. MacArthur Foundation Reports on Digital Media and Learning.

James, C. (2008). *Young people, ethics, and the new digital media: A synthesis from the Good Play project.* Boston, MA: Harvard University.

Jenkins, H. (2006). *Convergence culture: Where old and new media collide.* New York: New York University Press.

Jenkins, H., Purushotma, R., Clinton, K., Weigel, M., & Robison, A. J. (2006). *Confronting the challenges of participatory culture: Media education for the 21st century.* Chicago: The MacArthur Foundation.

Kirst, M. W., & Mazzeo, C. (1996). The rise, fall, and rise of state assessment in California: 1993–96. *Phi Delta Kappan, 78*(4), 319–323.

Lam, W. (2006). Culture and learning in the context of globalization; Research directions. *Review of Research in Education, 30,* 213–237.

Lancaster, T., & Clarke, R. (2008). How to succeed at cheating without really trying: Five top tips for successful cheating. In H. White (Ed.), *9th Annual Conference of the Subject Centre for Information and Computer Sciences,* pp. 121–125. Liverpool: University of Ulster.

Laucius, J. (2009, April 8). 'Wikipedia kids' ill prepared for universities, professors say. *The Ottowa Citizen.*

Lemke, J. L. (2000). Across the scales of time: Artifacts, activities, and meanings in ecosocial systems. *Mind, Culture, and Activity, 7*(4), 273–290.

Leu, D. J., O'Bryne, I., Zawilinski, J., McVerry, J. G., & Everett-Cacopardo, H. (2009). Expanding the new literacies conversation. *Educational Researcher, 38*(4), 264–269.

Lievrouw, L., & Livingstone, S. (Eds.). (2006). *Handbook of new media: Social shaping and social consequences.* London: Sage.

Lisbon Council. (2007). *Skills for the future*. Brussels: Lisbon Council.
Messick, S. (1994). The interplay of evidence and consequences in the validation of performance assessments. *Educational Researcher, 23*(2), 13–23.
Metzger, E., & Flanagin, A. (Eds.). (2008). *Digital media, youth, and credibility*. Cambridge, MA: MIT Press.
Mislevy, R. J., Steinberg, L. S., & Almond, R. G. (2003). On the structure of educational assessments. *Measurement: Interdisciplinary Research and Perspectives, 1*, 3–62.
Moss, P. A., Girard, B., & Haniford, L. (2006). Validity in educational assessment. *Review of Research in Education, 30*, 109–162.
Moss, P. A., Pullin, D., Gee, J. P., & Haertel, E. H. (2005). The idea of testing: Psychometric and sociocultural perspectives. *Measurement: Interdisciplinary Research and Perspectives, 3*(2), 63–83.
Moss, P., Pullin, D., Gee, J. P., Haertel, E., & Young, L. J. (2008). *Assessment, equity, and opportunity to learn*. Cambridge, UK: Cambridge University Press.
Partners in Educational Transformation. (2008). Transforming education: Assessing and teaching 21st century skills. Retrieved from http://www.atc21s.org/GetAssets.axd? FilePath=/Assets/Files/699792fd-4d41-44f2-8208-cbb3fccb6572.pdf
Partnership for 21st Century Skills. (2005). *Assessment of 21st century skills: The current landscape*. Tucson, AZ: Partnership for 21st Century Skills.
Partnership for 21st Century Skills. (2007a). *21st century skills professional development: A partnership for 21st century skills e-paper*. Tucson, AZ: Partnership for 21st Century Skills.
Partnership for 21st Century Skills. (2007b). *21st century skills assessment: A partnership for 21st century skills e-paper*. Tucson, AZ: Author.
Pellegrino, J. W., Chudowsky, N., & Glaser, R. (2001). *Knowing what students know: The science and design of educational assessment*. Washington, DC: National Academy Press.
Popham, W. J. (1997). What's wrong-and what's right-with rubrics. *Educational leadership, 55*, 72–75.
Popham, W. J. (2006). Phony formative assessments: Buyer beware! *Educational Leadership, 64*(3), 86–87.
Quellmalz, E. S., & Pellegrino, J. W. (2009). Technology and testing. *Science, 323*(5910), 75–79.
Rheingold, H. (2007). Using participatory media and public voice to encourage civic engagement. In L. Bennett (Ed.), *Civic life online: Learning how digital media can engage youth* (pp. 97–118). Cambridge, MA: MIT Press.
Rogoff, B., & Gardner, W. P. (1984). Adult guidance of cognitive development. In B. Rogoff & J. Lave (Eds.), *Everyday cognition: Its development in social contexts* (pp. 95–116). Cambridge, MA: Harvard University Press.
Ruiz-Primo, M. A., Shavelson, R. J., Hamilton, L., & Klein, S. (2002). On the evaluation of systemic science education reform: Searching for instructional sensitivity. *Journal of Research in Science Teaching, 39*(5), 369–393.
Scribner, S., & Cole, M. (1981). *The psychology of literacy*. Cambridge, MA: Harvard University Press.
Shavelson, R., & Towne, L. (Eds.). (2002). *Scientific research in education*. Washington, DC: National Academies Press.
Shepard, L. A. (2000). The role of assessment in a learning culture. *Educational Researcher, 29*(7), 4–14.
Shepard, L. A. (2007). Formative assessment: Caveat emptor. In C. A. Dwyer (Ed.), *The future of assessment: Shaping teaching and learning* (pp. 279–303). Mahwah, NJ: Erlbaum.
Shirky, C. (2008). *Here comes everybody: The power of organizing without organizations*. New York: The Penguin Press.
Shute, V. J., Ventura, M., Bauer, M. I., & Zapata-Rivera, D. (2009). Melding the power of serious games and embedded assessment to monitor and foster learning: Flow and grow. In U. Ritterfeld, M. Cody, & P. Vorderer (Eds.), *Serious games: Mechanisms and effects* (pp. 295–321). Mahwah, NJ: Routledge, Taylor and Francis.

Silva, E. (2008). *Measuring skills in the 21st century*. Washington, DC: The Education Sector.

Star, S. L., & Griesemer, J. R. (1989). Institutional ecology, 'translations' and boundary objects: Amateurs and professionals in Berkeley's Museum of Vertebrate Zoology, 1907–39. *Social Studies of Science, 19*(3), 387–420.

Steinkuehler, C. A., Black, R. W., & Clinton, K. A. (2005). Researching literacy as tool, place, and way of being. *Reading Research Quarterly, 40*(1), 95–100.

Street, B. (1984). *Literacy in theory and practice*. Cambridge, MA: Cambridge University Press.

Taasobshirazi, G., Anderson, K. A., Zuiker, S. J., & Hickey, D. T. (2006). Enhancing inquiry, understanding, and achievement in an astronomy multimedia learning environment. *Journal of Science Education and Technology, 15*, 383–395.

The New London Group. (1996). A pedagogy of multiliteracies: Designing social futures. *Harvard Educational Review, 66*(1), 60–92.

Towne, L., & Hilton, M. (Eds.). (2004). *Implementing randomized field trials in education: Report of a workshop*. Washington, DC: National Academies Press.

White House. (2009). *White House education agenda: January 2009*. Washington, DC: U.S. Government Printing Office.

Winerip, M. (2005, November 2). Are schools passing or failing? Now there's a third choice… both. *New York Times*.

Xenos, M., & Foot, K. (2008). Not your father's internet: The generation gap in online politics. In L. Bennett (Ed.), *Civic life online: Learning how digital media can engage youth* (pp. 51–70). Cambridge, MA: MIT Press.

Yancey, K. B. (2009). *Writing in the 21st century: A report from the National Council of Teachers of English*. Urbana, IL: NCTE.

Ysseldyke, J., & Tardrew, S. (2007). Use of a progress monitoring system to enable teachers to differentiate mathematics instruction. *Journal of Applied School Psychology, 24*(1), 1–28.

Chapter 9
Making Assessment Relevant to Students, Teachers, and Schools

Joseph A. Martineau and Vincent J. Dean

Abstract This chapter develops a model for an assessment and accountability system that reverses the trend of systems built upon a foundation of accountability—with sanctions for not meeting expected standards being the primary motivating feature for students, teachers, and schools to devise ways to avoid sanctions. The model developed in this chapter relies instead upon providing students, teachers, and schools with the necessary tools to achieve success as measured by student achievement and student growth based on multiple measures so that accountability is not a punitive measure, but a measure that assures that the tools are being used appropriately to assure success.

Keywords Accountability · Formative assessment · Interim benchmark assessment · Summative assessment · Balanced assessment · Classroom assessment · Standardized assessment · Professional development

9.1 Introduction

Schools, districts, and states have struggled for decades to provide standardized assessments that validly inform instruction. The fact that these systems have expanded greatly in terms of the number of grades and students included in statewide testing and accountability systems since the advent of the No Child Left Behind (NCLB) Act of 2001 (Law 107-110; 20 USC 6301; January 8, 2002) has not necessarily assured instructional improvement. The combination of a focus on sanctions for failure to make progress and the strained capacities at each level have contributed to massive resource expenditures with questionable legitimacy (Mintrop & Sunderman, 2009).

J.A. Martineau (✉)
Michigan Department of Education, Office of Educational Assessment & Accountability, Lansing, MI, USA
e-mail: martineauj@michigan.gov

V.J. Shute, B.J. Becker (eds.), *Innovative Assessment for the 21st Century*,
DOI 10.1007/978-1-4419-6530-1_9, © Springer Science+Business Media, LLC 2010

9.2 Transparency and the Failure of Relevance

A major challenge inhibiting the clear delineation of results from the standards-based reform movement articulated in NCLB is comparability of assessment results and accountability measures across states and over time. Requiring each state to be responsible for its own academic content and achievement standards, assessment system, and accountability model does not permit easy comparisons across state lines. Within states additional hurdles must be overcome in the effort to ensure that assessment results are instructionally relevant to teachers and students, and that accountability measures are capturing valid and reliable indicators of effective pedagogy and use of resources. Curriculum specialists, who are often responsible for leading the development of state content standards, may have significant differences of opinion, based on their training and experience, with state assessment experts responsible for measuring student attainment of these learning targets. The setting of achievement standards—the "bar" that defines proficiency for each content-area specific assessment (mathematics, science, etc)—has involved a variety of stakeholders with differing opinions about what a student must demonstrate in order to earn a passing score. Moreover, under NCLB regulations the number of proficient scores for some students with disabilities is capped to prevent schools from administering alternate assessments to large numbers of students.

Compounding these issues is the high degree of variability and sophistication found among state data systems. The national Data Quality Campaign (www.dataqualitycampaign.org) has identified ten critical elements for cohesive, longitudinal state data systems that are essential for tracking students from preschool through post-secondary education programs (also known as P-20). As of August 2009, only six states were able to support all ten data elements[1]. As states have received funds from the American Recovery and Reinvestment Act (ARRA) and applied for the US Department of Education's discretionary Race To The Top monies, they have been required to make a number of assertions to the federal government, such as confirming that the state either was on track to have, or would commit to developing, state data systems that would facilitate the collection and dissemination of P-20 information. Thurlow, Elliott, and Ysseldyke (2003) noted that common transparency problems include current state data systems and the reports provided to stakeholders from statewide testing. Together, the current implementation of these two critical pieces (state data and reporting systems) often contribute to the difficulty in understanding student performance.

An example of another federal push that serves as a comparable precedent for standardizing and improving state data and reporting transparency is the calculation

---

[1]The ten elements are: (1) statewide unique student identifier, (2) student-level enrollment data, (3) student-level test data, (4) information on untested students, (5) statewide unique teacher identifier with teacher/student match, (6) student-level course/transcript data, (7) student-level ACT/SAT/Advanced Placement test data, (8) student-level graduation/dropout data, (9) capacity to match P-12 and post-secondary data, and (10) data audit system (Data Quality Campaign, 2009).

of graduation rates. For many years, each state was permitted to define what constituted a "dropout" and had different means of capturing this in the state's data system. In some states a dropout was defined as any student who did not earn a high-school diploma in 4 years. In others, the graduation rate excluded students who changed schools during high school but were not picked up in the state data system when they enrolled in another community, regardless of whether or not they received a diploma in 4 years. Other states classified all students who received a GED through alternative education centers as dropouts, even though many institutions of higher education did not distinguish between a GED and a regular diploma. Only after the US Department of Education became involved and required all states to calculate and report graduation rates in the same manner did transparency and comparability become possible for the public.

In theory, the state-led movement to develop common academic standards organized by the National Governors Association (NGA) and the Council of Chief State School Officers (CCSSO) will facilitate transparency and comparability in assessment scores, and their subsequent use in accountability measures. However, this movement does not address an equally critical problem that may prevent common metrics from impacting student instruction on a large scale. That is, a number of assessment experts have noted with frustration the dearth of assessment literacy in the population of professional educators. Several presentations and panel discussions at the CCSSO 2009 National Conference on Student Assessment discussed how to remediate this problem (see CCSSO, 2009). Many teacher and school-administrator preparation programs contain no coursework specific to student assessment. Some education professionals, such as school psychologists, have a significant amount of assessment training. However, this is typically narrowly focused on individual student assessment for the purposes of determining special-education eligibility and is only partially germane to large-scale testing. Beyond the lack of training in assessment, very few educators leave their preparation programs equipped to deal with the complexities of state accountability models.

As assessment professionals and other educators engage in conversations across the nation about the next generation of assessments and accountability (e.g., holding schools and teachers accountable for individual student achievement growth), the absence of assessment literacy must be addressed. Resources put towards developing new and more informative methods of measuring student attainment of content will be money poorly spent if end users such as teachers are not equipped to appropriately use results and understand how results will be used for accountability. Other authors have questioned the appropriateness of using results from existing standardized instruments for measuring the effectiveness of teachers (e.g., Martineau, 2006; Popham, 2000; Schmidt, Houang, & McKnight, 2005). However, since recent federal reform efforts (e.g., Race To The Top grants) require that states have the capability to connect student achievement on standardized tests to specific teachers, it appears that the American education system will include holding educators accountable for assessment results as a component of measuring educational progress.

In many ways, one could argue that the current system used by State Education Agencies (SEAs) and Local Education Agencies (LEAs) is unbalanced. The focus on sanctions-based accountability informed by summative assessment results from secure instruments has been tremendous. This focus has come without integral supports for improving instruction. One might conclude that this system is not relevant to students, teachers, and schools for the purposes of improving student achievement. Building an assessment system with greater balance is a crucial component of educational reform that must be done well if improved student achievement is the ultimate desired outcome.

9.3 A Proposed Balanced Assessment (and Accountability) System

The idea of balanced assessment is a fairly new and relatively undefined phenomenon at state and federal levels. Redfield, Roeber, Stiggins, and Philip (2008) attempt to formalize a definition of balanced assessment. Their definition includes three types of assessment as components: formative assessment, interim assessment, and summative assessment. We add several components to this framework in an attempt to articulate a comprehensive system that truly provides a basis for informing instruction and improving student achievement.

First, we argue that a balanced assessment framework is unlikely to be useful for instructional purposes (i.e., be instructionally sensitive) unless it is based on a collection of content standards with specific characteristics (see Popham, 2008; discussed below). Second, we add professional development for pre-service and in-service educators to assure that the balanced assessment system truly improves teacher understanding of best practices in classroom assessment and assessment data use. Third, we expand from a balanced *assessment* system to a balanced *assessment and accountability* system to include appropriate uses of assessment data for accountability. Finally, we expand the three categories of formative, interim, and summative assessment into four categories: classroom formative assessment, classroom summative assessment, secure adaptive interim summative assessment, and secure adaptive summary assessment.

A schematic of the different components of a balanced assessment and accountability system and their interconnections is provided in Fig. 9.1. Each component of the balanced system in Fig. 9.1 is represented by a horizontal bar, showing in which aspect each of the individual pieces of the system are carried out. For example, note that the "assessment literacy standards for educator certification" box spans the formative, classroom summative, secure interim, and secure summary components, indicating that those standards must cover all four areas of assessment competence. In addition, Fig. 9.1 is intended to be symbolic in the following ways:

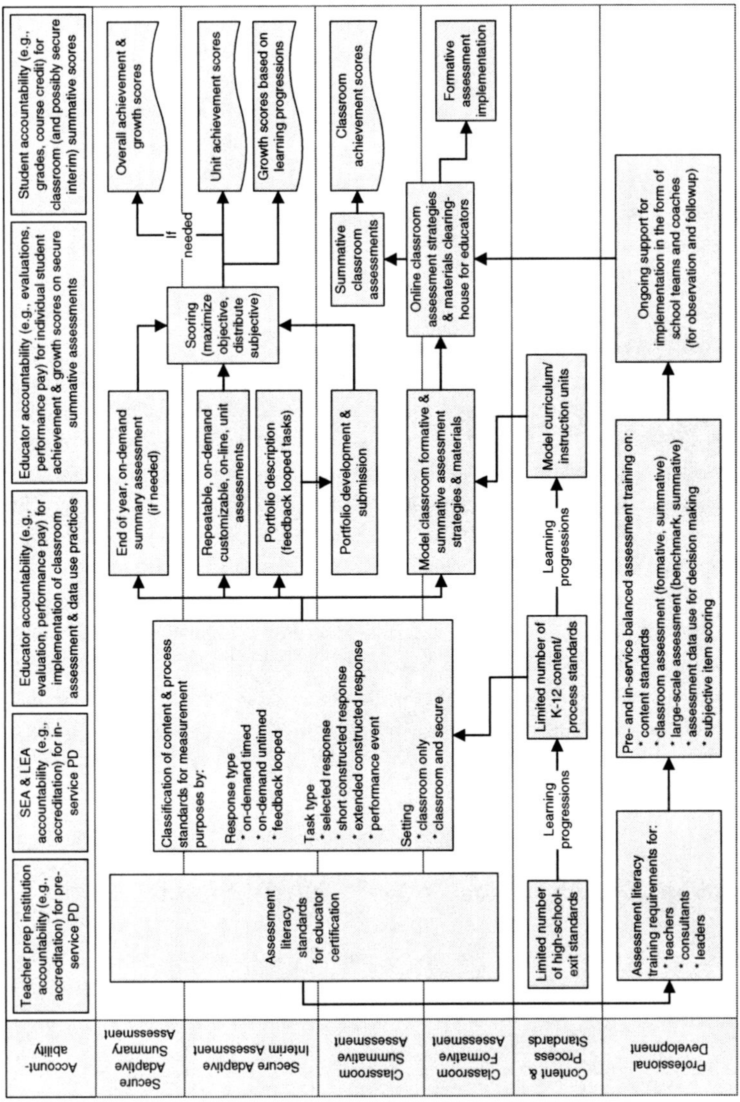

Fig. 9.1 Components and interconnections of a balanced assessment and accountability system

- The bedrock of the system is the professional development provided to educators to assure that they are equipped to work within the system.
- The foundation of the system must be coherent content and process standards, around which curriculum, instruction, and assessment must be developed to assure validity.
- Classroom formative assessment underlies all of the assessment components of the system—without which the stability and usefulness of the other assessment (and corresponding accountability) components are suspect.
- The system is protected by the umbrella of accountability (as described later in the chapter) to provide incentives to implement the system as intended, and to minimize unintended consequences for students, educators and schools.
- The system has only two entry points (as described later in the chapter): a limited number of high school exit goals, and assessment literacy standards for educator certification.
- The system has only three ultimate outcomes (all of which are measures of student achievement), represented by the symbol ⬦.
- The system has only two other critical goals—implementation of formative assessment, and ongoing support for school teams and coaches—which are intended to support the ultimate outcomes of student achievement. Note that accountability for implementation of these goals is included in the system.
- Inherent in the comprehensiveness and individualized nature of many components of the system is the capability to include all students (even students with disabilities and English language learners) in the system.
- Finally, the balanced assessment and accountability system requires a large-scale technical infrastructure for data collection, secure assessment delivery, hosting of a transparent and accessible model materials repository, and a transparent reporting structure capable of facilitating usefulness of the entire system. Note that all elements of the system feed into the accountability aspects, but adding the arrows from those elements to the accountability components would make the figure incomprehensible.

9.4 Describing and Explaining the Proposed System

We begin the discussion of the reasoning behind the proposed balanced assessment and accountability system from the two entry points to address the issue of why these are so important.

9.5 Entry Points

9.5.1 Entry Point 1: Limited Number of High-School Exit Standards

Thinking about innovative, balanced approaches to assessment begins first with rethinking what we measure. The same logic about assessment literacy holds true when applied to the academic content standards, or curricular targets, that assessments must evaluate. In other words, academic content standards are statements of the knowledge and skills that schools are expected to teach and students are expected to learn. Asking what the ultimate goals of education are is an appropriate way to being the development of these academic content standards.

Arguably, the end-game of public instruction is to have all students, as they exit secondary programs, prepared to enter college or the workforce (where the term "college" includes any kind of post-secondary education). Research by organizations such as ACT that are dedicated to measuring the achievement of secondary students has suggested that in the present, knowledge-based, global economy, college readiness and workforce readiness are highly comparable (ACT, Inc., 2006). By starting from the end-game of public instruction, we attempt to assure that a balanced system matches this goal by design (see Chapter 6 by Almond, this volume).

It is not only the benchmark against which high-school exit standards are measured that is important. The *number* of high-school exit standards is also of critical concern. Schmidt (2002) and Schmidt, McKnight, and Raizen (1997) characterized the state of the curriculum in the United States as very broad and very shallow. They suggest that a smaller number of standards will bring focus and coherence to education. Popham (2008) has criticized existing standards for the same flaw, indicating that in order for tests to be instructionally sensitive, the content standards should be sufficiently limited to allow for deep instruction and understanding of a focused number of topics rather than shallow instruction on a great range of topics. It is difficult to argue with the desire for students to attain a deep understanding of content, and it is also difficult to argue against having a clear (and not overwhelming) sense of what is expected of both educators and students.

Both of these concerns (a focus on the end-game, and reasonable limitations on the amount of content for deeper understanding) are in fact a significant motivation for the current common core of standards initiative led by NGA and CCSSO (2009). We believe that this effort is promising and may provide a strong entry point into a balanced assessment system.

Developing K-12 content standards. Developing easy-to-navigate documents showing the content standards not only in terms of the high school exit standards alone is insufficient. Clarity and ease of understanding are also important in the documents within and across preceding grade levels. This clarity should make obvious what content proficiency in each grade will lead to the ultimate outcomes. For example, the mathematical concept of place value can be found in many states' elementary standards. Since it is expected that this idea be mastered at a certain point, the concept is dropped at later grades and is replaced with other, more advanced targets. What is often missing, or left to local educators to determine for themselves, is how the concept of place value translates or contributes to the higher-order mathematics found in the higher grades. To the layperson (and often educators), it may appear that the idea of place value has disappeared in the content standards after, say, fourth grade. Without understanding how mastering ideas like place value contributes to deep understanding of more complex mathematics, educators are less able to determine where an individual student needs remediation. The way in which later content standards are built upon earlier concepts (e.g., place value) needs to be transparent and explicit.

Academic content standards need to be developed with a clear, vertically articulated sequence in mind. Educators and parents should be able to trace subject-specific content from kindergarten (or before) through post-secondary courses. Without a sequential understanding of how scientific, mathematical and literacy concepts build upon each other, stakeholders cannot make rational decisions about instruction or remediation. The next generation of content standards, and the documents created to accompany them, should communicate this transparently. This is essential in order to design a system of assessments that truly inform instruction.

Schmidt (2002); Schmidt et al. (1997) and Popham (2008) agree that coherent articulation of lower grade content standards to end-game goals is a necessary component of a rational and valid system. Other scholars (e.g., Martineau, Paek, Keene, & Hirsch, 2007; Wise, 2004) also comment that in order to measure student growth, this type of coherent progression from grade to grade is important. The key to developing assessments that are useful in helping practitioners and policymakers make appropriate decisions as to whether or not students are on track to meeting college- and workforce-readiness standards is to have a clear way to trace each content-specific construct across grade levels.

One field of research attempting to address this issue is the development of learning progressions[2]. Kennedy and Wilson (2007) presented a method for developing learning progressions, as did a National Research Council report (Duschl, Schweingruber, & Shouse, 2007). Since that time, the study of learning progressions has grown significantly, particularly with a conference dedicated specifically to learning progressions in science in 2009 (see presentation materials in LeaPS, 2009). And while developing formal, empirically-derived learning progressions is time consuming, beginning by working backward from the high-school exit standards to developmentally appropriate content standard progressions for younger children is desirable. In the interim, as the empirically-informed progressions are being developed, it is possible to use logical methods (e.g., based on expert opinion, such as described by Martineau et al., 2007; and Wise, 2004) to work backward to assure vertical coherence among K-12 content standards. It is also important to assure that the number of specific K-12 content standards supports instructional sensitivity by keeping the number manageable; thus deep instruction can be implemented, and deep understanding can be measured (see Popham, 2008; and Schmidt et al., 1996).

As noted by Porter, Polikoff, and Smithson (2009), while small core similarities exist in content standards developed to date by the states, significant variability also

---

[2] Wilson and Bertenthal (2006) define a learning progression (or progress map) as "a continuum that describes in broad strokes a possible path for the development of... understanding over the course of... education. It can also be used for tracking and reporting students' progress..." (p. 78). Doignon and Falmagne (see 1999) also described the development of knowledge spaces as a somewhat similar approach, positing, as a portion of the knowledge space, pre-requisite relationships among different subsets of a domain of knowledge.

is found across grades and aggregated standards. This creates major challenges for assessment teams charged with test development. Multiple pools of viable items must be updated or undergo substantial revision each time the content standards change. Educators have similar challenges as they attempt to align their curricular materials with standards that appear to be in a constant state of flux.

We argue that if the content standards are few, clear, and high-level, leading to well-articulated outcomes, educators will readily see the relevance of the content standards, and will in turn be able to better focus their efforts in such a way that students will understand where they are going, and why it is important to get there (for more on this topic, see the section on formative assessment implementation). While some may argue that this might lead to inappropriately narrowing the curriculum, other scholars have made strong arguments that the current state of curriculum standards is too broad and shallow to achieve deep understanding or to achieve comprehensive measurement of desired outcomes (see Popham, 2008; and Schmidt et al., 1996).

Developing model curriculum units. When the high-school exit standards (e.g., college-and career-readiness standards) and K-12 content standards have been developed, the development of model curriculum units can then take place. While individual teachers may choose to adopt, adapt, or ignore the model curriculum units, the development of those units provides educators with a high quality starting point. These model units should be available transparently to any educator who is responsible for teaching the content standards. The pouring of the foundation of the system is then complete, providing stability for the rest of the system.

9.5.2 Entry Point 2: Assessment Literacy Standards for Educator Certification

Any system built to be balanced will only be effective if those carrying out the activities within it are equipped with the knowledge and skills needed to perform their functions. Therefore, the second entry point into the system is equally critical. If educators are underprepared to develop and implement formative *and* summative classroom assessment activities, they will be unable to make data-based decisions to prepare students for success on secure, high-stakes tests (see Stiggins, 2002). It is difficult to exaggerate the importance of this point: the absence of educator assessment literacy is akin to medical doctors knowing how to diagnose illness only when a condition is already serious.

If educators are underprepared to use assessment data (whether from classroom or secure assessments), data-based decision making will be either poorly informed or nonexistent. Therefore, in the system schematic, the assessment literacy standards cover all phases of assessment. These literacy standards are built on the bedrock of professional development in assessment literacy and delivered to educators in both the pre-service and in-service arenas. We argue that it should not only be individual teachers who are prepared in assessment literacy, but also school leadership (to provide the necessary support for professional development and implementation by teachers) and ancillary staff who serve in consulting roles (to provide the necessary support to sustain the professional development for and implementation by teachers).

We also argue that educators should receive training in several aspects of the system. First, as a foundation, educators need to know and be able to do the same things that they will expect their students to know and do. Once that level of content competency has been established, educators should be trained in the use of classroom assessment, both formative and summative. The information gained from such smaller scale instruments—which may include locally developed curriculum-based, criterion-referenced components—should facilitate focused, intensive formative feedback cycles. Research has shown that substantive, frequent, formative feedback can translate into significant gains in achievement (e.g., Black & Wiliam, 1998; Bloom, Hastings, & Madaus, 1971; and Shute, 2008). This will enable teachers to use classroom assessment practices to look both forward and backward along the sequence of content mastery in order to develop efficient lesson plans and modify them as appropriate.

While high-quality classroom assessment practices are critically important for teachers to understand, it is also important for educators to understand the appropriate use of large-scale, secure assessment data for decision making. In particular, classroom teachers may use secure assessment results to validate or fine-tune their classroom assessment and instruction practices, whereas educators in consulting or leadership roles may use the secure assessment results for programmatic and policy-planning purposes. Knowing how to use the data in appropriate ways is critical to assure that data-based decisions are accurately informed.

In order to support the secure assessment components of the system as well as the improvement of the quality of classroom assessment practice, educators should be trained in the development and appropriate use of rubrics for the scoring of extended student work projects. Understanding the principles of accurately rating student work will not only help educators in providing formative feedback to their students, but also in increasing the reliability and validity of classroom grading practices, and will allow for individual educators to be integrally involved in rating extended student work samples for the secure assessments produced by students of other educators in other locations.

Finally, the development of teams of educators within schools (including teachers, leaders, and consultants) to provide feedback on assessment and instruction practices is important to protect the sustainability of the system. Without a supporting community, it is unlikely that implementation of the balanced assessment and accountability system will penetrate deeply into the wider educational system (see Fixsen, Blase, Horner, & Sugai, 2009).

The existence and implementation of professional development around high quality assessment practices and the sustainability offered by school-based teams including leaders, consultants, and teachers provides the bedrock the system will need to be stable. Only after grounding the system on the bedrock of professional development and laying the foundation of coherent content standards does it make sense to talk directly about the assessment components of the system.

9.6 Developing the Assessment Components of the System

9.6.1 Classifying Content and Process Standards

A critical first step in developing the assessment components of the balanced system is to review the K-12 content standards in order to classify them in terms of: (a) the timeframe students should have to respond, (b) the most appropriate methods to measure student achievement of the standards, and (c) the most appropriate setting for measuring student achievement of those standards. Our experience in large-scale assessment has made clear the need for these three types of classification.

First, some content standards seem best suited to an on-demand response from students (e.g., adding two two-digit numbers, finding the main idea of a story). These on-demand appropriate tasks can be further broken down into a few that should be strictly timed (e.g., fluently performing mathematical computations, fluently reading aloud) versus those for which strict timing is not needed. Other content standards imply that a feedback-looped task is needed (meaning tasks that require multiple rounds of student work and educator review, such as, pre-writing, drafting, and revising a report), rather than on-demand assessment. Specifying the appropriate timing for each content standard is likely to make the system more relevant to educators and students because they will be able to see the logical connection between the instructional goals and the timeframe within which responses are gathered.

Second, multiple methods exist for measuring student achievement of content standards: traditional selected response items (e.g., multiple choice, multiple selection, true/false), short constructed response items (e.g., short answer, brief computations), extended constructed response items (e.g., essays, reports), and performance events (e.g., carrying out a set of activities or conducting an experiment). Clearly, some content standards are more appropriately measured by one of these methods than by others. Delineating the appropriate tools for measurement will also increase relevance for educators and students by assuring connections between the content standards and the activities upon which accountability is based.

Third, some content standards are best assessed using informal procedures (e.g., regular classroom assignments) rather than typical secure assessment procedures (e.g., annual summative assessments). For instance, content standards that imply oral processing or feedback loops with teachers may be very difficult to implement in a secure environment where sharing tasks with educators may be viewed as a security breach. It is important to note that feedback looping as used in this chapter is defined as multiple rounds of feedback.

9.6.2 Developing Model Classroom Strategies and Materials

Based on model curriculum units and the classification of content standards, model classroom formative and summative assessment strategies and materials can be developed. Our experience with small-scale implementation of a balanced assessment system in Michigan has been that one of the largest obstacles to implementation is the lack of model materials for high-quality classroom assessment. Our experience has also shown that when formative assessment training is provided, one of the first questions that comes up is "now what do I do about grading?" Because many teachers are used to grading and including all student work in summative assessment scores (e.g., final grades), the idea of not using a majority of student work (e.g., not using every homework assignment or pop quiz) for grading is uncomfortable[3]. Therefore, we suggest that clear divisions be made in the model strategies and materials to assure that both formative and summative needs are met.

Classroom formative assessment. To clarify some of the muddy waters surrounding the use of the term *formative assessment*, we adopt a formal definition. The basis for this definition comes from a comprehensive review of the literature on effective formative assessment by the CCSSO Formative Assessment of Students and Teachers (FAST) State Collaborative on Assessment and Student Standards (SCASS). Popham (2008) modestly revised the CCSSO FAST SCASS definition to make clearer the role of students in formative assessment:

> Formative assessment is a planned process in which assessment-elicited evidence of students' status is used by teachers to adjust their ongoing instructional procedures or by students to adjust their current learning tactics (p. 6).

We adopt this definition with some clarifications. That is, while formative assessment may be adjusted to the particular circumstances, the phrase "planned process" is key because in planning to use formative assessment, teachers intend to gather information about student understanding rather than information gathering being a purely spontaneous act.

We also argue that formative assessment results should not be used for accountability purposes in any way (including grading, teacher evaluations, or school evaluations). When assessment results are put to such uses, they cease to be formative because they are being used in a summative manner (e.g., for accountability/grading). This is critical because formative use allows for low-stakes evaluation rather than high-stakes evaluation—of both teachers and students—and the transition from low- to high-stakes use changes the nature of the activity and responses, and thus alters the interpretation of results.

---

[3] For example, in many classrooms all student work is graded in such a way that a student who ultimately meets the instructional goals at the end of a unit still achieves a low unit grade because s/he struggled with early work on that content. Such a student should be identified as having met the expectations based on final performance, *regardless* of early performance.

In addition, formative assessment is not only about educator knowledge and skills. To maximize the impact of formative assessment on ongoing instruction students need to be integrally involved in the process. They need to understand the goals of each unit of instruction, what is necessary to arrive at the goals from where they are, and when they have achieved the goals.

Another necessary clarification is that item banks and online test delivery systems are relatively inflexible systems in terms of the types of data gathering methods, and by themselves do not integrally involve students in understanding the goals of instruction, nor do they have sufficient flexibility to provide targeted, diagnostic feedback how for all types of content. While astute educators can integrate these tools *where appropriate* into formative assessment, these tools fit better into the interim/benchmark portion of a balanced assessment system, as described below. Many test vendors indicate that their relatively inflexible systems are "formative," and therefore this distinction needs to be made clear (see, for example, ACT, Inc., 2009a; CTB/McGraw-Hill, 2009; Data Recognition Corp, 2009; Educational Testing Service, 2009; Northwest Evaluation Association, 2009; Pearson Educational Measurement, 2009; and Questar Assessment, Inc., 2009).

To facilitate ongoing adjustment of instruction toward meeting instructional goals, feedback must be immediate or near immediate. Feedback may be formal or informal (e.g., informal verbal checks for understanding versus formal [self-]evaluation of understanding), but in order to be formative needs to be immediate or near immediate to provide for timely adjustment. Embedding technology into the formative assessment process can facilitate such timely feedback. For example, if students are able to enter self-assessments into an online system for immediate aggregation and reporting, instructional adjustments can be made in near real time. Another example might be a classroom computer system in which checks for understanding can be developed either in advance (as a part of the planned process) or entered dynamically (as a modification to the planned process), and students can enter their selected or free responses for immediate aggregation and reporting.

Model strategies and materials for accomplishing this type of formative assessment need to be developed so that educators are able to see examples of high-quality formative assessment in use.

Classroom summative assessment. Because it is important to get a good, relatively objective sense of where a student is before he or she takes a secure test that may be used for accountability purposes, classroom summative assessment remains a critical component of the system. For example, a final project or a final classroom test on a particular unit of instruction may be helpful in assessing whether students are ready to take the secure unit test. Model strategies and materials for classroom summative assessments should also be provided for educators to get a relatively objective look at how their students will do on the secure tests with similar types of tasks. Alignment of classroom assessment to the content standards that will be measured on the secure tests (in terms of both formative and summative classroom assessments) provides the needed support for adequate achievement on the secure tests. Such model strategies and materials will make assessment more relevant to classroom teachers and to students by creating clearer links between instructional goals and measurement.

9.6.3 Developing a Clearinghouse for Classroom Assessment Strategies and Materials

The development of model strategies and materials should be only the beginning. Individual educators may develop innovative new strategies and materials for classroom assessment aligned with the secure tests. To capitalize on educator efforts and creativity, a clearinghouse should be developed where individual educators can add their materials to the model materials, with peer review (social network) ratings from other educators who have implemented the strategies and materials. In this way, educators would be able to share successful experiences, and try different methods when existing models or practices are not working.

An example illustrating one method that could be applied to a clearinghouse of model materials can be found in an initiative called EdSteps (www.edsteps.org), a venture created by the CCSSO and supported by the Bill and Melinda Gates Foundation that several states have joined as participants. This project is designed to collect thousands of examples of student work, have them evaluated by a large variety of stakeholders, and then publish scales of performance (from novice to expert) with accompanying samples of student work.

The intent is that these scales will provide teachers, students, and parents with meaningful ways to assess individual progress and a plethora of examples of specific skills in order to inform instruction. Example work and scales will be collected and generated for three areas: Writing, Global Competency, and Curiosity and Creativity. This is an example of an innovative way to leverage the work of consortia in ways that could not be matched by an individual state. If a similar process were applied to mathematics and English language arts, statewide assessments could be constructed with robust scoring mechanisms that would lead to concrete examples of the types of work or responses that lead to improved scores.

9.6.4 Implement Classroom Assessment Strategies and Materials

Based on model strategies and materials in the clearinghouse, educators can then adopt, adapt, or create their own strategies for formative and summative classroom assessment. The formative assessment implementation, based on sound professional development and on sound model strategies and materials, will support achievement of classroom instructional goals, and adequate performance on the summative assessments (e.g., adequate achievement scores), making the entire system relevant and desirable to students and educators because such a system supports improved achievement and success rates.

9.6.5 Developing the Secure Assessment Components

Once classroom assessment professional development has been provided, and model strategies and materials are available, it then makes sense to create secure, high-stakes assessments. Educators at that point would be equipped with the knowledge and supports needed to improve student achievement of instructional goals and their success rates on the secure assessments.

In the proposed system, all secure assessments are given in an adaptive manner whenever possible. We define an adaptive environment as in Sands, Waters, and McBride (1997), where large pools of test items are available with wide-ranging levels of difficulty so that each student's achievement is measured by items tailored to the students' individual level of achievement. While each student gets a different set of test items, each student can still receive a set of items that measures achievement on the same content standards as every other student.

Tailored testing has the significant advantage that fewer items can generally be used to obtain measurement precision that is both high and comparable for each student. The use of frequent adaptive testing lends itself better to measuring student growth not only in an overall sense (e.g., obtaining a measure of knowledge of mathematics), but also on specific content topics (e.g., understanding multiplying fractions). In a standards-based environment where each content standard must be included, a large item pool is required with significant variation in difficulty levels for each content standard against which achievement is measured. By having the assessments administered in an adaptive manner (which requires a technical solution), students not only receive a tailored test, but can receive near immediate feedback on their level of achievement on test questions that can be scored objectively.

In cases where subjectively scored test questions are to be administered, adaptive testing does not make as much sense because the advantage of rapid turnaround is diminished. Still, with distributed scoring (discussed below), or automated scoring (see Shermis, 2010, this volume), turnaround times can be significantly reduced even for subjectively scored test questions.

Individualized Assessment Made Relevant with Technology. Developing adaptive assessments is crucial in ensuring that the data yielded from them are relevant. By definition, adaptive assessments must be highly sensitive to the unique status of the learner. Dean, Burns, Grialou, and Varro (2006) noted that historically, individual students have often been assessed with instruments and in contexts that are standardized and foreign, begging the question of instructional relevance. This problem is compounded as State Education Agencies (SEAs) attempt to address the needs of diverse learners. Students with disabilities and English language learners are umbrella terms that cover a myriad of conditions and circumstances for which traditional standardized assessment programs are ill-equipped. State policies regarding inclusion of these special populations vary considerably (Albus & Thurlow, 2007; Lazarus, Thurlow, Lail, Eisenbraun, & Kato, 2006).

Under NCLB, all SEAs have been expected to develop accommodated (e.g., Braille) or translated (e.g., Spanish) versions of their assessments, and to meet the rigorous technical requirements designed to ensure comparability (see US Department of Education, 2007). These costly processes provide access for more students to the current types of statewide assessments, but do not yield instructionally relevant results that are any better than those provided for students taking the regular test, because they are arguably insensitive to individual learners (see Popham, 2008).

The administration and development of adaptive assessments will most likely be facilitated by effectively leveraging technology. The potential benefits of administering assessments via computer include more efficient administration, eliminating printing and shipping costs, quicker scoring, and generating results more quickly. In addition to these fiscal and logistical advantages, technology provides the best means of developing assessment system components that are tailored to the individual. Thompson, Thurlow, and Moore (2003) noted that computer-based tests have the capacity to incorporate features designed to enhance accessibility for students with disabilities and English language learners. If developed appropriately, such tests can provide each student with more individualized control over accommodations that are familiar and appropriate.

Before we describe the development of secure assessments, and how they fit in the system, it is necessary to discuss what we mean by student achievement on an assessment.

Rigorous, realistic and relevant achievement standards. In the earlier section on content standards, we indicated that the lines between college- and workforce-readiness have been blurred. The homogeneity that represents lends itself toward more meaningful standards-based reform *only if* the content standards are clear and sequentially articulated, a system of assessments is designed to measure them thoroughly, and the achievement standards (i.e., how we define proficiency or mastery) are rigorous, realistic and relevant in regard to the skills all students will need.

Academic achievement standards are explicit definitions of how students are expected to demonstrate attainment of the knowledge and skills of the content standards. Achievement standards have three key components that describe the levels or categories they are designed to represent along the continuum of performance on the assessment. These components are: (1) the category label (e.g., Proficient); (2) the performance level descriptor (i.e., a narrative description of what a student needs to display on the assessment to land in a particular category); and (3) the range of scale scores that psychometrically corresponds to each category.

Unfortunately, policymakers at several levels have succumbed to the temptation to compare achievement standards across tests. In an effort to wring the water of comparability from the stones represented by instruments developed for different purposes based on different content, stakeholders have been inundated with statistical and psychometric comparisons that are inappropriate. One example of this is the efforts supported by the National Assessment Governing Board (NAGB) to compare the National Assessment of Educational Progress (NAEP) to the summative achievement tests administered by individual states (see Cronin, Dahlin, Adkins, & Kingsbury, 2007; National Center for Education Statistics, 2007; and Bandeira de Mello, Blankenship, & McLaughlin, 2009). These comparisons have fueled arguments that state tests are not as rigorous as the NAEP. However, since they do not measure the same content, have a different design, were developed for different purposes, have dramatically different achievement standards based on different policy objectives, and are not given at the same time of year, comparing them is highly misleading. The use of common content and achievement standards across states has the potential to address this issue, if the consortia being developed function as intended.

The comparisons do, however, generate considerable debate about how to validate achievement standards that are meaningful and predictive of success in college and the workforce. Earlier in this chapter, we mentioned the emerging body of research suggesting that students must display proficiency on similar skills, regardless of which post-secondary path they pursue. Those skills are articulated in the content measured by instruments, but as this pertains to the achievement standards, another conversation is warranted. How much of this content does a student need to master in order to be successful? Where should the bars be set in terms of drawing the lines between advanced, proficient and not proficient? Does one set of achievement standards or bars work for everything or should we have different sets based on post-secondary setting (e.g., junior college, 4-year institution, workforce, etc.)?

Secure adaptive summary assessments. In order to set valid and logical achievement standards across the system, the secure adaptive high-school exit test must be developed first. Based on student performance on that assessment, prediction of college and/or workplace success should be carried out, with an acceptable threshold identified as the target cut score in each subject area for high-school exit. While ACT, Inc. (ACT, Inc., 2009b; and Allen & Sconing, 2009) has developed methods for creating college-readiness benchmarks, ACT's research has been based on averages across a variety of post-secondary institutions, rather than being able to identify specific readiness levels for, say post-secondary institutions in the West, South, Midwest, Northeast, etcetera, or for community colleges, 4 year institutions, and the like. It would be helpful to have those thresholds defined for the multiple types of institutions in different regions to see how widely these might vary before setting a single cut score identifying college and workforce readiness, or deciding multiple cut scores are appropriate.

In addition, although ACT has conducted research showing that college and workforce readiness are not appreciably different (2009b), including prediction of work success in different types of employment would also be helpful in identifying different possible cut scores. And while this introduces its own complexities (4-year ready, technical school ready, 2-year ready), it avoids the need for dividing the achievement scale into multiple subjectively described ranges. Reporting can be done in terms of how far above or below a particular cut score a student achieves. All students would take a high-school exit exam, not for a diploma, but to determine whether he or she has met the high-school exit achievement standards in each subject. To assure application to all students, alternate exit examinations should be developed for students with significant cognitive or sensory impairments, in order to permit valid and reliable determinations of whether or not these students have met achievement criteria deemed relevant for them by appropriate stakeholders. This does leave the difficulty of identifying an acceptable level of achievement at high school exit, since external criteria such as college and workforce readiness may be difficult to define for students with significant cognitive disabilities.

Following the development of the high-school exit exam, the K-11 end-of-year assessments should be developed. Based on the assumption that maintaining the *status quo* in K-11 education will lead to equal pass rates across grades on the high-school exit exam for students in the pipeline, cut scores on the K-11 assessments can be extrapolated downward from the high-school exit exam to give identical pass rates to those observed on the high-school exit exam. No other cut scores need be developed as no other external criteria besides college and workforce readiness were identified for setting cut scores on the high-school exam. Reporting can be done in terms of how far above or below a cut score a student is. While this method of setting a standard is unorthodox, it eliminates the conflict of interest that skews current standard setting methods in which educators who will be held accountable for student achievement set the cut scores. In addition, because this method requires the assumption described above, this method is a 1-year stopgap measure. After 2 years of measuring student performance with these instruments, cut scores can be determined without the *status quo* assumption by identifying cuts that give at least a 50% (or more, depending upon policy objectives) probability of success on the next year's test, again working downward from the high school exit cut score(s) or benchmark(s).

Secure adaptive interim assessments. Once the summary assessments have been developed, the secure adaptive interim assessments may be developed for grades K-12. Except in grade 12, acceptable performance on the secure interim assessments can exempt students from having to take the end-of-year tests.

These interim assessments need to be repeatable (within reason), so that students have more than one opportunity to pass each interim assessment. With adaptive assessment allowing for high levels of accuracy for each student (Sands et al., 1997), the effect of measurement error on increasing false positives from repeated measurement can be minimized. In addition, these assessments need to be customizable to cover the content standards addressed in a specific unit of instruction to allow for educators to either use the model curriculum units or develop their own units combining any number of content standards to fit their students.

Based on scores and sub-scores taken from the end-of-year tests, prediction equations can be developed to create scores on the unit assessments based on the probability (solely for performance on the unit) that a student would meet or exceed a cut score on the overall end-of-year assessment. These become useful in multiple ways: they can predict sufficiently far in advance how a student is likely to perform on the overall assessment for intervention; they provide more detail than an overall score, and they provide a basis for pre- and post-testing for measuring student growth on a finer grain.

Acceptable performance on these unit (interim) assessments could be defined as achieving a 50% prediction of acceptable performance or higher on the end-of-year test. Or, it could be defined as higher than 50%, to assure adequate overall achievement. Once a student achieves an adequate score on all unit tests, the student can be exempted from the end-of-year test. However, any student who does not demonstrate sufficient achievement on any unit test (after one or more attempts) would be required to take the complete end-of-year test to demonstrate adequate overall achievement. To assure that the system is working properly, a small sample of students exempted from the assessment should be required to take the end-of-year test to assure that exempted students do indeed pass the overall test at an acceptable rate. As described further in the accountability section, only the summative (interim) unit tests need be used for accountability for students who have demonstrated adequate achievement on all unit tests.

By not only having classroom assessment results to go on, but also knowing at the end of each unit the classroom pass rates (or rates of other defined populations such as English language learners), the system becomes more transparent and relevant to both educators and students. Such feedback loops allow for data to be returned to both educators and students before it is too late to address high-stakes lack of achievement.

Developing and administering secure feedback-looped tasks. Because content standards including higher-order skills will likely require feedback-looped tasks, a special process is also needed for developing and administering such tasks as a part of interim or summative assessments (e.g., using samples of revised student work in summative measures)[4]. The tasks can be developed in a secure environment, but should be administered in the classroom to allow for feedback looping. The products developed during those tasks can then be included in a portfolio scored by different educators to avoid the conflict of interest of an educator rating students' work for which he or she will be held accountable.

Scoring. Objectively scored test questions will not be appropriate measurement tools for some content standards. However, each content and process standard should be carefully evaluated to determine whether it is possible to develop test questions measuring that content that can be scored objectively. Because subjectively scored test questions (such as constructed response items and performance tasks) introduce many additional sources of measurement error (see Lane & Stone, 2006), it is important to minimize the amount of subjectively scored items to the degree possible while maintaining validity. The minimization of subjectively-scored items also decreases the turnaround time for score reporting. This is not to imply that subjectively-scored tasks should not be used if they are appropriate. What this implies is that with new technological capabilities and some creativity, tasks that previously would have been scored subjectively might now be scored objectively either through artificial intelligence (see Shermis, 2010; Shute, 2007) or by creatively developing new types of tasks using new technology platforms (e.g., simulation of performance tasks) that can be scored objectively.

---

[4] This does not move feedback-looped tasks out of the formative and summative classroom assessment arenas. This simply acknowledges the need to include feedback-looped tasks in the secure assessments as well.

In cases where content standards clearly must be measured using subjectively scored test questions, the professional development provided to educators can be leveraged to reduce turnaround time and to provide beneficial experience to individual educators. Using a distributed scoring system, portfolio tasks and other constructed response tasks can be scored by teachers in different parts of the state or country. Traditional scorer training and monitoring would be needed (see Lane & Stone, 2006), but teacher involvement in scoring would be maximized, and their experiences in scoring student work products would be helpful in benchmarking the work students produce for them.

Innovative formats for performance tasks and twenty-first century skills. As these various types of assessment are developed, and content standards are classified in order to determine which item types are most suitable, exploring possible new item formats is appropriate. As noted above, traditional multiple-choice formats are suitable for measuring certain content standards, but are less appropriate for assessing others that require deeper responses to gauge mastery. Towards that end, truly innovative assessments must utilize a variety of item formats if the data yielded from them are intended to accurately reflect level of mastery.

Items that measure, or provide students with the opportunity to demonstrate, rich understanding of *content-specific processes* must supplement those measuring simple knowledge of facts. For example, some states have science content standards that call for students to show they can conduct an experiment. Multiple-choice items can capture whether or not a student knows the proper steps, and constructed-response items (requiring a written response) may permit the student to articulate how he or she would conduct the experiment. However, neither of these formats permits the student to demonstrate understanding of experimentation to the same degree that could be observed if he or she were required to conduct a brief experiment through a performance task.

Chief among the factors in considering what types of item formats would constitute a significant improvement over those in the present array of statewide assessments is the cost. The resources expended on developing different types of items (e.g., open-ended constructed response vs. multiple-choice) vary less than the resources expended on scoring different types of items. Scoring constructed-response items, typically done by having a trained person apply a standardized rubric to the respondent's answer, is vastly more expensive than scoring multiple-choice items via sheets where answers are bubbled in and sent through high-speed scanners.

Looking again at the rapid evolution of technology, computer-based testing has the potential to revolutionize how we think of test items. The ability to assess students in dynamic ways that are more representative of real-life situations through embedding a variety of digital media such as audio and/or video files within items could engage students in more robust ways (Sireci & Zenisky, 2006). However, a significant amount of research remains to be conducted on whether or not including rich media elements adds value to items. Additionally, the inclusion of more complex item components like video introduces new challenges in the creation of accommodated and translated versions of the tests.

While technological advancements make development of innovative item types that can be scored both objectively and subjectively more likely, two ideas must remain at the fore: (1) new item types are experimental and should not be used for high-stakes purposes until validated, and (2) to assure that adequate reliability and cost-effectiveness are maintained, every attempt to create item types that can be scored objectively should be made before resorting to developing new types of subjectively-scored items.

9.7 Accountability

With the bedrock in place, the foundation set, and the structure of the system created, the protective umbrella of accountability can be put into place. Without accountability, there are no strong incentives for the system to work as it is intended. Several important components of accountability are found within the system.

9.7.1 Accountability Components

Teacher preparation institutions. Each teacher preparation institution needs to be held accountable for providing high-quality pre-service preparation in assessment literacy standards in order to be accredited. Doing so will provide the incentive needed to make assessment literacy a valued component of pre-service preparation.

State and local education agencies. Each state and local education agency needs to be held accountable for providing in-service professional development (PD) in assessment literacy standards. This can be done by assuring that approved state-level provision of PD is included in requirements for federal approval of state testing programs, and assuring that approved LEA-level provision of PD is included in school accountability/accreditation standards. Doing so will assure support at upper and middle-level management levels of the education system for adequate PD in assessment literacy.

Educators. Educators need to be held accountable not for the results of their classroom assessment practices, but for their level of implementation of those practices and the degree to which they use data for instructional decision making. This can be done by requiring that educator evaluations include measures of the implementation of these practices.

Educators also need to be held accountable, in part, for achievement scores of students who are on track, and growth for students who are not on track to meeting the ultimate goals of college or workforce readiness. Scholars have expressed concerns about attributing either achievement or growth to individual educators (Martineau, 2006; McCaffrey, Lockwood, Mariano, & Setodji, 2005). However, if individual educators consistently show similar results on valid and reliable measures with different groups of students (and with significant intervention for educators with a poor showing), only then does it makes sense to apply consequences (both positive and negative) in terms of performance pay and performance evaluations. While this may be aversive to individual educators, we believe this is an appropriate balance between fairness toward educators and accountability for student achievement. The student-growth component of educator evaluations should be based only on secure interim and summative assessment scores to reduce the conflict of interest inherent in educators being involved in scoring assessments for which they will be held accountable.

Separate components of educator evaluations should include supervisory evaluations of their implementation of sound assessment practices, use of data for instructional decision making, and other important educational practices and outcomes.

Students. Since the advent of grading, students have been held accountable for their achievement, so it may seem strange to include this component in the system. However, formalizing the appropriate achievement for which students should be held accountable is helpful. Students should not be held accountable for formative assessment results because doing so would undermine their purpose. Students should clearly be held accountable for summative classroom achievement scores (e.g., final projects, teacher-developed tests), and *could* be held accountable for secure interim achievement test scores. Students should not be held accountable for secure summary assessments as the information provided by the once-yearly summary assessments is also provided in greater detail in the secure unit assessments.

9.7.2 Combining Achievement and Growth for Accountability

Scholars have criticized existing accountability systems based on student achievement as not recognizing extraordinary improvement (see many of the chapters in Lissitz, 2005, 2006; and Millman, 1997). Consequently, some scholars have suggested replacing the achievement-based accountability models with growth-based models requiring 1 year of growth for 1 year of instruction rather than achieving a set performance standard (see Sanders, Saxon, & Horn, 1997).

However, there is a significant problem with this approach. That is, if a student starts below grade level, and only 1 year of growth is expected for 1 year of instruction, then the student's goal for the next year is to remain equally far behind as he or she was the previous year. In order to achieve the end-game policy objective (college and workforce readiness) for all students, students who are not on track to meet the end-game policy objective must improve their standing (or make more than 1 year of growth for 1 year of instruction). Some scholars have addressed this by creating growth models that measure "progress toward a standard" (see Martineau, & Betebenner, 2006; Thum, 2002). In such models, students who are not on track to achieving the end-game policy objective must have a growth measure. However, when modeling growth toward meeting an ultimate, rigorous expectation, growth scores are not needed for students who have demonstrated they are on track to meeting the ultimate goal (as measured by the secure assessments).

Because of this, it is possible to eliminate once-yearly testing for students who score adequately on the unit sub-tests. It is, of course, possible for any student to take the year-end assessment to find out exactly where they stand and calculate a growth score. However, it is not necessary to do so. The only students for whom a growth score is necessary are those students who do not demonstrate adequate performance on each unit (interim) test. These are either students who have fallen behind from adequate overall performance the previous year, or those whose achievement was not satisfactory the previous year and is not satisfactory in the current year. This assures that students who have fallen behind this year have a baseline against which to measure growth the next year, and assures that students whose achievement was inadequate the previous year and have not yet achieved an acceptable score this year can have a growth score calculated.

In other words, in the proposed balanced system, the ultimate outcome (college and workforce readiness) is sufficiently rigorous that schools should receive credit for any student scoring proficient; as well as receiving credit for any student on a trajectory of progress toward meeting the ultimate goal by high-school exit. There is no need to measure growth for students already proficient (i.e., on track to meet a rigorous desired outcome).

9.8 Conclusion

In our view, the most valuable contribution of this chapter is not in the development of a coordinated and balanced assessment and accountability system, although we do see that as important. What is a sea change is turning the typical, current assessment and accountability system on its head.

Traditional systems are built upon the bedrock of accountability, assuming that consequences for poor performance will sufficiently motivate schools and educators to try harder, or to find or invent the tools to do whatever is necessary to improve student achievement. However, the "whatever is necessary" is not defined, and can include any number of good, bad, or ugly approaches that may or may not work.

By making professional development (on the content standards, assessment literacy, and use of data) the bedrock of the proposed new system, it provides educators with the tools and supports to implement what is necessary to improve student achievement. In addition to the bedrock of professional development, the foundation of a smaller number of coherent, logically-sequenced content standards against which student achievement is measured provides a more realistic and attainable goal for instruction and measurement.

In addition, the tools provided to educators to meet accountability goals are enhanced by creating and providing a clearinghouse filled with model materials and strategies for sound classroom assessment and instructional practice. By fully implementing an interim assessment component within the system, educators also receive timely feedback on how students are likely to perform on the overall assessment before it is too late to provide remediation on specific sub-topics. In addition, administering pre and post unit tests will allow educators to see the impact of their instruction on student achievement with sufficient frequency to determine whether any changes need to be made to their approaches. While the system as described provides these tools, it continues to allow educators to innovate with new tools and practices, and to see timely impact data based on their implementation of those innovations.

Finally, by tying all goals to the ultimate outcome of college and career readiness, the relevance of the system can be clearly seen by both educators and students.

Some are likely to continue to oppose the use of accountability as a part of a system. However, by providing tools to educators to facilitate success on relevant accountability goals, the accountability components of the system change in function. Accountability pressures move from motivating educators to grasp at unproven tools toward motivating the implementation of tools that are proven, meaningful to educators and students, provided with appropriate pre- and in-service professional development, and which produce timely feedback. Thus, they transform from being fearful motivators to protectors of the system.

References

ACT, Inc. (2006). *Ready for college and ready for work: Same or different?* Iowa City: Author. Available at http://www.act.org/research/policymakers/reports

ACT, Inc. (2009a). *Formative item pools.* Retrieved December 1, 2009, from http://www.act.org/qualitycore/itempools.html.

ACT, Inc. (2009b). *The condition of college readiness 2009.* Iowa City: Author. http://www.act.org/research/policymakers/reports

Albus, D. A., & Thurlow, M. L. (2007). *English language learners with disabilities in state English language proficiency assessments: A review of state accommodation policies (Synthesis Report 66).* Minneapolis, MN: University of Minnesota, National Center on Educational Outcomes.

Allen, J., & Sconing, J. (2005). *Using ACT assessment® scores to set benchmarks for college readiness.* ACT Research Report 2005-3. Iowa City: Author. Retrieved December 1, 2009, from http://www.act.org/research/researchers/reports/pdf/ACT_RR2005-3.pdf

Bandeira de Mello, V., Blankenship, C., & McLaughlin, D. H. (2009). *Mapping state proficiency standards onto NAEP scales: 2005–2007 (NCES 2010-456).* Washington, DC: National Center for Education Statistics, Institute of Education Sciences, US Department of Education.

Black, P., & Wiliam, D. (1998). Assessment and classroom learning. *Assessment in Education,* 5(1), 7–73.

Bloom, B. S., Hastings, T., & Madaus, G. (1971). *Handbook of formative and summative evaluation of student learning.* New York: McGraw-Hill Book Company.

CTB/McGraw-Hill. (2009). *LAS links benchmark assessments.* Retrieved December 1, 2009, from http://www.ctb.com/products/product_accessory.jsp?Current_Page=1&FOLDER%3C%3Efolder_id=1408474395292399&ASSORTMENT%3C%3East_id=1408474395213825&CONTENT%3C%3Ecnt_id=10134198673323014

Council of Chief State School Officers & National Governors Association. (2009). *The future of student assessment.* Program of National Conference on Student Assessment, Los Angeles. Retrieved December 5, 2009, from http://www.ccsso.org/content/pdfs/NCSA%202009%20Final%20Web%20Program.pdf

Council of Chief State School Officers, & National Governors Association. (2009). *Common core state standards available for comment*. Retrieved November 28, 2009, from http://www. nga.org/portal/site/nga/menuitem.6c9a8a9ebc6ae07eee28aca9501010a0/?vgnextoid=6d50c211 06ec3210VgnVCM1000005e00100aRCRD&vgnextchannel=6d4c8aaa2ebbff00VgnVCM100 0001a01010aRCRD

Cronin, J., Dahlin, M., Adkins, D., & Kingsbury, G. G. (2007). *The proficiency illusion*. Washington, DC: Thomas B. Fordham Institute.

Data Quality Campaign. (2009). *10 essential elements of a state longitudinal data system*. Retrieved 12/5/2009 from http://www.dataqualitycampaign.org/survey/elements

Data Recognition Corp. (2009). *Online testing*. Retrieved December 1, 2009, from http://www.data recognitioncorp.com/PageContent.aspx?Ref=es2OnlineTesting

Dean, V. J., Burns, M. K., Grialou, T., & Varro, P. J. (2006). Comparison of ecological validity of learning disabilities diagnostic models. *Psychology in the Schools, 43*(2), 157–168.

Doignon, J. -P., & Falmagne, J. -C. (1999). *Knowledge spaces*. New York: Springer.

Duschl, R. A., Schweingruber, H. A., & Shouse, A. W. (Eds.). (2007). *Taking science to school: Learning and teaching science in grades K-8*. Washington, DC: National Academies Press.

Educational Testing Service. (2009). *Item banks*. Retrieved December 1, 2009 from http://www. ets.org/portal/site/ets/menuitem.1488512ecfd5b8849a77b13bc3921509/?vgnextoid=f55aaf5e 44df4010VgnVCM10000022f95190RCRD&vgnextchannel=c1f1253b164f4010VgnVCM100 00022f95190RCRD

Fixsen, D. L., Blase, K. A., Horner, R., & Sugai, G. (2009). *Scaling up evidence-based practices in education*. Scaling Up Brief #1. Chapel Hill: The University of North Carolina, FPG, SISEP.

Kennedy, C. A., & Wilson, M. (2007). Using progress variables to map intellectual development. In R. W. Lissitz (Ed.), *Assessing and modeling cognitive development in schools: Intellectual growth and standard setting*. Maple Grove, MN: JAM Press.

Lane, S., & Stone, C. A. (2006). Performance assessment. In R. L. Brennan (Ed.), *Educational measurement* (pp. 387-431). Westport, CT: American Council on Education, Praeger.

Lazarus, S. S., Thurlow, M. L., Lail, K. E., Eisenbraun, K. D., & Kato, K. (2006). *2005 state policies on assessment participation and accommodations for students with disabilities* (Synthesis Report 64). Minneapolis, MN: University of Minnesota, National Center on Educational Outcomes. Retrieved [today's date], from the World Wide Web: http://education. umn.edu/NCEO/OnlinePubs/Synthesis64/

LeaPS. (2009). *Proceedings of the learning progressions in science conference*, June 24–26: Iowa City, IA. Retrieved November 28, 2009, from http://www.education.uiowa.edu/ projects/leaps/proceedings/Default.aspx

Lissitz, R. L. (Ed.). (2005). *Value added models in education: Theory and applications*. Maple Grove, MN: JAM Press.

Lissitz, R. L. (Ed.). (2006). *Longitudinal and value added models of student performance*. Maple Grove, MN: JAM Press.

Martineau, J. A. (2006). Distorting value added: The use of longitudinal, vertically scaled student achievement data for growth-based value-added accountability. *Journal of Educational and Behavioral Statistics, 31*(1), 35–62.

Martineau, J. A., & Betebenner, D. W. (2006). *A hybrid value table/transition table model for measuring student progress*. Paper presented at the 36th annual national conference on large-scale assessment of the Council of Chief State School Officers (CCSSO), San Francisco.

Martineau, J. A., Paek, P., Keene, J., & Hirsch, T. (2007). Integrated, comprehensive alignment as a foundation for measuring student progress. *Educational Measurement: Issues & Practice, 26*(1), 28–35.

McCaffrey, D. F., Lockwood, J. R., Mariano, L. T., & Setodji, C. (2005). Challenges for value-added assessment of teacher effects. In R. Lissitz (Ed.), *Value added models in education: Theory and applications* (pp. 111–141). Maple Grove, MN: JAM Press.

Millman, J. (Ed.). (1997). *Grading teachers, grading schools: Is student achievement a valid evaluation measure?* Thousand Oaks, CA: Corwin Press.

Mintrop, H., & Sunderman, G. L. (2009). Predictable failure of federal sanctions-driven account-ability for school improvement – and why we may retain it anyway. *Educational Researcher*, *38*(5), 353–364.
National Center for Education Statistics. (2007). *Mapping 2005 state proficiency standards pnto the NAEP scales* (NCES 2007-482). US Department of Education. Washington, DC: Author.
Northwest Evaluation Association. (2009). *NWEA's measures of academic progress is selected as a state approved formative assessment in Colorado.* Retrieved December 1, 2009, from http://www.nwea.org/about-nwea/news-and-events/nweas-measures-academic-progress-selected-state-approved-formative-assess
Pearson Educational Measurement. (2009). PASeries formative assessments from Pearson Education reviewed by National Center on Student Progress Monitoring. Retrieved December 1, 2009, from http://www.pearsoned.com/pr_2007/022007.htm
Popham, W. J. (2000). *Testing! Testing! What every parent should know about school tests.* Needham Heights, MA: Allyn & Bacon.
Popham, W. J. (2008). *Transformative assessment.* Alexandria, VA: ASCD.
Porter, A. C., Polikoff, M. S., & Smithson, J. (2009). Is there a de facto national intended cur-riculum? Evidence from state content standards. *Educational Evaluation and Policy Analysis*, *31*(3), 238–268.
Questar Assessment, Inc. (2009). Touchstone Applied Science Associates, Inc. and Rally! Education announce partnership to develop Testpower, a web-based instructional assessment product line. Retrieved December 1, 2009, from http://www.questarai.com/AboutUs/News/PressReleases/Pages/pr051706_tasa_and_rally_education_announce_partnership_to_develop_testpower.aspx
Redfield, D., Roeber, E., Stiggins, R., & Philip, F. (2008). *Building balanced assess-ment systems to guide educational improvement.* A background paper for the keynote panel presentation at the National Conference on Student Assessment of the Council of Chief State School Officers, June 15, 2008, Orlando, FL. Retrieved from http://www.ccsso.org/content/PDFs/OpeningSessionPaper-Final.pdf
Sanders, W. L., Saxon, A. M., & Horn, S. P. (1997). The Tennessee value-added assessment system: A quantitative, outcomes-based approach to educational assessment. In J. Millman (Ed.), *Grading teachers, grading schools: Is student achievement a valid evaluation measure?* (pp. 137–162). Thousand Oaks, CA: Corwin Press.
Sands, W. A., Waters, B. K., & McBride, J. R. (1997). *Computerized adaptive testing: From inquiry to operation.* Washington, DC: American Psychological Association.
Schmidt, W. H. (2002). *The quest for a coherent school science curriculum: The need for an orga-nizing principle.* East Lansing: Education Policy Center at Michigan State University. Retrieved November 28, 2009, from http://ustimss.msu.edu/coherentscience.pdf
Schmidt, W. H., Houang, R. T., & McKnight, C. C. (2005). Value-added research: Right idea but wrong solution? In R. Lissitz (Ed.), *Value added models in education: Theory and applications* (pp. 145–164). Maple Grove, MN: JAM Press.
Schmidt, W. H., McKnight, C. C., & Raizen, S. A. (1997). *A splintered vision: An investigation of US science and mathematics education.* Dordrecth: Kluwer Academic Publishers.
Shermis, M. D. (2010, this volume). Automated essay scoring in a high stakes testing environment. In V. J. Shute & B. J. Becker (Eds.), *Innovative assessment for the 21st century: Supporting educational needs.* New York: Springer.
Shute, V. J. (2007). Tensions, trends, tools, and technologies: Time for an educational sea change. In C. A. Dwyer (Ed.), *The future of assessment: Shaping teaching and learning* (pp. 139–187). New York: Lawrence Erlbaum Associates, Taylor & Francis Group.
Shute, V. J. (2008). Focus on formative feedback. *Review of Educational Research*, *78*(1), 153–189.
Sireci, S. G., & Zenisky, A. L. (2006). Innovative item formats in computer-based testing: In pursuit of improved construct representation. In S. M. Downing & T. Haladyna (Eds.), *Handbook of test development.* Mahwah, NJ: Lawrence Erlbaum Associates, Inc.

Stiggins, R. J. (2002). Assessment crisis: The absence of assessment FOR learning. *Phi Delta Kappan, 83*(10), 758–765.

Thompson, S., Thurlow, M., & Moore, M. (2003). *Using computer-based tests with students with disabilities* (Policy Directions No. 15). Minneapolis, MN: University of Minnesota, National Center on Educational Outcomes. Retrieved [today's date], from the World Wide Web: http://education.umn.edu/NCEO/OnlinePubs/Policy15.htm

Thum, Y. M. (2002). *Measuring progress towards a goal: Estimating teacher productivity using a multivariate multilevel model for value-added analysis.* Santa Monica, CA: Milken Family Foundation.

Thurlow, M. L., Elliott, J. L., & Ysseldyke, J. E. (2003). *Testing students with disabilities: Practical strategies for complying with district and state requirements.* Thousand Oaks, CA: Corwin Press, Inc.

US Department of Education. (2007). Standards and assessments peer review guidance: Information and examples for meeting requiremetns of the No Child Left Behind Act of 2001. Washington, DC: US Department of Education, Office of Elementary and Secondary Education. Retrieved December 1, 2009, from http://www.ed.gov/policy/elsec/guid/saaprguidance.pdf

Wilson, M. R., & Bertenthal, M. W. (Eds.). (2006). *Systems for state science assessment. Committee on test design for K–12 science achievement.* Washington, DC: The National Academies Press.

Wise, L. (2004). *Vertically-articulated content standards.* Retrieved June 5, 2006, from http://www.nciea.org/publications/RILS_LW04.pdf

Chapter 10
Automated Essay Scoring in a High Stakes Testing Environment

Mark D. Shermis

Abstract This chapter discusses the use of automated essay scoring (AES) as a possible replacement for an annual statewide high-stakes writing test. The examples provided are drawn from development work in the state of Florida, but might apply to any state in the United States. In the first section, literature associated with the frequency, costs, and consequences of high-stakes testing is reviewed. In the second section, automated essay scoring is introduced and a description of how it works as an assessment tool is provided. In the third section, an example of how AES is used as an instructional tool is given and I argue for a tighter integration of assessment with instruction. Finally, I propose that AES actually replace the high-stakes testing program for accountability (and other) purposes, and provide a list of advantages for proceeding in this fashion.

Keywords Automated essay scoring · High-stakes assessment · Writing assessment · Writing instruction · Testing · Computer-based testing

10.1 The Need for Change in Testing Practices

Just how much assessment is required to ascertain that a skill or knowledge domain is mastered remains a matter of considerable debate. However, there is consensus that US school children are exposed to many more high- and low-stakes tests than ever before (Shermis & Di Vesta, in press). No Child Left Behind (No Child Left Behind Act of 2001, 2002) spurred the acceleration of state accountability testing programs and increased the number of tests to which students are exposed annually. Popham (2002) has criticized this trend on the basis of three arguments: *curricular reductionism* (the tendency to ignore skills not assessed on the high-stakes test), *test-focused drilling* which he suggests is "boring" at best, and the tendency to promote

M.D. Shermis (✉)
College of Education, The University of Akron, Akron, OH, USA
e-mail: shermis@uakron.edu

V.J. Shute, B.J. Becker (eds.), *Innovative Assessment for the 21st Century*,
DOI 10.1007/978-1-4419-6530-1_10, © Springer Science+Business Media, LLC 2010

academic dishonesty on the part of both students and teachers because the stakes for poor performance are so high.

Most statewide testing programs administer their assessments in February or March, and some informal estimates suggest that teachers spend 6–8 weeks focused exclusively on preparing students to take the annual high-stakes achievement test. Moreover, most statewide testing programs spend between 2 and 3 days to simply administer the exams. Finally, the results from these tests are not generally available to schools until late May, limiting their utility to accountability purposes only. They cannot be employed for student placements or for diagnostic purposes.

What if an assessment technique could be integrated with instruction, administered on a regular basis, could provide instant feedback, could be used for diagnosis and placement in addition to accountability, could be reliable and valid, and would cost no more, or, perhaps even less than the standard high-stakes pencil-and-paper test? Most policy makers and testing professionals would be at least intrigued by the possibility of such a substitute. The remainder of this article discusses such a possibility for the domain of writing using a measurement technology known as automated essay scoring (AES).

10.2 Automated Essay Scoring

Automated essay scoring is the evaluation of written work via computer-based analysis. Initial research restricted AES to English, but the measurement technology has been extended to Japanese (Kawate-Mierzejewska, 2003, March), Hebrew (Vantage Learning, 2001), Bahasa Malaysia (Vantage Learning, 2002), and other languages. AES interfaces are predominantly internet-based, though some implementations use CD-ROMs.

Most AES packages place documents within an electronic portfolio. The programs provide a holistic assessment of the writing which can be supplemented by trait scores based on an established rubric, and may provide qualitative critiques through an analysis of a variety of features in the text (for example, grammatical errors and discourse structure). Most evaluations of AES systems compare system rating predictions with human ratings as the criterion for scoring accuracy, though some systems permit validation against other sources of information (i.e., a psychology text book for prompts related to psychological principles).

Ellis Page first proposed that computers might relieve some of the grading burden for elementary and secondary school teachers in a seminal article published in *Phi Delta Kappan* (Page, 1966). Page, a former high school English teacher, argued that teachers were reluctant to make writing assignments because of the amount of time they would be required to spend grading them. So, for instance, every time a 10th grade writing instructor gives a writing assignment to all of her classes, she is likely to have 125 papers to grade (5 classes × 25/students per class). Page found that, on average, secondary students only received about three writing assignments per semester in *writing* classes, and reasoned that the use of AES would lead to more, and consequently, better writing (Truman, 1995).

Page and his colleagues at the University of Connecticut developed a functional automated essay scoring engine (Project Essay Grade; PEG) in 1973 that possessed good psychometric characteristics, but the technology was well ahead of its time (Ajay, Tillett, & Page, 1973). In the mid-1970s there were only three mechanisms to get information into computers - either via a mounted magnetic tape, paper tape, or through 80-column punched cards. Both technologies were cumbersome for mass use in transferring essays into the computer for grading. So although the "proof of concept" had been demonstrated, not until almost 30 years later did Page resurrect the technology with a web-based version that could have widespread use (Shermis, Mzumara, Olson, & Harrington, 2001).

10.2.1 How Automated Essay Scoring Works

Consider the following statement:

> I couldn't quite remember how to throw a boomerang, but it eventually came back to me.

A few of you who just read this statement are smirking (or groaning) at what you have correctly identified as a pun. It is a clever play on words that most people would quickly identify without further clarification or elaboration. However, the computer would simply see a compound sentence (*but*) with a subject (*I*), a verb (*could remember*), and predicate (*boomerang*). From the computer's standpoint, the first part of the sentence can only be related to the second part in terms of its syntactical structure, but not underlying meaning. So for example, "boomerang" can be related to "it" and "I" can be related to "me", but the underlying pun which is the relationship between "remember", "boomerang", and "back to me" is lost. The point here is that computers do not "understand" written messages in the same way that humans do, a consideration that may be unnerving until one reflects on ways alternative technologies achieve similar results. For instance, cooking was once associated primarily with convection heating, a form of heating external to the food. But thinking "outside the box", it can be seen that the same outcome can be achieved by a technology not based on convection, but on molecular activity within the uncooked items (i.e., the microwave oven).

The computer scores essays according to statistical and linguistic models of what human raters consider desirable and undesirable elements given a writing sample. Collections of these elements are referred to as "traits", the intrinsic characteristics of writing called "trins" (Page & Petersen, 1995). The specific elements are called proxies or "proxes" (Page & Petersen, 1995).

The differentiation of "trins" and "proxes" is parallel to that of "latent" and "observed" variables in the social sciences. For example, the score on an IQ test might be thought of as a "prox" (specific element) for the underlying characteristics of the "trin" (conceptualization) intelligence.

AES software packages include computer programs that analyze the essay text to identify hundreds of prox variables ranging from simple to complex. For example, a deceptively simple variable is *essay length*. Although raters value this attribute, the relationship to good writing is not linear but rather logarithmic (i.e., raters value the amount of writing output up to a point, but then they look for other salient aspects of writing once the quantity threshold is met). Similarly, the number of occurrences of the word *because* is a relevant feature. Although seemingly superficial, it importantly serves as a proxy for the beginning of a dependent clause. And this, in turn, is reflective of sentence complexity. Each prox is coachable (i.e., you could instruct individuals to write extended text with a lot of *becauses* in it), but it turns out that most models are composed of 40+ proxes (some of which are consolidated) and one could argue that if a person had mastery of the 40 different aspects of writing, any measuring stick would show that the person was a good writer.

When human raters provide the criterion against which rating performance is judged, AES engines use a statistical model developed employing the following (ideal) procedures: (1) Obtain a sample of 300–500 essays with (4–8) human ratings on each essay (i.e., sometimes referred to as the "training set"); (2) Randomly select (approximately 300) essays and regress the human ratings against the feature set of available proxes from various computational analyses of a text; (3) Use a subset of consolidated feature variables, or the factor structure underlying a set of feature variables, in order to formulate a regression equation. The equation does not have to have a linear basis, but linear models are easier to explain. (4) Cross-validate the regression equation on the 200 remaining essays to obtain information about system accuracy and to determine if the original regression line has suffered from "shrinkage" and the model has been over-fit.

A few comments are worth noting from the procedures identified above. First, most models are developed on ratings from two to three raters, not four to eight. The fewer the raters on which the models are built, the lower the correlations between the scores the computer assigns and the writer's true score. When two to three raters are used, the human-human reliabilities and computer-human reliabilities are about the same. When more humans are used in model building, the human-computer correlations are often higher than the human-human correlations. Second, models using stepwise multiple regression will generally result in accounting for a higher proportion of overall variance. However, if one believes that some underlying model norms exists for the type of writing (or the type of writers), then a forced variable order to the regression may have a more theoretical appeal.

Writing applications that offer automated essay scoring are typically composed of two parts. The first component is an electronic portfolio where students obtain the writing assignments, use writing tools to compose their essays, write their response to a prompt, and receive quantitative and qualitative feedback. Quantitative feedback is provided either as a holistic score (usually ranging from one to six, with six representing the best writing) or scores from trait ratings where the trait represents some "trin" of interest (e.g., content, creativity, style, mechanics, organization). Some programs provide a narrative of how the score level should be interpreted. Qualitative feedback is best exemplified by the *Criterion*[SM] package from the Educational Testing Service. This product uses a technique known as *discourse analysis* (Burstein, Marcu, & Knight, 2003) which essentially is a "conversation" between the writer and the computer. The computer summarizes what it has formulated as the key structural points made by the writer. If the writer believes the summary to be incorrect, the content of the essay can be changed and resubmitted. The computer will then re-summarize the modified essay. The process typically iterates until the summary provided by the computer matches the intent of the writer or the writer gives up trying. Teachers also use the electronic portfolio to create their writing assignments, provide their own comments on student writing (independent of what the computer might generate), and monitor their students' progress.

The second component is the AES engine itself. For all users the AES component is transparent in that they only see the results of the AES engine in the form of writing scores and commentary from within the electronic portfolio. We make the distinction here because the score validity of the AES evaluation process is a key concern.

Presently AES programs are available from four major vendors. These include *Criterion*[SM] from the Educational Testing Service (containing portfolio creation capabilities, and *e-rater*®, an AES system), *Project Essay Grade*[TM] (*PEG*; an AES system only) from Measurement, Inc., the *Intelligent Essay Assessor*[TM] (IEA; an AES system only) from Pearson Knowledge Technologies, and *My Access!*® (both a portfolio and *IntelliMetric*®, an AES system). In the following paragraphs a detailed description of the *IntelliMetric*® system from Vantage Learning is provided. Available space limits a similar description of the other AES systems, though these can be found elsewhere (Shermis & Burstein, 2003; Shermis, Burstein, & Leacock, 2006).

10.2.2 *IntelliMetric*®

IntelliMetric®, much like other AES systems, emulates processes demonstrated by human scorers (Vantage Learning, 2003). It draws on the traditions of cognitive processing, artificial intelligence, natural language understanding and computational linguistics in the process of evaluating written text.

IntelliMetric® incorporates a feature extractor that identifies more than 500 semantic, syntactic, and discourse level features to reflect/represent the syntactic and grammatical structure of the language in which the essay is written. Each sentence is analyzed with regard to its parts of speech, vocabulary, sentence structure, and concept expression. Several techniques are employed to extract meaning from the text including morphological analysis, spelling recognition, collocation grammar, and word boundary detection. It also includes a 500,000 word unique vocabulary and 16 million word "concept net" which are referenced to form an understanding of the text. A concept net maps out relationships among words in a fashion similar to that employed by latent semantic analysis (Landauer & Dumais, 1997).

The information gleaned is then used by a series of independent mathematical judges, or mathematical models, to "predict" the human expert scores which are optimized to produce a final predicted score.

Rather than relying on a single "judge", *IntelliMetric*® employs multiple mathematical judges ("virtual judges") which vary depending on whether a linear or non-linear prediction solution is desired; in *My Access!*® the number of judges is six. Nevertheless, the judges all share certain things in common: at the highest level, features extracted from the text are associated with the scores assigned in the training set in order to make accurate scoring judgments about essays with unknown scores. Judges differ with regard to the specific information used to score an essay and more importantly with regard to the underlying mathematical model used to make judgments. Several statistical methodologies are used to create judges. In the development stage for a new prompt or topic, this step actually creates the mathematical models or "judges" to be used. After the models have been created, this step would simply apply the mathematical rules to a novel essay response.

The primary source of information used to obtain the approximately 400 features (i.e., proxes) used for model building is the set of sample essays on which the engine has been trained. In addition, reliance on the word "concept net" permits linking words thematically or by function. For example, it might recognize that *car* and *automobile* are semantically similar, even though only the word *car* was used in the training essays.

The *IntelliMetric*® scoring model is optimized when the essays represent various cut-points across a rubric. Multiple raters evaluate each essay to increase reliability. It is important that essays represent each scale point on the rubric; having 25 or more essays at each scale point produces the best results, however strong models have been calculated with as few as 3 essays representing each of the end points of the scale. The spread of essay scores essentially maximizes the variability of the essays and allows for a more efficient weighting process.

As mentioned previously, the empirical models can be adjusted in a variety of ways. For instance, the *IntelliMetric*® technology can be set to flag "bad faith" essays (e.g., inappropriate use of vulgar language), to check for plagiarism, or to identify the writer's intent to do harm to him or herself or to others.

Information from previous models can be employed to adjust or supplement information from current models. This can be particularly helpful when trying to create scoring models where samples are small and the writing model is likely to conform to some existing set of parameters.

IntelliMetric® uses a multi-stage process to evaluate responses. First, *IntelliMetric*® is exposed to a subset of responses with known scores from which it derives knowledge of the scoring scale and the characteristics associated with each score point. Second, the model reflecting the knowledge derived is tested against a smaller set of responses with known scores to validate the model developed. Third, after making sure that the model is scoring as expected, the model is applied to score novel responses with unknown scores. Using Vantage Learning's proprietary Legitimatch™ technology, responses that appear off topic, are too short to score reliably, do not conform to the expectations for edited American English, or are otherwise unusual are identified as part of the process.

IntelliMetric® evaluates an essay in significantly less than one second; however, to provide a better understanding of how *IntelliMetric*® works, this process is divided into steps presented in the following diagram (Fig. 10.1) accompanied by a short description.

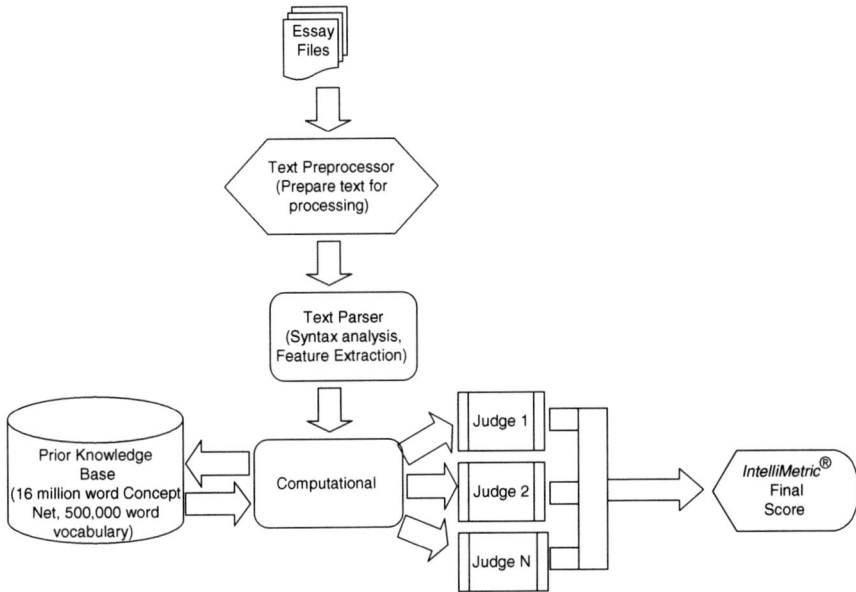

Fig. 10.1 *IntelliMetric*® architecture (Used by permission)

Step 1: Create essay files. *IntelliMetric*® requires that essays be provided in electronic form (i.e., Plain ASCII Text or Unicode for character-based languages). Essay responses can either be transcribed versions of handwritten essays, or more commonly essays entered electronically. *IntelliMetric*® can accept information as an individual response or as a "batch" of many responses. Increasingly, information is submitted using the Internet as part of a broader educational application, such as *My Access!*®.

Step 2: Pre processing. After the information has been received in electronic form, *IntelliMetric*® prepares the information for further analysis. This pre-processing stage makes sure that all materials are in a form that is readable and understandable by *IntelliMetric*®. The preprocessor removes extraneous characters and corrects formatting.

Step 3: Analyze text. Once converted to a usable form, the text is then parsed using Vantage's patented Natural Language Processing engine to understand the syntactic and grammatical structure of the language in which the essay is

written. Each sentence is analyzed with regard to its parts of speech, vocabulary, sentence structure, and concept expression Several patented techniques
are used to make sense of the text including morphological analysis, spelling
recognition, collocation grammar, and word boundary detection (Vantage
Learning, 2003). A 500,000 unique word vocabulary and 16 million word
concept net are consulted to form an understanding of the text.

Step 4: Calculate information. After all the feature information has been
extracted from the text, it is translated into numerical values to support com-
putation of the mathematical models. This process relies on a variety of
statistical techniques and computational linguistics to create the more than
500 features described earlier. A randomly selected subsample of essays is
removed for cross-validation.

Step 5: Evaluate text based on virtual judges (mathematical models). The information obtained as a result of Step 4 is used as a basis to determine one
or more mathematical models to make a judgment about the score to be
assigned to an essay response. Rather than relying on a single "judge" or
mathematical model, *IntelliMetric*® employs multiple mathematical judges
("virtual judges") based on a variety of techniques. Using a proprietary mathematical model, *IntelliMetric*® integrates the information obtained from the
judges to yield a single accurate, reliable and stable score. This is much like
human scoring situations where multiple scorers evaluate an essay response
and some model must be applied to integrate those diverse opinions. The
randomly selected sample that was held out from the original model construction is then used to create a separate model. The original and hold-out
models are compared for model overfitting (i.e., shrinkage).

Step 6: Resolve multiple judges' scores and cross-validate.

10.2.3 Reliability and Validity of Automated Essay Scoring Systems

As is true with most performance assessments, the indices for reliability and validity are generally lower than those associated with multiple-choice tests, but fall well
within the realm of psychometric acceptability. And, as Bennett and Bejar (1998)
point out, attempts to maximize reliability of performance assessments may undermine validity. For example, if raters are asked to concentrate their attention on,
say, six traits of writing, the consequence may be that they ignore other aspects
essential to differentiating good from poor writing performance. Issues of reliability
and validity with human raters are covered elsewhere (Cizek & Page, 2003; Keith,
2003).

10.2.4 Reliability

Most of the literature on reliability for objective tests is focused on either measures
of internal consistency or changes in test performance over time (test-retest). These

ways of assessing reliability are irrelevant in the context of automated essay scoring since, for example, test-retest reliability is perfect under machine scored conditions (i.e., you will get the same score for the essay no matter when you ask the automated essay scorer to evaluate it). In a performance assessment, such as AES, where the criterion is drawn from human ratings, the concern is not so much that the ratings are "reliable", but rather that the raters are in agreement with one another regarding their observations. So it is possible to have perfect covariation among a set of ratings (i.e., perfect reliability), but little in the way of actual agreement.

Accordingly, two indices are commonly provided for agreement: exact and adjacent. Exact agreement is an estimate of the level of agreement either among a set of raters or among both an AES engine and set of raters' evaluation of writing. If, for example, a six-point scale was used, a "3" from Rater A and a "3" from Rater B would count as a "match" for the purposes of calculating exact agreement.

Adjacent agreement stipulates that scores from adjacent categories are equivalent. So a "3" from Rater A and a "4" from Rater B, on the hypothetical six-point scale, are viewed as equivalent. This tradition arises from the way in which human scored essays are often handled. With discrepancies of more than one point between two raters, a third rater resolves the disagreement. Otherwise the ratings are found to be close enough to make a decision about the overall quality of writing.

Most of the evidence suggests that reliabilities of AES evaluations are equivalent to or higher than reliability with human raters (Elliot, 2003; Landauer, Laham, & Foltz, 2003; Shermis, Koch, Page, Keith, & Harrington, 2002; Shermis et al., 2001). All AES engines have obtained exact agreements with humans at about 85% and adjacent agreements in the mid-high 90% range–slightly higher than the agreement coefficients for trained expert-human raters. The slight edge for AES may be a function of the fact that the statistical models are often based on more raters than one would typically find in a human rating enterprise.

10.2.5 Validity

A variety of trait rubrics have emerged as the standard by which to assess writing performance. Most mainstream efforts coalesce into the "Big Five": content, creativity, style, mechanics, and organization (Page, 2003). One popular trait rubric for the assessment of writing is the 6+1 Traits[TM] from the Northwest Regional Education Laboratory, which focuses on the following: ideas, organization, voice, word choice, sentence fluency, and conventions (Northwest Educational Research Laboratories, 1999).

Despite these efforts, the discipline is unable to articulate a "gold standard" of the constituents of good writing, or even for good writing at various developmental levels. Even if a "gold standard" were to be formulated, it is unclear that human raters could adhere to it without some modification. For example, in one high-stakes statewide accountability assessment, the rubric allows for expressions

of non-standard English dialects without penalty. However, after many years of trying, the State Department of Education concluded that it was impossible to train
human raters to read such essays without undervaluing them. The point here is that
human evaluators may at times apply subjective criteria regardless of any written
standards.

One way in which the construct validity of automated essay scoring has been
assessed is through confirmatory factor analysis. Shermis et al. (2002) used confirmatory factor analysis (CFA) with data from a Project Essay Grade study on
386 essays, each evaluated by six judges. The normal standard for such comparisons is "pairs of judges." Accordingly, five CFAs were performed to compare the
PEG ratings with all possible pairs of human judges. The Amos 4.0 (Arbuckle,
1999) computer program, and maximum-likelihood estimation using the raw data
were employed in this analysis. Five separate covariance analyses were conducted
to avoid overlapping judge pairs. For each analysis, there was one latent variable, the
presumed true essay score, and four measured variables (three judge pairs and the
PEG ratings). Model identification was achieved by constraining the unstandardized
factor loading for the first judge pair to 1. Thus, the first analysis compared judge
pairs 1&2, 3&4, and 5&6 to PEG ratings, the second CFA compared judge pairs
1&3, 2&5, and 4&6 to PEG ratings, and so on. All five models showed a good fit
to the data using conventional criteria (e.g., Goodness of Fit and Comparative Fit
Indices above .95).

For the five CFAs, the standardized loadings for the human judge pairs ranged
from .81 to .89, with a median loading of .86. In comparison, the loading of PEG
ratings on the latent essay true score were .88 to. 89 (*Mdn* = .89). Thus, the computer
ratings of essays appeared to be at least as valid a rating as ratings from *pairs* of
human judges.

Keith (2003) examined the convergent and discriminant validity of seven PEG
data sets in the following way. He took the statistical models from each data set
and used each one to predict the score outcomes on the other data sets, and then
correlated the score results. The results across data sets, which differed on a number of variables (essay content, writing populations, number of essays, and number
of judges), are summarized in Table 1 (see Appendix A). Convergent validity coefficients ranged from .69 to .90 demonstrating that the model was accounting for
common variance.

Overall, AES has done as well as or better than humans on the psychometric
issues in the rating of essays for high- and low-stakes tests. Since humans typically
form the ultimate criterion in AES, replications of human errors can contribute to
decrements in overall reliability and validity. As was alluded to in the example with
ratings of non-standard English, AES may be able to overcome some of the biases
that humans bring to the assessment enterprise.

Many of the variables defined in the statistical model for AES are "coachable"
but their combination is what contributes to high essay scores in most models. If one
had mastery of all or a good portion of them, one would most likely be deemed a
"good writer." Interestingly, when attempts have been made to generate "bad faith"

essays intended to "trick" the AES engine into giving a poor essay a good score, it has been found that a poor essay can get a good score, but only good writers can generate the "bad faith" essay that does so (Shermis et al., 2002).

While the purpose of this study is to describe and validate the use of AES, it is interesting to note that a few studies have shown that automated essay writing interventions have also had a positive impact on writing production. In a national study using *e-rater*, Attali and Burstein (2004) observed improvements in essay development, and rating scores based on subsequent revisions of *e-rater*-evaluated submissions. Shermis, Burstein, and Bliss (2004) used the same technology, but in an urban setting only, and found improvements in essay production and reductions of numbers and types of errors over subsequent essay submissions. The aforementioned studies help establish the linkage between automated essay scoring and scoring in typical writing instruction; a form of empirical validity beyond face validity.

In two different statewide evaluations of AES, both Stemmer (2006) and Rich et al. (2008) have found promising results using AES for assessment and instruction. Rich and her colleagues found that students who used AES, and who used it more often, performed better on both formative and summative writing tasks than those who did not. Significant improvements were found with students having access to four or more sessions with automated essay scoring. Shermis, Garvan et al. (2008) found significant improvements in writing production and a significant decrease in writing errors in as few as seven AES sessions.

10.3 Electronic Portfolio Applications

10.3.1 My Access!®

My Access!® is a web-based instructional writing product that provides students enrolled in grade 4 through higher education with the opportunity to develop their writing skills within an electronic portfolio-based environment. The web-based application is divided into two capabilities—an electronic portfolio in which teachers can manage, and students can respond to, writing prompts, and an automated essay scoring engine that provides feedback on writing performance.

Teachers can create a writing assignment from a large pool of over 1,300 unique prompts covering grades 4 through higher education, including narrative, persuasive, informative, literary, and expository genres. In order to provide an integrated writing instruction tool, the prompts are aligned to major textbook series as well as other core and supplemental programs selected by districts, are aligned to state standards, and provide cross-curricular writing opportunities in areas such as science, math, social studies, history, music, and physical education. In addition to the prompts available in *My Access!*®, teachers may create an unlimited number of their own prompts for use in the system.

Teachers may guide the students through pre-writing activities and review exemplar papers for the prompts available within *My Access!*®. Students can receive feedback from the system during the writing process as well as upon submission for a score based on the *My Access!*® rubric. After submitting an essay, the student receives immediate feedback from *IntelliMetric*® and can also receive feedback from his/her teacher.

My Access!® provides both a holistic (overall) score and analytical (trait) scores in the areas of Focus and Meaning; Content and Development; Organization; Language, Use and Style; and Mechanics and Conventions. An online portfolio is maintained for every student using *My Access!*®. All original drafts, scores, revisions, comments from teachers, reflective journal entries, and *IntelliMetric*® feedback are accessible at any time. Feedback can be provided in English as well as a variety of other languages. Teachers and administrators are also able to view these portfolios at the individual, class, school, or higher aggregate level.

In addition to the online portfolio of student responses, scores, comments, journals, and teacher comments, *My Access!*® provides additional writing instruction materials and tools.

Students have access to a variety of tools:

1. Writer's Checklist to help guide the student through the writing process.
2. Scoring rubrics to self-assess their writing through the process.
3. MyEditor to provide grammatical comments, suggestions, and explanations of rules. This tool is available at multiple levels of difficulty and language in order to be most effective for the student.
4. MyTutor providing software tutor-assisted feedback at three different developmental levels and in multiple languages.
5. Word counter to keep track of essay length.
6. Word banks to assist in the selection of appropriate words for use in an essay of a particular genre.
7. Spell checker to assist in the proper spelling of words used in the essay.
8. Venn diagrams and other graphical pre-writing tools to assist in the formulation and organization of ideas to be included in the essay.

Teachers have access to a variety of reports to view the students' writing and feedback in almost any manner. In addition, the teacher has ultimate control over the tools available to the students while writing essays. For example, if it is important that the students do not receive any help with spelling, the spell checker can be turned off for any particular assignment. Also, the teacher has final control over the scores provided to the student. If the teacher wishes to adjust a score provided by *My Access!*®, the teacher can enter in the final score in addition to specific feedback. Administrators also have access to customized reporting to obtain frequency distributions, historical summaries, and roster reports. Figures 10.2 and 10.3 illustrate, respectively, computer screen shots that show how students would input an essay in to *My Access!*® and how a teacher would generate a classroom report based on *My Access!*® data.

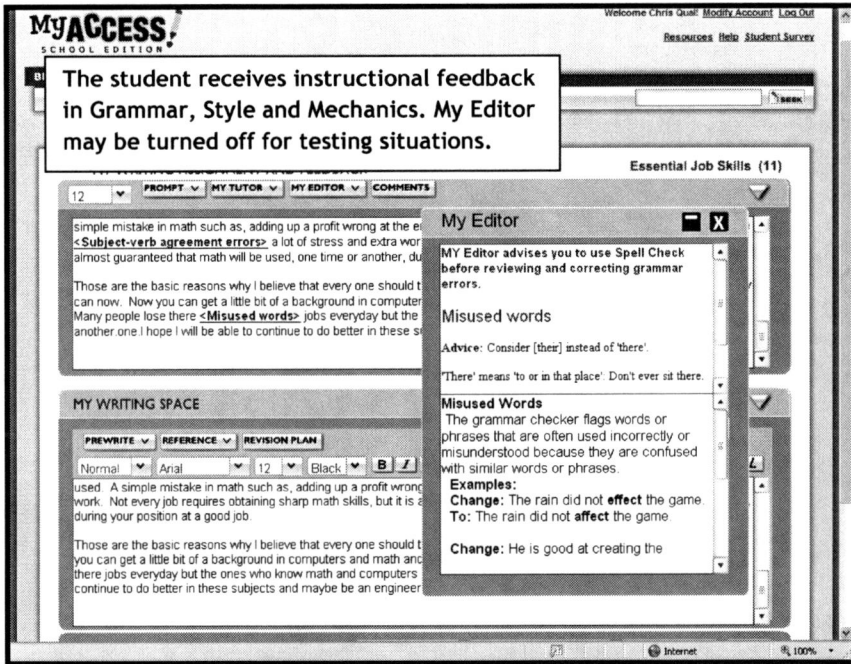

Fig. 10.2   *My Access!*® editing screen illustrating how students enter and edit their essays (Used by permission)

10.3.2   Computer-based Testing and Vulnerable Populations

While paper-and-pencil tests have played a predominant role in high-stakes assessments, a number of states (Kansas, Virginia, North Carolina, Indiana, Oregon, West Virginia) have moved to computer-based testing (CBT) for a variety of reasons. CBTs reduce paper, printing, shipping, and administration costs, improve security of the testing enterprise, and result in immediate test scores (Poggio, Glasnapp, Yang, & Poggio, 2005). Most of these conversions, however, are direct substitutions for multiple-choice tests. The results of CBT comparability studies have changed over time. Early reviews (Mazzeo & Harvey, 1988) suggested a number of situations in which examinees might be disadvantaged by CBTs, including lack of familiarity with computers, difficult item content, and awkward testing formats (e.g., questions based on a separate reading passage). However, as computer access has become more ubiquitous and as test designers have been able to take advantage of increased computer capabilities, later studies have shown minimal differences between outcomes for CBTs and paper-and-pencil tests (Pommerich, 2004; Puhan, Boughton, & Kim, 2007).

Unfortunately, only a few of the comparability studies have examined the impact of the technology on vulnerable populations, including ethnic minorities, students

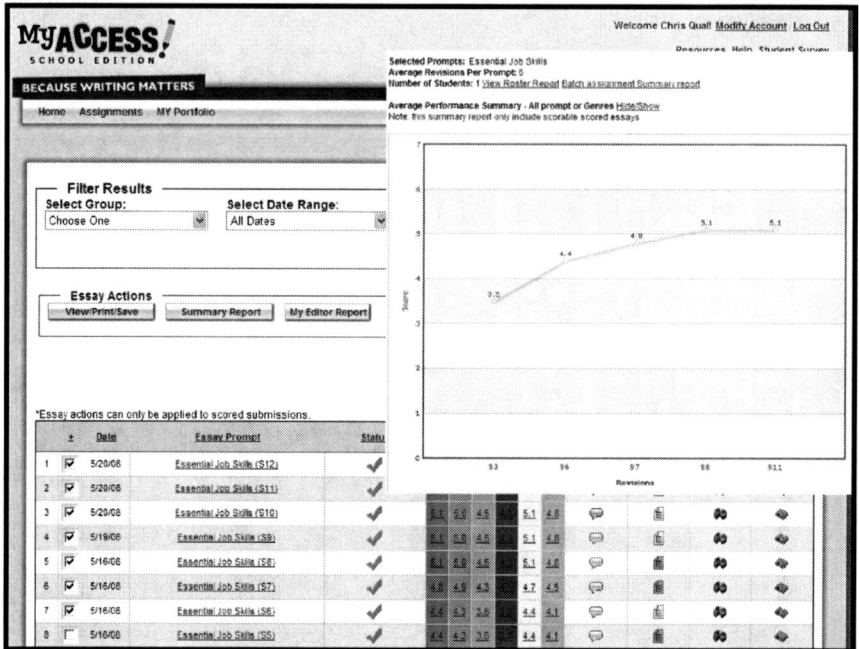

Fig. 10.3 *My Access!*® report screen showing student performance over time (Used by permission)

in special education programs, English language learners (ESL students), and those from lower SES groups. For example, in an evaluation of the Kansas statewide CBTs in mathematics, Poggio et al. (2005) found no significant differences between CBTs and paper-and-pencil tests for 7th-grade examinees in the general student population and by gender. However, comparisons with children in lower SES groups (i.e., students receiving free or reduced lunches) or special education programs performed worse on the computer-based assessments. The correlations of CBT scores with their paper-and-pencil test scores were very high, however.

10.4 A Proposal

So here is the proposal: rather than administer a high-stakes writing test in the Spring of each year, administer about 15 AES-scored essays throughout the year (it could be more). The electronic portfolio could monitor student progress from the beginning of the year throughout to the end. Towards the end of the year, average the scores for the last three writing assignments and use it as the accountability measure for the domain of writing. To keep the process secure, the topics for the last three prompts can be controlled by the state department of education and released on a strict schedule.

To be sure, there are issues that have to be addressed and studies to be conducted before this is possible. For example, norms would have to be created at each grade level and ostensibly for each prompt genre. For example, one might have a different norm for a persuasive prompt (low content valence) than for a narrative prompt (higher content valence) (Shermis, Shneyderman, & Attali, 2008). One would have to create studies that would examine the equivalency of AES scores to their pencil-and-paper counterparts. In addition, the impact of this testing procedure on vulnerable populations (i.e., ESL, free/reduced lunch, special education, minority groups) would have to be evaluated. Note that vulnerable populations typically perform at levels lower than their non-vulnerable counterparts, but the disadvantage with AES may be less than with pencil-and-paper tests.

10.4.1 Potential Benefits

Integration, Not Competition, with Instruction—Assessment that Informs Instruction. Consider the use of AES as an instructional tool that is integrated into a writing curriculum. Students might have weekly writing assignments in which they use pre-writing tools[1] to organize their thoughts, then write on a topic where the difficulty level of the prompt has been pre-calibrated. Students might also have access to writing tools (thesaurus, dictionary, writing guide) that they could consult as they create their responses. The computer provides diagnostic feedback which in turn prompts the student to make a revision and re-submission. Students can iterate in this fashion until they reach some performance threshold or are satisfied that they have created their best work. Teachers can focus their instructional attention on students who seem to be struggling with some aspect of the writing enterprise. Figure 10.4 illustrates a hypothetical growth curve for a writing student with some interesting features.

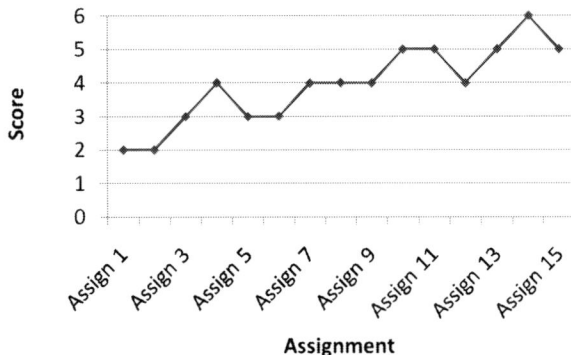

Fig. 10.4 A hypothetical writing growth curve using automated essay scoring

---

[1] Both *My Access!*® and *Criterion*SM already contain pre-writing tools.

Several advantages accrue through the use of multiple measures over time rather than relying on one high-stakes test to ascertain student performance. First, because AES feedback is instantaneous and diagnostic, both the student and teacher can focus their efforts on potential areas of improvement. For example, the student can experiment with changes to text in an effort to enhance the writing outcome and receive instantaneous feedback regarding the modifications. Second, because the prompts are normed on statewide samples, teachers have a relative picture of how a student's writing compares to that of others at the same grade level or within the same writing genre. This would be useful for placement purposes. Third, with experience, teachers can begin to develop a set of realistic expectations regarding when an intervention of this nature might take hold for a particular student with a specific set of skills or challenges. This level of weekly performance monitoring is less likely without the aid of technology.

Cost. In discussing the expenses associated with standardized testing, Phelps (2000) identifies two cost sources: gross and marginal. The gross costs are those encumbered in creating, administering, and scoring the tests. Prior to the implementation of NCLB, the GAO estimated that nationally over 20,000,000 person hours were invested in activities associated with district- and state-level testing enterprises (Phelps, 2000). On an annual basis, the state of Florida spends approximately $34 M on their *FCAT* K-12 testing programs, all of which is directed to their accountability mission.

Additionally, once summative writing prompts have been utilized for high-stakes summative assessment, they can be "released" by the state into a bank of formative writing prompts to be used to inform instruction, thus maximizing the initial investments in training and calibration of the AES engine. By providing released prompts for formative use, this eliminates the need to continuously build, train, and calibrate prompts for other uses, e.g. build once, use many times.

Conclusion

Clearly there are hurdles to overcome before the vision of replacing tests with instructional technology that can double as a test will be realized. For example, not all school districts have ubiquitous access to technology. Some districts have computers in unsecure labs, some districts place computers in individual classrooms. Some children have access to technology at home, others only encounter it in schools or libraries. Currently no state or national norms exist for automated essay scoring, and the technology's impact on vulnerable populations has to be evaluated. Each state engages in a process to assess impact on vulnerable populations (and usually there is some), but the impact varies from assessment to assessment. While the potential for automated essay scoring is clearly evident, a number of challenges must be addressed before it would even be prudent to proceed. However, these are all challenges for which solutions are known.

Automated Essay Scoring Vendors

http://www.ets.org/criterion
http://www.vantagelearning.com
http://www.pearsonkt.com

Acknowledgment Based on a paper presented at the annual Florida State University Dean's Assessment Conference in Tallahassee, FL, October, 2008. I would like to thank Harry Barfoot from Vantage Learning, Inc. for a summary information on *IntelliMetric*® and *My Access!*® and for permission to use the screenshots associated with the Vantage Learning software. The opinions expressed in this paper are those of the author and may not necessarily represent opinions held by either Vantage Learning, Inc. or the Florida Department of Education. I am also indebted to two anonymous reviewers for their valuable contributions to the manuscript and providing invaluable, helpful insights.

References

Ajay, H. B., Tillett, P. I., & Page, E. B. (1973). *Analysis of essays by computer (AEC-II)* (No. 8-0102). Washington, DC: US Department of Health, Education, and Welfare, Office of Education, National Center for Educational Research and Development.

Arbuckle, J. (1999). *Amos user's guide 4.0.* Chicago: SmallWaters.

Attali, Y., & Burstein, J. (2004). *Automated essay scoring with e-rater V.2.0.* Paper presented at the Annual Meeting of the International Association for Educational Assessment, Philadelphia, PA.

Bennett, R. E., & Bejar, I. I. (1998). Validity and automated scoring: It's not only the scoring. *Educational Measurement: Issues and Practice, 17*(4), 9–17.

Burstein, J., Marcu, D., & Knight, K. (2003). Finding the WRITE stuff: Automatic identification of discourse structure in test-taker essays. *Special Issues on Advances in Natural Language Processing, IEEE Intelligent Systems, 18*(1), 32–39.

Cizek, G. J., & Page, B. A. (2003). The concept of reliability in the context of automated essay scoring. In M. D. Shermis & J. Burstein (Eds.), *Automated essay scoring: A cross-disciplinary perspective* (pp. 125–145). Mahwah, NJ: Lawrence Erlbaum Associates, Inc.

Elliot, S. (2003). *IntelliMetric*®: From here to validity. In M. D. Shermis & J. Burstein (Eds.), *Automated essay scoring: A cross-disciplinary perspective* (pp. 71–86). Mahwah, NJ: Lawrence Erlbaum Associates, Inc.

Kawate-Mierzejewska, M. (2003, March). *E-rater software.* Paper presented at the Japanese Association for Language Teaching, Tokyo.

Keith, T. Z. (2003). Validity and automated essay scoring systems. In M. D. Shermis & J. Burstein (Eds.), *Automated essay scoring: A cross-disciplinary perspective* (pp. 147–168). Mahwah, NJ: Lawrence Erlbaum Associates, Inc.

Landauer, T. K., & Dumais, S. T. (1997). A solution to Plato's problem: The latent semantic analysis theory of acquisition, induction, and representation of knowledge. *Psychological Review, 104,* 211–240.

Landauer, T. K., Laham, D., & Foltz, P. W. (2003). Automated scoring and annotation of essays with the Intelligent Essay Assessor. In M. D. Shermis & J. Burstein (Eds.), *Automated essay scoring: A cross-disciplinary perspective* (pp. 87–112). Mahwah, NJ: Lawrence Erlbaum Associates, Inc.

Mazzeo, J., & Harvey, A. L. (1988). *The equivalence of scores from automated and conventional educational and psychological tests: A review of the literature* (No. 88-8 College Board). Princeton, NJ: Educational Testing Service.

No Child Left Behind Act of 2001, Public Law No. 107-110 115 Stat 1444-1446 C.F.R. (2002).

Northwest Educational Research Laboratories. (1999). *6+1 traits of writing rubric.* Retrieved December, 1999, from, http://www.nwrel.org/eval/pdfs/6plus1traits.pdf

Page, E. B. (1966). The imminence of grading essays by computer. *Phi Delta Kappan, 48,* 238–243.

Page, E. B. (2003). Project Essay Grade: PEG. In M. D. Shermis & J. Burstein (Eds.), *Automated essay scoring: A cross-disciplinary perspective* (pp. 43–54). Mahwah, NJ: Lawrence Erlbaum Associates, Inc.

Page, E. B., & Petersen, N. S. (1995). The computer moves into essay grading: Updating the ancient test. *Phi Delta Kappan, 76*(7), 561–565.

Phelps, R. P. (2000). Estimating the cost of standardized student testing in the United States. *Journal of Education Finance, 25*(3), 343–380.

Poggio, J., Glasnapp, D. R., Yang, X., & Poggio, A. J. (2005). A comparative evaluation of score results from computerized and paper and pencil mathematics testing in a large scale state assessment program. *Journal of Technology, Learning, and Assessment, 3*(6). Retrieved from http://www.jtla.org

Pommerich, M. (2004). Developing computerized versions of paper-and-pencil tests: Mode effects for passage-based tests. *Journal of Technology, Learning, and Assessment, 2*(6). Retrieved from http://www.jtla.com

Popham, W. J. (2002). An impending avalanche of achievement testing. *Harvard Education Letter, 18*(3), 1–3.

Puhan, P., Boughton, K., & Kim, S. (2007). Examining differences in examinee performance in paper and pencil and computerized testing. *Journal of Technology, Learning and Assessment, 6*(3). Retrieved from http://www.jtla.org

Rich, C. S., Harrington, H., Kim, J., & West, B. (2008, March). *Automated essay scoring in state formative and summative assessment.* Paper presented at the American Educational Research Association, New York.

Shermis, M. D., & Burstein, J. (2003). *Automated essay scoring: A cross-disciplinary perspective.* Mahwah, NJ: Lawrence Erlbaum Associates.

Shermis, M. D., Burstein, J., & Bliss, L. (2004, April). *The impact of automated essay scoring on high stakes writing assessments.* Paper presented at the annual meetings of the National Council on Measurement in Education, San Diego, CA.

Shermis, M. D., Burstein, J., & Leacock, C. (2006). Applications of computers in assessment and analysis of writing. In C. A. MacArthur, S. Graham & J. Fitzgerald (Eds.), *Handbook of writing research* (pp. 403–416). New York: Guilford Publications.

Shermis, M. D., & Di Vesta, F. (in press). *Contemporary classroom assessment.* Lanham, MD: Rowman & Littlefield.

Shermis, M. D., Garvan, C. W., & Diao, Y. (2008, March). *The impact of automated essay scoring on writing outcomes.* Paper presented at the National Council on Measurement in Education, New York.

Shermis, M. D., Koch, C. M., Page, E. B., Keith, T., & Harrington, S. (2002). Trait ratings for automated essay grading. *Educational and Psychological Measurement, 62*(1), 5–18.

Shermis, M. D., Mzumara, H. R., Olson, J., & Harrington, S. (2001). On-line grading of student essays: PEG goes on the web at IUPUI. *Assessment and Evaluation in Higher Education, 26*(3), 247–259.

Shermis, M. D., Shneyderman, A., & Attali, Y. (2008). How important is content in the ratings of essay assessments? *Assessment in Education: Principles, Policy & Practice, 15*(1), 91–105.

Stemmer, P. (2006, February). *Online MEAP.* Paper presented at the Michigan School Testing Conference, Ann Arbor, MI.

Truman, D. L. (1995, April). *"Teacher's helper": Applying project essay grade in english classes.* Symposium conducted at the annual meetings of the American Educational Research Association, San Francisco, CA.

Vantage Learning. (2001). *A preliminary study of the efficacy of IntelliMetric* ® *for use in scoring Hebrew assessments*. Newtown, PA: Vantage Learning.

Vantage Learning. (2002). *A study of IntelliMetric* ® *scoring for responses written in Bahasa Malay* (No. RB-735). Newtown, PA: Vantage Learning.

Vantage Learning. (2003). *How does IntelliMetric* ® *score essay responses* (No. RB-929). Newton, PA: Vantage Learning.

Chapter 11
Assessing Change in Learners' Causal Understanding Using Sequential Analysis and Causal Maps

Allan C. Jeong

Abstract New methods and software tools are needed to assess the quality of learners' causal maps (maps that convey a learner's understanding of complex phenomena) and the quality of learners' discourse used to help justify changes and refinements in learners' causal maps. New methods and software tools are needed to assess the dialog move sequences observed in group discourse that trigger changes in causal maps and to measure and visualize across time the extent to which changes in causal maps of the individual or collective group progress toward group consensus and target maps. The software tool called jMAP was developed to enable learners to individually produce and submit causal maps, download and aggregate the maps of other learners. It also generates aggregated maps to reveal similarities between individual/group maps, the percentage of maps sharing particular causal links, average causal strength assigned to each link, and degree of match between the maps of the collective group and the target/expert diagram. jMAP also supports the use of sequential analysis to measure and visualize (with transitional state diagrams) how learner's causal maps change over time and how dialogic processes of argumentation conducted in online discussions trigger changes in learner's causal maps. This chapter presents findings from two case studies to illustrate how jMAP can be used to support the assessment of causal understanding, and to identify areas for future research and development.

Keywords Argumentation · Causal maps · Causal reasoning · Sequential analysis

11.1 Introduction

Each one of us holds different beliefs and theories about the world. Learners' theories can be conceived, articulated, and assessed more efficiently in the form of causal maps—networks of events (nodes) and causal relationships (links) between

A.C. Jeong (✉)
Department of Educational Psychology and Learning Systems,
Florida State University, Tallahassee, FL, USA
e-mail: ajeong@fsu.edu

V.J. Shute, B.J. Becker (eds.), *Innovative Assessment for the 21st Century*,
DOI 10.1007/978-1-4419-6530-1_11, © Springer Science+Business Media, LLC 2010

events—than in the form of linearly written text. Some causal maps may be more accurate than others—depending on the presence and/or absence of supporting evidence; and some maps and the causal links within the maps may be more or less firmly held—depending on both the strength of the supporting evidence and the strength of specific causal relationships. Furthermore, causal maps are not fixed and unchanging. Instead, they are incomplete and constantly evolving; may contain errors, misconceptions, and contradictions; may provide simplified explanations of complex phenomena; and may often contain implicit measures of uncertainty about their validity (Seel, 2003). As a result, causal maps can change, but usually not randomly. That is, we presume that events trigger and provide the impetus for change. Causal maps and other similar forms of visual representations are being increasingly used to help assess learners' understanding of complex domains and/or learners' progress towards increased understanding (Nesbit & Adesope, 2006; Spector & Koszalka, 2004). However, the methods and software tools to measure how learner's maps change over time (Doyle & Radzicki, 2007; Ifenthaler & Seel, 2005) and how specific events (e.g., pedagogical discourse) trigger changes in learners' causal maps (Shute, Jeong, & Zapata-Rivera, in press) have not yet been adequately addressed.

To address some of these methodological challenges, Ifenthaler and Seel (2005) used transitional probabilities to determine how likely learners' maps (when examined as a whole) changed in structural similarity across eight different time periods. Raters were given a specially designed questionnaire to determine if a learner's map at one point differed in structure from the learner's map produced from the most previous point in time. The study found that maps were most likely to change in structure at the early stages of the map construction process with the likelihood of changes dropping from one version to the next. However, Ifenthaler, Madsuki, and Seel (2008) found that changes in scores on seven of nine measures of structural quality (e.g., total number of links, level of connectedness, average number of incoming and outgoing vertices per node) had no correlation to the degree to which the learners' maps matched the expert map. Not surprisingly, the one aspect of the learners' maps that did correlate to learning was the number of links shared between the learner's map and the expert map. These findings altogether suggest that measures used to gauge changes at the global level (where the unit of analysis is the map as a whole) and measures that are not scored in relation to a target map (e.g., expert or collective group map) may have little or no value when used to assess learners.

One alternative approach is to measure changes at a more micro-level by using the node-link-node as the unit of analysis and unit of comparison between learners' and target maps. At this level, we can examine how likely links between specific nodes change from one state to another (e.g., strong vs. moderate vs. weak vs. no causal *impact*; or high vs. moderate vs. low *probability/likelihood*) as maps change over time. We can also see to what extent the observed changes in the values of each causal link converge towards the target causal link values present in the target map. For example, we expect that the causal link values for links representing learner's misconceptions (e.g., erroneous links *not* observed in the target map) or learners' shallow understandings (e.g., links between two nodes not directly related and/or better explained by inserting a mediating node) will converge towards a value of 0 (no causal link) over time, following close examination and critical discussion of the causal relationships. At the same time, the expectation is that the causal link values of the links *not* observed in a learner's map (but present in the target map) will progress from a value of 0 to the value observed in the target map. Using the node-link-node as the unit of analysis enables us to precisely examine how and to what extent observed changes in targeted links help and/or inhibit learners from achieving the target learning outcomes (e.g., more accurate, deeper, precise understanding). Furthermore, this approach enables us to examine how specific interventions and instructional events (e.g., depth of argumentation, the production of supporting evidence) affect the direction and magnitude of changes across links that are either missing or present and at the same time links that are valid or invalid.

To explore the strengths and limitations of using the node-link-node as the unit of analysis, this chapter presents a software tool called jMAP that can be used to identify differences between learners' causal maps, initiate collaborative argumentation to produce justifications for proposed causal links, and produce changes in learners' causal maps that better reflect/represent complex phenomena (see Fig. 11.1). Similar to the Cognizer program produced by Nakayama and Liao (2005), jMAP enables learners to individually produce causal maps (with numerically weighted links) thus reducing unwanted biases and the influence of other learners (Doyle et al., 2007). Once learners submit their maps, they can download and aggregate maps of all or

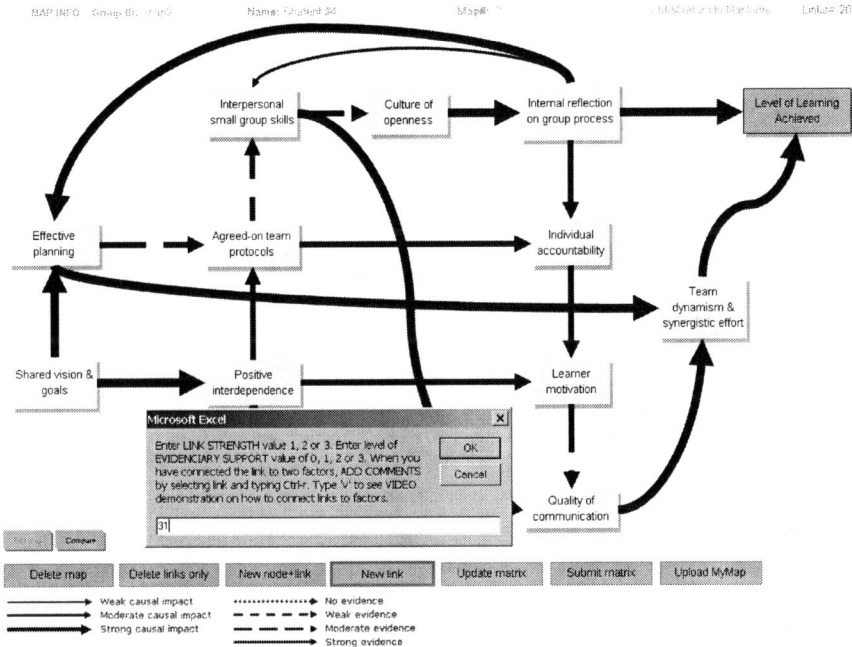

Fig. 11.1 Causal map produced in jMAP using weighted links to specify strength of each causal relationship and *dotted links* to specific level of confidence or evidentiary support

selected learners to capture the group's collective understanding. Unique to jMAP is that the learner can generate matrices to compute and report the percentage of learners' maps that share each causal link (including the average strength of each link observed across all learners' maps), and can superimpose his/her own causal diagram over the aggregate map to visually identify similarities and differences among the causal maps of all learners (Jeong, 2008).

Some of the other unique functions of jMAP enable researchers and teachers to: (a) graphically superimpose an *individual* learner's map over the expert/target map to visually identify and highlight changes occurring over time in the causal maps of an individual or group of learners; (b) determine the extent to which the observed changes progress toward a target or collective model; (c) determine precisely where, when, and to what extent changes occur in the causal links within the causal maps; and most importantly (d) identify and measure how and to what extent specific events (e.g., viewing consensus data, discussing evidence, engaging in specific and critical discourse patterns) trigger changes in the causal links between various states (e.g., strong, moderate, weak, and no causal link) as demonstrated in Fig. 11.2.

The following sections in this chapter present the findings from two case studies. The first study illustrates how sequential analysis can be used to build stochastic

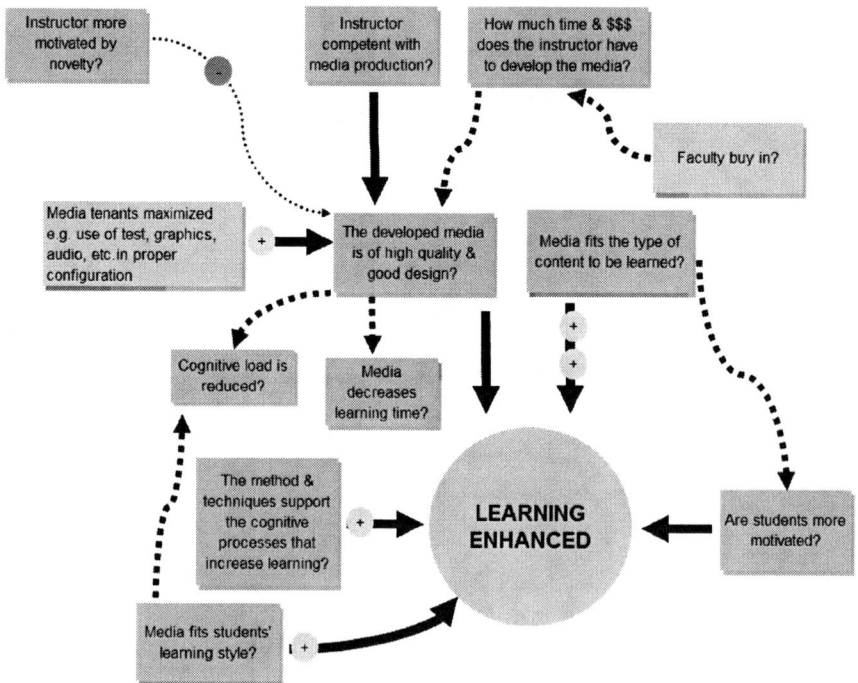

Fig. 11.2 A learner's map depicting a view of *media's relation to learning* with positive (+) and opposing (−) evidence and differential link strengths

models that assess how specific learning events affect the way learners change causal links in their causal maps. The second study serves to evaluate some of the potential advantages and issues when using software tools like jMAP to support learning and assessment. In the end is a brief discussion of possible directions for future research and development.

11.2 Assessing Change in Causal Maps with Sequential Analysis

An initial case study was conducted to develop and test the jMAP software and its ability to help us *visually* and *quantitatively* analyze how causal maps change over time. Specifically, this study assessed how the causal links between nodes changed in strength values (i.e., no link, weak, moderate, and strong) in learners' causal maps after learners reviewed readings and discussed related issues in an online threaded discussion. Most of all, this study examined how particular events (the presence of evidentiary support derived from group discussions and readings) affected how learners changed the causal strength values of the causal links presented in their causal maps.

11.2.1 Method

Twelve graduate students in the Instructional Systems program at Florida State University participated in a weeklong online discussion on the topic *Technologies and Media in Distance Education*. Students were assigned a set of readings and were required to post at least six contributions to the discussion forum across the 1 week period. Each student produced three concept maps representing their current beliefs of the functional/causal relationships among ten variables related to the topic. In this study, the ten variables were selected by the course instructor. Four learners did not submit one or more of the maps (for reasons unknown) and as a result, the maps of eight learners were used in this study to illustrate the tools and methodology.

The students' objectives were to describe the conceptual differences between media, technology, and instructional methods, and to state criteria for making decisions about the selection and use of delivery systems. To achieve these objectives, students were presented readings from which to extract arguments, counter-arguments, explanations, and supporting/opposing evidence to bring into an online team debate over the claim that, "One's choice of media (text, graphics, audio, and video) significantly increases student learning". Before, during, and after the team debates, each student was required to draw causal maps to convey their evolving understanding of how media affects learning. The maps were completed at three specific times during the week: (a) before reading and discussions, (b) in the middle of the week following initial discussions, and (c) at the end of the week following the conclusion of the discussions. Students were individually assigned to debate during the first 3 days on one side of the issue, and then asked to debate for the opposite side of the issue on the last three days. The readings were given to learners to reveal two opposing views: (a) media makes no difference on learning, and (b) media does make a difference.

In each causal map, learners could vary the density of each link (weak = low width, moderate = moderate width, strong = highest width) to convey the level of impact one variable has on another variable. Students judged the strength of each causal link based on empirical evidence presented in the readings (e.g., the reported effect sizes or the percent difference or increase in learning). In addition, learners specified the direction (+ or –) and amount of evidence (if available) to support and justify the causal links presented in their maps. The experiment coded all maps by hand and recorded each observed causal link into adjacency matrices—one matrix for each student map. For example, the cell in row 2 column 6 in Fig. 11.3 shows that the student believes that a causal relationship exists between "novelty" and "media quality" (e.g., when an instructor uses new media for the first time, its novelty tends to motivate instructors to produce higher quality media). The first digit in the cell signifies that the causal relationship is weak (1 = weak, 2 = moderate, 3 = strong). If a second digit appears, the second digit signifies that the learner possessed some knowledge of evidence to support this causal relationship.

Nodes	Novelty	InstructorCompetence	$$$	MediaFitsContent	LearnStyle	MediaQuality	CognitiveProcess	DecreaseTime	CogLoad	StudentMotivation	Outcome
Novelty						1 1					
InstructorCompetence						3					
$$$						2					
MediaFitsContent										2	3 2
LearnStyle									2		3 1
MediaQuality								2	2		3
CognitiveProcess											3 1
DecreaseTime											
CogLoad											
StudentMotivation											3
Outcome											
ProperMediaCombo						3 1					
FacultyBuyIn			2								

Fig. 11.3 Adjacency matrix of links and number of evidentiary support derived from the learner's causal map with the addition of "new nodes" inserted in the last two rows. Note: The first digit in each cell signifies the strength of causal impact (blank, 1, 2 or 3) that one node (listed in *left column*) has on another node (listed in the *top row*). The second digit (1 or blank) signifies whether the learner possesses evidence to support the proposed causal relationship

Table 11.1 Message tags and definitions of message tags

Msg tag	Description of message tag
+	If you are on the SUPPORTING team, ALL your posted messages must include the + tag before each message label
–	If you are on the OPPOSING team, ALL your posted messages must include the—tag before each message label
ARG1 ARG2 ARG3	ARGUMENT: Identifies a message that presents *one and only one* argument or reason to support your team's position. Number each posted argument by counting the number of arguments already presented by your team. Example argument supporting use of threaded discussions over use of chat rooms: +ARG2 *ProducesDeeperDiscussions*
EXPL	EXPLANATION: Identifies a response that provides additional support or sub arguments, explanation, clarification, or elaboration in response to a previous message: +*EXPL CanParticipateInMultipleThreads*
BUT	CHALLENGE: Identifies a response that questions/challenges the merits, logic, relevancy, validity, accuracy or plausibility of a claim or challenge: –*BUT MultipleThreadsProducesCognitiveOverload*
EVID	EVIDENCE: Identifies a response that provides proof or evidence to verify or establish the validity of an argument or challenge: +*EVID DiscussionThreadsAre50%LongerOnAverage*

In the online debates, learners were required to post specific messages and responses (see Table 11.1) to a threaded discussion (Fig. 11.4) hosted in Blackboard, a course management system. In each posting, learners inserted a corresponding tag into the subject heading to explicitly identify the function of each posting (Jeong & Juong, 2007). As a result, each posting served one and only one function at a time. Included with each tag was a + and – symbol to identify team position. Students were required to follow this protocol to receive points for participating in the week long debate. At any time, learners could return to their postings to insert the appropriate tags into the message headings.

11.2.2 Data for Sequential Analysis

To analyze the data recorded in the adjacency matrices for each learner's causal map, jMAP was developed and used to sequentially tabulate data from the adjacency matrices to capture observed changes in causal strength values between learners' maps produced on Monday versus Thursday and Thursday versus Sunday. The sequential data was imported into the Discussion Analysis Tool or DAT (Jeong, 2005a, 2005b) to produce a frequency matrix (Fig. 11.5) to reveal patterns in the changes observed in links that possessed vs. did not possess evidentiary support. The frequencies reported in the upper left quadrant of the matrix were used to compute the transitional probabilities (or relative frequencies) for changes in strength

☐	⊟ SUPPORT statement because...	Student names	Sat Oct 2, 2004 11:18 am
☐	⊟ +ARG#1 MedialsButAMereVehicle	Student names	Mon Oct 4, 2004 8:47 pm
☐	⊟ -EVID MedialsButAMereVeh...	Student names	Tue Oct 5, 2004 7:09 pm
☐	⊟ +But RelativityTheory...	Student names	Tue Oct 5, 2004 9:43 pm
☐	-But RelativityThe...	Student names	Sat Oct 9, 2004 10:12 am
☐	-BUT Whataboutemotions?	Student names	Tue Oct 5, 2004 9:53 pm
☐	+EVID DistEdEffectiveAsF2F	Student names	Tue Oct 5, 2004 10:40 pm
☐	-BUTMediaamerevehicle	Student names	Wed Oct 6, 2004 8:19 pm
☐	⊟ +EVID MooreConcurs	Student names	Wed Oct 6, 2004 10:07 pm
☐	+EXPLMediaSelectionCo...	Student names	Sun Oct 10, 2004 12:35 am
☐	⊟ -BUT WellChosenEffect...	Student names	Sun Oct 10, 2004 4:31 pm
☐	+But SupportingRes...	Student names	Sun Oct 10, 2004 5:37 pm
☐	⊟ -BUTMediaismorethenamere...	Student names	Fri Oct 8, 2004 5:30 pm
☐	+BUT SupportingEviden...	Student names	Sat Oct 9, 2004 8:51 am
☐	-BUT LearningNotSimplyAP...	Student names	Mon Oct 11, 2004 9:54 am
☐	⊟ +ARG2 Standards for teaching	Student names	Wed Oct 6, 2004 1:48 pm
☐	+But Clarification?	Student names	Sun Oct 10, 2004 5:39 pm
☐	⊟ +ARG3 MediaUnrelatedtoLearn...	Student names	Wed Oct 6, 2004 3:12 pm
☐	⊟ -BUTMediaUnrelatedtoLear...	Student names	Wed Oct 6, 2004 8:26 pm
☐	⊟ +BUT MediaSelection	Student names	Thu Oct 7, 2004 9:20 am
☐	-BUT MediaSelection	Student names	Sun Oct 10, 2004 11:21 am
☐	+EVID MethodNotMedia	Student names	Wed Oct 6, 2004 11:04 pm
☐	⊟ -BUT MediaUnrelatedtoLea...	Student names	Sat Oct 9, 2004 10:59 am

Fig. 11.4 Team debate with message tags in an online threaded discussion board. Note: Digits signify causal link strength/impact presented with and without supporting evidence

	0 - no evid	1 - no evid	2 - no evid	3 - no evid	0 - with evid	1 - with evid	2 - with evid	3 - with evid	Parent node
0 - no evid	295	4	7	8	0	5	7	9	407
1 - no evid	1	1	0	0	0	1	1	0	7
2 - no evid	2	0	3	1	0	0	1	1	16
3 - no evid	2	0	1	4	0	0	0	0	17
0 - with evid	0	0	0	0	0	0	0	0	0
1 - with evid	0	0	0	0	0	6	0	1	15
2 - with evid	2	0	0	0	0	0	5	0	18
3 - with evid	1	0	0	1	0	0	2	12	32
	303	5	11	14	0	12	16	23	512

Fig. 11.5 Frequency matrix with reported number of observed changes in strength values between revised and previous causal maps

values observed when causal links were *not* presented with supporting evidence. The probabilities of a change between each of the possible strength values in causal links *with* supporting evidence were computed by combining the cell frequencies from the other three quadrants of the frequency matrix (when evidence was presented in the previous and/or current map). The DAT software was then used to create the transitional state diagrams in Fig. 11.6 to visually convey and compare the observed transitional probabilities between causal links with versus without supporting evidence.

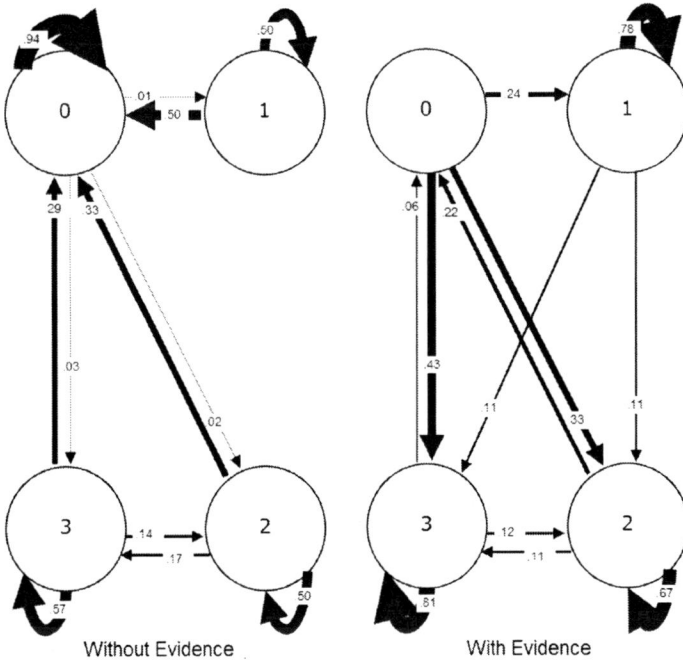

Fig. 11.6 Transitional state diagrams revealing the direction and likelihood of changes in causal strengths when links are presented without vs. with supporting evidence

11.2.3 Findings

The sequential analysis of causal link values revealed that evidentiary support strongly influenced how likely a student retained or eliminated a causal link between specific variables on each successive revision of their causal maps. Overall, links presented without evidence were more likely to change to lower strength values in subsequent revisions to the map, whereas links presented with supporting evidence were more likely to remain the same or increase in strength values.

For example, the left diagram in Fig. 11.6 shows that when *no* evidence was present to justify a causal link, the causal links that were assigned a strength value of one (1 = weak impact) were changed to a strength value of zero (None = no impact) 50% of the time (based on the examination of all changes observed between the first and second *and* between the second and third causal maps). In contrast, the right diagram shows that when causal links were presented with evidence, the links with strength values of one were much more likely to remain the same (78% instead of 50%), with 11% of the values *increasing* from weak to moderate impact and 11% of links increasing from weak to strong impact. A similar pattern can be seen in the causal links that were assigned strength values of two and three. A Chi-Square test can be used to test for significant differences between specific links that were presented with versus without supporting evidence.

11.2.4 Implications

These findings illustrate how sequential analysis and state diagrams (Fig. 11.6) can be used to assess changes in learners' causal understanding and learning trajectories by analyzing how causal links (examined across all learners) change in strength values (i.e., no link, weak, moderate, and strong). Furthermore, these findings illustrate how sequential analysis can be used to assess how particular learning or learner events (providing student access to empirical data or learner's knowledge of evidentiary support) affect the directions in which learners change the causal strength values of the causal links presented in their causal maps and the likelihood of such changes.

The methods and software tools presented here are intended to make the assessment of causal understanding and the process of argumentation more feasible and less labor intensive. The same tools and methods can be used to assess the learner's ability to engage in high level argumentation measured in terms of the observed number of message-response exchanges performed when cross examining the proposed causal relationships between nodes and the accuracy of the presented evidence (as illustrated in the next case study). The tools can then be used to assess how learners are able to apply the insights gained from argumentation to justify and validate changes/revisions to causal link values, and to assess how the changes converge towards target values observed in the expert map or the map of the collective group.

11.3 Assessing Argumentation and Effects on Causal Maps

The second case study illustrates how jMAP and the described methods can be used to assess learners' ability to engage in specific forms of argumentation and their ability to apply these forms of argumentation to construct better causal maps. Furthermore, this study also illustrates how jMAP can be used to compare causal maps between learners, identify differences between learners' maps and initial/current consensus on map links, and to initiate and structure learners' discussions in ways that might help to improve their causal maps. This study addressed the following research questions:

1. *What are the effects of consensus observed in initial maps on the level of consensus in subsequent maps?* When learners use jMAP to determine which causal links are shared most among everyone's initial maps, are the most commonly shared links more likely to remain in learners' subsequent maps than the less commonly shared links?
2. *What is the relationship between initial levels of consensus and level of argumentation?* Do learners engage in more argumentation when a causal link is more or less commonly shared between learners? In other words, do higher or lower levels of initial consensus trigger higher levels of argumentation?
3. *What are the effects of argumentation levels on consensus in subsequent maps?* Do high levels of argumentation lead to higher or lower levels of consensus in maps produced subsequent to group discussions/debates?

11.3.1 Method

Participants. Nineteen graduate students (8 male, 11 female) enrolled in an online course on computer-supported collaborative learning at a large southeastern university participated in this study. The participants ranged from 22 to 55 years in age, and the majority of the participants were enrolled in a Master's level program in instructional systems/design.

Procedures. The course examined factors that influence success in collaborative learning and instructional strategies associated with each factor. In week 2, learners used a Wiki webpage to share and construct a running list of factors believed to influence the level of learning or performance achieved in group assignments. Students classified and merged the proposed factors, discussed the merits of each factor, and voted on the factors believed to exert the largest influence on the outcomes of a group assignment. The votes were used to select a final list of 14 factors that learners individually organized into causal maps.

In week 3, students were presented six example maps to illustrate the desired characteristics and functions of causal maps (e.g., temporal alignment, parsimony). Students were provided the jMAP program (pre-loaded by the instructor with nodes for each of the 14 selected factors) to construct their first causal diagram (map 1). Map 1 allowed students to graphically explain their understanding of how the selected factors influence learning in collaborative settings. Using the tools in jMAP, learners connected the factors with causal links by: (a) creating each link with varying densities to reflect the perceived *strength* of the link (1 = weak, 2 = moderate, 3 = strong); and (b) selecting different types of links to reveal the level of evidentiary support (from past personal experiences) for the link. Personal maps were completed and electronically uploaded within a 1-week period to receive class participation points (class participation accounted for 25% of the course grade). The maps were also used to complete a written assignment describing one's personal theory of collaborative learning (due week 4, and accounting for 10% of the course grade).

Using jMAP, the instructor *aggregated* all the initial maps ($n = 17$) that were submitted by students. Two students did not submit their maps for reasons unknown. The matrix in Fig. 11.7 was shared with students to convey to the students the percentage of maps that possessed each causal link. The links enclosed in boxes in the right side of the figure are *common links* observed in 20% or more of the learners' maps. For example, the causal link between 'Individual Accountability' and 'Learner Motivation' was observed in 47% of learners' maps. To select this 20% cut-off criterion, the instructor ran multiple aggregations of the learner maps at different cut-off criterion until the instructor felt that a sufficient number of links were identified on the right side of Fig. 11.7 to help discriminate between links that were more versus less shared between learners. Presented in the left side of the figure are the mean strength values of links observed in 20% or more of the maps. The highlighted values reveal links that are present or absent in the expert's map (i.e., dark shaded cells with values = links shared and strength values match, lightly shaded with values = links shared with non-matching values, lightly shared boxes with no values = missing target links).

In week 9, learners were shown the matrix in Fig. 11.7 with the percentage of maps (map 1) that possessed each link. Students posted messages in online threaded discussions to explain the rationale and justification for each proposed causal link. Each posted explanation was labeled by learners with the tag 'EXPL' in message subject headings. Postings that questioned or challenged explanations were tagged with 'BUT.' Postings that provided additional support were tagged with 'SUPPORT.' In weeks 9 and 10, learners searched for and reported quantitative findings from empirical research into a group Wiki that could be referenced and used later to determine the instructional impact of each factor.

Students received instructions on how to use jMAP to *superimpose* their own map over the aggregated group map (Fig. 11.8) to visually identify similarities and differences between their own maps and the collective conception of the causal relationships between factors and outcomes. For example, Fig. 11.8 reveals the similarities and differences between an individual student's first map (student #4) and the group map (g1) generated by the aggregation of all the maps produced by all students at the first time period. The course instructor used jMAP to superimpose his expert map over the group map produced at time period one (g1) and in time period two (g2) by using the control keys (ctrl-h, ctrl-j, ctrl-k) to toggle between maps g1 and g2. By using the navigational tools to toggle between the two group maps, the instructor was able to visually and quantitatively observe the progression of changes averaged across all the students' maps in order to assess the extent

Percent of Maps with Given Links (n = 17)

Mean Link Values

$n = 17$ (mean scores rounded to zero decimals)
Selection criteria: 20% or more of maps with given links

Row/column variables:
- Shared vision & goals
- United team spirit
- Effective planning
- Learning style of group members
- Access to resources
- Culture of openness
- Agreed-on team protocols
- Internal reflection on group process
- Learner motivation
- Individual accountability
- Interpersonal small group skills
- Positive interdependence
- Quality of communication
- Team dynamism & synergistic effort
- Level of Learning Achieved

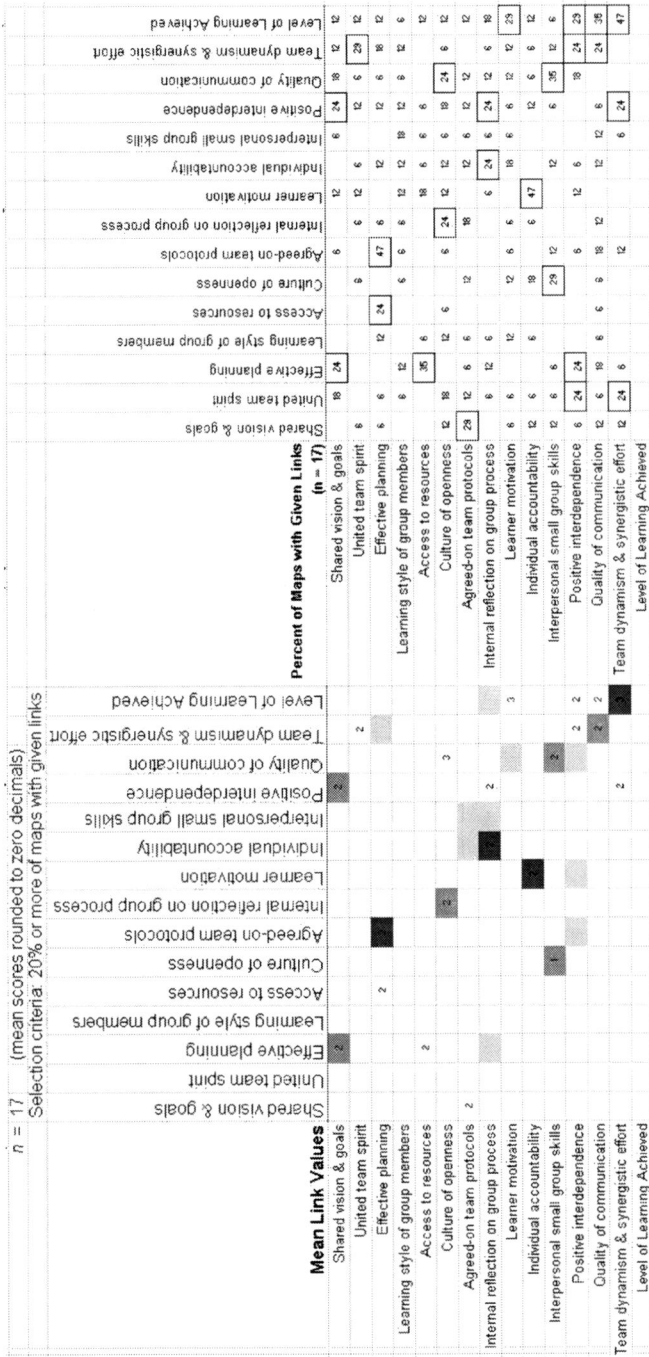

Fig. 11.7 Mean causal link strengths across all maps and percent of maps with given links

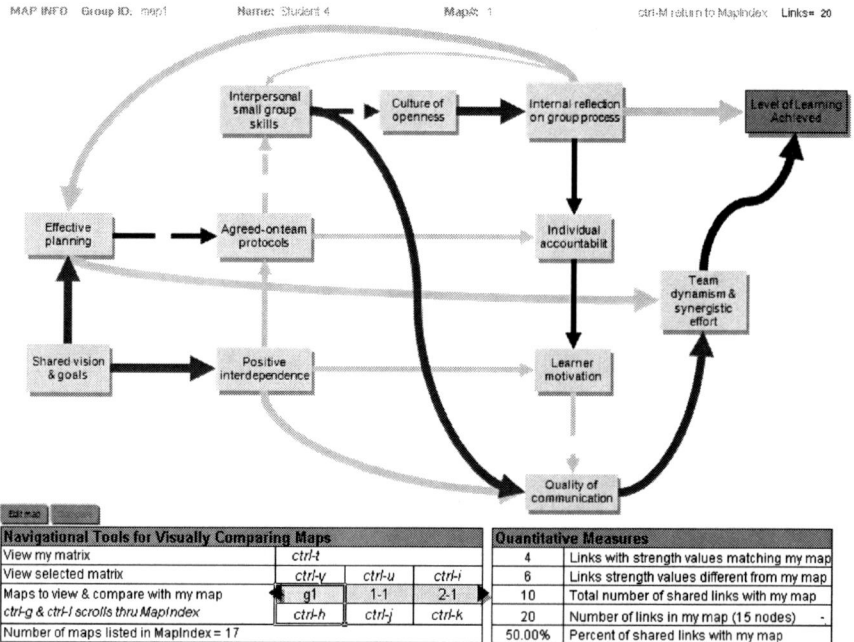

Navigational Tools for Visually Comparing Maps			
View my matrix	ctrl-t		
View selected matrix	ctrl-y	ctrl-u	ctrl-i
Maps to view & compare with my map	g1	1-1	2-1
ctrl-g & ctrl-l scrolls thru MapIndex	ctrl-h	ctrl-j	ctrl-k
Number of maps listed in MapIndex = 17			

Quantitative Measures	
4	Links with strength values matching my map
6	Links strength values different from my map
10	Total number of shared links with my map
20	Number of links in my map (15 nodes)
50.00%	Percent of shared links with my map

Fig. 11.8 Visual comparison of student 4's first map with the aggregated group map (g1) with *darker links* revealing matching causal strength values, *lighter links* revealing shared links (differing in values), and *light gray links* revealing missing links

to which the observed changes converged towards the expert map. Jeong (2008) presents more detailed information on how to use jMAP to visualize and animate progressive changes in maps created by a select learner (or group of learners) across multiple time periods relative to a target map.

In week 10, students reviewed the discussions from week 9. Within a discussion thread for each examined link, learners posted messages to report whether they rejected or accepted the link (along with explanations). At the end of week 10, each student posted a revised causal diagram based on their analysis of the arguments presented in class discussions (see Fig. 11.8).

Data Analysis. To measure the level of change in learners' maps, link frequencies from each learner's second map ($n = 15$) were aggregated to determine the percentage of maps that shared each link. Differences in the reported percentages between maps 1 and 2 were computed and appear in Fig. 11.9. Overall, the percentages in 19 of the 24 commonly shared links (in boxes) increased by an average of 26%. Four of these shared links (in gray-shaded boxes) changed by an average of –10.75%.

The level of critical discourse produced within each discussion on each link was determined by the number of observed EXPL-BUT, BUT-BUT, BUT-EXPL or SUPPORT, and BUT-SUPPORT exchanges. Challenges to explanations, and explanatory responses to challenges were used as a measure of critical discourse

Change in percentage of maps sharing links in map 2 from map 1	Shared vision & goals	United team spirit	Effective planning	Learning style of group members	Access to resources	Culture of openness	Agreed-on team protocols	Internal reflection on group process	Learner motivation	Individual accountability	Interpersonal small group skills	Positive interdependence	Quality of communication	Team dynamism & synergistic effort	Level of Learning Achieved
Shared vision & goals	-11		64			-6	6	-6			0	14	-18	-12	-12
United team spirit	-6					-6	-6	-6	-6			-6	0	14	1
Effective planning	0	-6		-12	14		40	-6		7		7	-6	-18	-12
Learning style of group members	-6	-6				-6	-6	-6	-12	-12	-5	-12	-6	-12	-6
Access to resources	6	6	8	-6			6	-11	-6	-6	-6				-12
Culture of openness	-6	-18		-12	-6		-6	-11	-12	-12	0	-18	45	0	-12
Agreed-on team protocols	-17	1	-6	-6		1		1		-6	0	-6	13	6	-12
Internal reflection on group process	6	-6	-6	-6					-6	14	-6	14	-6	-6	7
Learner motivation	-6	0	6	-6		-6	-6	-6		-18	0	-6	-12	1	21
Individual accountability	-12	-6		-6			-11	-6	40			-12	-6	0	-6
Interpersonal small group skills	-6	-6	-6		8	-12		-6				0	52	1	-6
Positive interdependence	-6	33	14				7		-6	0			-18	1	2
Quality of communication	-12	-6	-18	-6	-6	0	-18	7		-12	-12	-6		70	-4
Team dynamism & synergistic effort	-12	14	-6				-12	6			-6	-11	6		28
Level of Learning Achieved								6					6		

Fig. 11.9 Change in percent of maps sharing selected links

because explanations, when generated in direct response to conflicting viewpoints, have been shown to improve learning (Pressley et al., 1992). Pearson correlations between variables are presented below.

11.3.2 Findings

Effects of consensus observed in initial maps on level of consensus in subsequent maps. Based on links ($n = 24$) that were observed in 20% or more of students' maps and discussed by students on the discussion board, the correlation (Table 11.2) between the percentage of students that shared a causal link in the first map and the average change in the percentage of students that shared the causal links was not significant ($r = -0.09$, $p = 0.68$). The opinions of the majority did not appear to influence learners' decisions to include or exclude causal links into their revised maps. This suggests that the use of jMAP to reveal the similarities and differences between students' maps did not promote group think.

Relationship between initial agreement and level of critical discourse. The correlation ($n = 24$) between the percentage of students that shared a causal link in

Table 11.2 Correlations ($n = 24$) between level of initial agreement, critical discourse, and change in percent of learners sharing each causal link

		LevelAgree	CritDisc	%Change	Expl	But	Support	Expl-But	But-Ex/Sup	But-But	Expl-Sup
LevelAgree	r	1	0.39	-0.09	0.23	0.33	0.29	0.33	0.37	0.18	0.15
	signif		0.06	0.68	0.27	0.12	0.17	0.12	0.08	0.41	0.48
CritDiscource	r	0.39	1	-0.15	0.34	0.92	0.12	0.87	0.92	0.49	0.14
	signif	0.06		0.48	0.11	0.00	0.58	0.00	0.00	0.01	0.53
PercentChange	r	-0.09	-0.15	1	0.06	0.17	0.31	0.05	-0.17	0.22	0.39
	signif	0.68	0.48		0.79	0.42	0.14	0.81	0.44	0.30	0.06

the first map and the level of critical discourse that was generated by students to examine the strength of each causal link approached statistical significance ($r = 0.39$, $p = 0.06$). The students engaged in more critical discussion over the causal links when the causal links were shared by more students rather than less students. This finding suggests that students did not simply accept or give into the status quo. Conversely, the finding also suggests that students exhibited some tendency to engage in *less* critical discussion over the causal links when the casual links were shared by *fewer* students. One possible explanation for this finding may be that the causal links shared by the fewest number of students where those that exhibited the most obvious flaws in logic and as a result, these links did not warrant much debate to omit the causal link from the causal maps.

Effects of argumentation on changes in agreement in subsequent maps. No significant correlation was found between the level of critical discourse over each causal link and the change in the percentage of maps sharing each casual link ($r = -0.15$, $p = 0.48$). This finding suggests that the level of critical discourse over each causal link neither increased nor decreased the percentage of students that rejected a causal link.

Post-hoc analysis on the individual effects of each of the four types of exchanges (all of which were aggregated and used to measure the level of that critical discourse) revealed the frequency of EXPL-SUPP exchanges observed in discussions over each link were moderately and positively correlated ($r = 0.39$, $p = 0.06$) with changes in the percentage of students that shared each causal link. Supporting statements that were specifically posted in direct response to other learners' causal explanations (e.g., presenting supporting evidence, simple expression of agreement) were the types of events/exchanges that were most likely to persuade learners to adopt new links into subsequent causal maps. This finding is consistent with the findings from the first case study in which causal link strength values were more likely to remain the same or increase in value when links were supported with evidence. Also worth noting here is that the frequency of supporting statements alone observed in discussions over each causal link (without regard to what messages they were posted in response to) revealed a similar correlation but of lesser statistical significance ($r = 0.31$, $p = 0.14$). This suggests that message-response exchanges as opposed to simple message frequencies alone can provide more explanatory power when analyzing the effects of critical discourse on causal understanding.

11.3.3 Implications

The findings in this second case study illustrate how jMAP can be used to assess the impact of critical discussions or other types of learning events on learners' causal understanding. When used as a research tool, jMAP provides insights into the processes of learning (e.g., causal understanding) and insights into how specific processes (e.g., EXPL-SUPP) lead to specific learning outcomes/behaviors. At the same time, this case study illustrates how jMAP can help learners work collaboratively to build and refine causal understanding. Learners can identify similarities and differences in their causal understanding relative to others. Then they can use the differences as the starting point to discuss and explore the causal relationships.

11.4 Directions for Future Research

The findings in the two case studies reported above are not conclusive given the limited sample size. Nevertheless, these studies illustrate how the demonstrated tools and methods can be used to assess how causal understanding evolves over time and how specific processes of discourse (including processes of scientific inquiry) influence causal understanding. More research is needed to identify the specific discourse processes (and interventions designed to foster critical discussions) that can trigger changes in causal links—particularly changes that converge towards the expert and/or the group model.

To further facilitate research on processes that support causal understanding, online discussion boards can be integrated into jMAP to automatically create discussion threads for each causal link observed in learners' causal maps, to seed discussions with learners' initial explanations, to support message tagging, and to compile and report scores that measure certain qualities observed in the group discussions for any given set of causal links. Such a system could be used by instructors to assess not only the quality of learners' causal maps and understanding, but also the quality of learners' discourse and its impact on their causal understanding. Additional functions can be added to jMAP to recognize nodes that are indirectly linked via mediating nodes to fully account for observed differences between learner and expert maps. Another useful function would be one that can identify/measure to what extent and in what temporal direction changes in causal links propagate subsequent changes in adjacent links—a measure that could be used to determine to what extent learners are able to systematically break down and reflect on causal relationships. To examine this issue in more detail, a function can be added to jMAP that captures and logs every action performed in jMAP as learners construct their maps.

In addition, refinements to the jMAP user interface will be necessary to make map construction easier, more intuitive, and less time consuming if systems like jMAP are to be used in school-based applications—particularly for learners at younger ages. Instructions and guidance on how to conceptualize a coherent causal map/model (e.g., temporal flow, parsimony) should be embedded directly into the jMAP interface to assist learners that lack the skills needed to construct a causal map.

References

Doyle, J., Radzicki, M., et al. (2007). Measuring change in mental models of complex systems. In H. Qudrat-Ullah, J. M. Spector, & P. I. Davidsen (Eds.), *Complex decision making: Theory and practice* (pp. 269–293). Berlin and Heidelberg: Springer.
Ifenthaler, D., & Seel, N. M. (2005). The measurement of change. Learning-dependent progression of mental models. *Technology, Instruction, Cognition and Learning, 2*(4), 317–336.

Ifenthaler, D., Iskandaria, M., & Seel, N. M. (2008). *Tracking the development of cognitive structures over time*. Paper presented at the American Educational Research Association 2008 conference, New York.

Jeong, A. (2005a). *Discussion analysis tool*. Retrieved May 2009, from http://mailer.fsu.edu/~ajeong/DAT

Jeong, A. (2005b). A guide to analyzing message-response sequences and group interaction patterns in computer-mediated communication. *Distance Education, 26*(3), 367–383.

Jeong, A., & Juong, S. (2007). Scaffolding collaborative argumentation in asynchronous discussions with message constraints and message labels. *Computers & Education, 48*, 427–445.

Jeong, A. (2008). *jMAP*. Retrieved July 24, 2008, from http://jmap.wikispaces.com

Nakayama, V. K., & Liao, J. (2005). An outline of approaches to analyzing the behavior of causal maps. In V. K. Nakayama & D. J. Armstrong (Eds.), *Causal mapping for research in information technology* (pp. 368–377). Hershey, PA: Idea Group Publishing.

Nesbit, J., & Adesope, O. (2006). Learning with concept and knowledge maps: A meta-analysis. *Review of Educational Research, 76*(3), 413–448.

Pressley, M., Wood, E., Woloshyn, V. E., Martin, V., King, A., & Menke, D. (1992). Encouraging mindful use of prior knowledge: Attempting to construct explanatory answers facilitates learning. *Educational Psychologist, 27*(1), 91–109.

Seel, N. M. (2003). Model-centered learning and instruction. *Technology, Instruction, Cognition and Learning, 1*(1), 59–85.

Shute, V. J., Jeong, C., & Zapata-Rivera, D. (in press). Using flexible belief networks to assess mental models. In B. B. Lockee, L. Yamagata-Lynch, & J. M. Spector (Eds.), *Instructional design for complex learning*. New York: Springer.

Spector, J. M., & Koszalka, T. A. (2004). *The DEEP methodology for assessing learning in complex domains (Final report to the National Science Foundation Evaluative Research and Evaluation Capacity Building)*. Syracuse, NY: Syracuse University.

Chapter 12
Development and Use of a Tool for Evaluating Teacher Effectiveness in Grades K-12

Alysia D. Roehrig and Eric Christesen

Abstract In a culture of accountability, reliable and valid tools are needed for assessing the quality of teaching in grades K-12. The results of a seminal series of qualitative studies describing exemplary classrooms were inductively categorized to create such a tool–the Classroom AIMS Instrument–which assesses *A*tmosphere, *I*nstruction, *M*anagement and *S*tudent Engagement. The more consistently teachers incorporated practices observed in exemplary classrooms, the more highly and consistently engaged were their students. Confirmatory factor analysis (CFA) for the Management category confirmed a two subcategory model. Results of the CFAs for Atmosphere, Instruction, and Student Engagement suggested moderately good fit after minor modifications to six, five and single factor models, respectively. While initial results are promising, suggestions for additional validation research are made.

Keywords Classroom observation techniques · Effective teaching · Learner engagement · Classroom climate · Instruction · Management

12.1 Introduction

In the late 1970s and early 1980s, researchers attempted to identify those teaching behaviors (or processes) that correlated with gains in student achievement (products). The results of this process-product methodology showed that several generic teaching or classroom practices were related to higher student achievement. For example, smooth lesson pacing and transitions were associated with greater achievement gains as well as classroom management (e.g., Anderson, Evertson, & Brophy, 1979). Process-product methodology, however, fell out of favor as many scholars began to embrace more complex views of teaching. These scholars argued that

A.D. Roehrig (✉)
Department of Educational Psychology and Learning Systems,
Florida State University, Tallahassee, FL, USA
e-mail: aroehrig@fsu.edu

V.J. Shute, B.J. Becker (eds.), *Innovative Assessment for the 21st Century*,
DOI 10.1007/978-1-4419-6530-1_12, © Springer Science+Business Media, LLC 2010

effective teaching was more than simply employing a few, key generic instructional practices. Instead, effective teachers employed their knowledge—of subject matter, pedagogy, and students—to plan for, enact, and evaluate their classroom instruction (e.g., Berliner, 1988; Shulman, 1986; Sternberg, 1998). To capture this complexity, researchers shifted to using qualitative methods, which they believed were more capable of capturing how teachers' thinking and beliefs influenced their actions (e.g., Wharton-McDonald, Pressley, & Hampston, 1998).

Recent accountability demands in education, particularly related to the No Child Left Behind Act (NCLB) of 2001, have refocused researchers' attention on finding ways to quantify teacher quality and tie it to student achievement. Many researchers are now engaged in varied efforts to define and operationalize classroom teaching and teacher knowledge. Although researchers have developed many tools for assessing teacher quality—including direct observation, logs of classroom performance, and surveys of knowledge—teacher behaviors in the classroom are the most robust predictors of student achievement gains (Kennedy, 1999). This is because more proximal factors such as teacher behaviors have been found to have stronger direct effects on student achievement than more distal teacher characteristics such as knowledge and beliefs (Muijs & Reynolds, 2002). Teachers' classroom practices are assessed most accurately via direct observation, and such assessments are better predictors of student achievement than teacher self-reports (Kennedy, 1999).

Prior to 2000, only a few comprehensive classroom observation tools focused on instructional techniques as well as classroom management and motivational climate for the elementary grades. The majority of the well-known measures were developed to evaluate preschool and sometimes kindergarten environments (e.g., ECERS; Harms, Clifford, & Cryer, 1998; ECCOM; Stipek, 1996). While a few existing classroom observation tools attempted to quantify some of the more complex characteristics of classroom practices in elementary school, prior to the development of the Classroom AIMS Instrument described in this chapter, these earlier tools were not very comprehensive. For example, the Classroom Observation Rubric focused only on the use of constructivist teaching practices in science instruction (Burry-Stock & Oxford, 1993). The Assessment of Practices in Early Elementary Classrooms (APEEC) covered more broad-ranging classroom contexts and dealt with the physical environment, the instructional context, and the social context (Hemmeter, Maxwell, Ault, & Schuster, 1998). The APEEC, however, covered only 16 characteristics and relied, in part, on teacher interviews in addition to observations for rating. Weller's Teacher Performance Assessment Instruments (TPAI) evaluated 14 competencies including teaching plans and materials, classroom procedures, and interpersonal skills. The TPAI, which has well established reliability and validity, and other comprehensive observation tools (e.g., Cloud-Silva & Denton, 1988; Stulac et al., 1982) were developed for the assessment of minimal teaching competencies (Lavely, Berger, Blackman, Follman, & McCarthy, 1994). In contrast, the Classroom AIMS Instrument was developed for the assessment of exemplary competencies.

In this chapter, we describe the development and initial validation of a classroom observation tool for the purposes of evaluating teacher effectiveness. The

Classroom AIMS Instrument was developed to advance the teacher quality observational assessment literature in a several ways. The Classroom AIMS Instrument is comprehensive and evaluates multiple domains associated with exemplary teaching. While initially developed with a focus on reading achievement and student engagement, it evaluates many forms of effective instruction (e.g., direct instructional approaches, modeling, peer tutoring, discovery learning, etc.) that may be applicable across content areas. The Classroom AIMS Instrument also incorporates elements of the classroom community, motivational tone, and classroom management. This instrument provides some of the most stringent criteria available for assessing the quality of teacher practices. The criteria were developed from studies of teachers who not only were able to help their students make exceptional literacy achievements but also were able to keep students highly engaged during the learning process (e.g., Pressley, Allington, Wharton-McDonald, Block, & Morrow, 2001). The AIMS model is an extension of exemplary teacher research.

12.1.1 Exemplary Teacher Research

The Classroom AIMS Instrument was developed from a qualitative analysis of the classroom practices of teachers who succeeded in maintaining high levels of student engagement and corresponding literacy improvements in students from a range of socio-economic backgrounds (Allington & Johnston, 2002). The types of practices used by these more successful or "exemplary" teachers cover the broad range of classroom life (i.e., classroom atmosphere, classroom instruction, classroom management, and student engagement) and are not focused solely on reading instruction (e.g., Bogner, Raphael, & Pressley, 2002; Day, Boothroyd, Johnston, & Cedeno, 1999; Day, Woodside-Jiron & Johnston, 1999; Allington & Johnston, 2002; Dolezal, Welsh, Pressley, & Vincent, 2003; Johnston, Powers, & Costello, 1999; Morrow, Tracey, Woo, & Pressley, 1999; Pressley, Allington, et al., 2001, 2003, 2002; Pressley, Wharton-McDonald et al., 2001; Roehrig, Pressley, & Sloup, 2001; Wharton-McDonald et al., 1998).

As part of the exemplary teacher research that led to AIMS, the behaviors characteristic of exemplary primary teachers (i.e., teachers with students who were highly and consistently engaged in learning and were working above grade level in literacy activities) as well as those characteristic of teachers who were less effective (i.e., their students demonstrated low engagement and performed at or below grade level in reading achievement) were identified. The effective-teacher researchers cited in the preceding paragraph used a grounded theory approach (Strauss & Corbin, 1998) to examine teaching behaviors and discover what excellent teachers do to motivate their students, especially in the area of literacy. In general, these studies conformed to the following process: Researchers requested that local school administrators "nominate teachers who they believed were outstanding in promoting literacy in their... students as well as teachers who were more typical of district standards" (Pressley et al., 2002, p. 77). The researchers did not blindly accept the schools' nomination or appraisal of teacher effectiveness; effectiveness was confirmed by multiple observers who made multiple unobtrusive observations of the nominated teachers in their classrooms. Classrooms were observed until no new patterns or insights emerged.

The classrooms differed in the degree of student engagement observed. Variation in student engagement was associated with differences in achievement, measured in several different ways: in terms of the level of books read, quality of writing, as well as, in some studies, standardized test performance (Allington & Johnston, 2002; Pressley, Allington, et al., 2001). Some teachers were effective; their students were consistently engaged in reading and writing and by the end of the year could write several pages with good mechanics and spelling as well as read books above grade level. Two other groups of teachers were less effective, with student engagement either more variable between students and over time (typical teachers) or consistently low (ineffective teachers). The amount and quality of student reading and writing were similarly less impressive for these groups. In addition, the standardized reading test scores of exemplary grade 1 teachers' students were above grade-level and higher than in less effective classrooms (Pressley, Allington, et al., 2001). Similarly, grade 4 students also "made better than average reading progress during their year" (i.e., more than 1 year of growth) when in exemplary classrooms (Allington & Johnston, 2002, p. 233).

More engaging, more effective teachers taught differently than less effective teachers. Exemplary teachers taught many skills, emphasized literature, provided numerous reading and writing opportunities during literacy and content instruction, matched student competencies with task demands (increasing the demand as students improved) monitored student efforts, provided scaffolding as needed, encouraged students to be self-regulated, and made many cross-disciplinary connections (e.g., Pressley et al., 2002). Exemplary teachers also motivated their students by creating comfortable, stimulating, cooperative, effort-focused atmospheres. They challenged and engaged their students by incorporating interesting, authentic tasks while demonstrating strategic problem solving and scaffolding students. These teachers maintained very high expectations for their students' learning and carefully monitored student understanding. Effective teachers essentially saturated their classrooms with motivating practices (e.g., Bogner et al., 2002; Dolezal et al., 2003). Finally, exemplary teachers were outstanding classroom managers (for a review of the exemplary teacher research see Pressley et al., 2003). The Classroom AIMS Instrument includes measures of diverse exemplary teaching behaviors, incorporating instruction, motivation and management in the classroom.

12.1.2 Development of the Classroom AIMS Instrument

Qualitative analysis of the results of the exemplary teacher research conformed to the following process (Roehrig, Dolezal, Welsh, Bohn, & Pressley, 2002). An inclusive list of exemplary teaching practices described in the qualitative teacher studies was compiled. Repetitive items were removed or combined, and all items describing behaviors not found in exemplary classrooms were worded negatively (e.g., Teacher does NOT allow off-task disruptions). Next, these items were sorted, and using grounded theory analysis (Strauss & Corbin, 1998), categories were inductively developed and relationships between categories identified. Thus, the original categories of teaching practices resulting from earlier qualitative studies were dismantled and recombined.

The general process of coding was as follows. First, we labeled items with descriptors that were grouped into categories. Second, we reexamined the original items to confirm or recategorize membership until no new subcategories emerged. And third, we looked for connections between subcategories to identify overarching categories. The 185 initial items were consequently organized into 31 initial subcategories (e.g., Classroom is a Democratic Place, Focus on Effort, Teacher Modeling, Engaging Content, and Establishing Behavioral Self-Regulation/Routines) subsumed under three overarching categories of Atmosphere, Instruction, and Management.

Three rounds of agreement checks were conducted to further verify the item groupings. Once item wording and category labels for this initial categorization scheme were agreed upon, the validity of these groupings was evaluated by having two additional reviewers independently sort the items under the group labels to determine how accurately others could recreate the categories. One reviewer was familiar with terms, related literature, and classrooms of previously identified exemplary teachers, having participated in data collection for some of the exemplary teaching studies. She was given the items listed individually on index cards, as well as a set of labels and their organization, and was asked to sort the items into the scheme of categories and subcategories. Her placement of items into the three main categories was perfectly aligned with the original coders' placement, and her placement of items into subcategories was nearly identical: 100% of Management items, 85% of Atmosphere items, and 92% of Instruction items were subcategorized in perfect agreement with the original coders' categorization scheme. The other new reviewer, who had not been involved in exemplary teacher data collection and was not familiar with the literature, also was given the same sorting task. Her agreement with the original coders on the overarching categories was lower: 80% of Management items, 62% of Instruction items, and 74% of Atmosphere items were subcategorized in perfect alignment with the original coders. The items categorized and subcategorized differently by these two additional reviewers were reconsidered and, based on this feedback, revisions were made to categorizations, subcategory labels, and item wordings. In order to increase transparency, especially for those not familiar with the literature, category definitions and item examples were added.

After these revisions, the items entered a second round of coding. During this round, Roehrig et al. (2002) reduced the 31 initial subcategories to 27 and finally to 21 and left the three overarching categories intact. The two extra reviewers from the first round were asked to (a) review the most recently revised categories/subcategories/items, (b) point out any areas of confusion or disagreement, and (c) make suggestions for improvements. The list of categorized items also was given to two more new reviewers for additional sorting: both were unfamiliar with the exemplary teacher research and literature. The goal was to develop an instrument that was self-explanatory and accessible to anyone with an interest in teachers and students. Based on the alternative categorizations and feedback of the reviewers, the subcategorization and wording of items were further refined. During the third round of coding, three of the original reviewers were presented with the refined list of categorized items. These reviewers were asked to evaluate the changes and provide additional feedback about the items. Comments were again taken into consideration, and further minor adjustments were made. The highly iterative process resulted in minor changes to the initial overarching categories (Atmosphere, Instruction, and Management) developed in the first round of coding.

During these later stages of coding, the instrument also was used to evaluate teachers. The use of the instrument revealed problematically worded items. These items either were revised or eliminated. The instrument thereby was reduced to 163 teacher practices and 7 student outcomes that were typical of early-primary teachers, who had highly engaged students doing lots of reading and writing at or above grade level. Each individual item, subcategory, and category associated with being an exemplary teacher, however, still needed to be validated by experts. Nineteen experts in early-primary grades research and eight expert teachers (many of whom were identified in earlier qualitative research in exemplary teaching), were contacted to provide feedback on the items and their organization. These experts rated the items and categories on a 3-point scale, where 1 meant an exemplary teacher would not emphasize that practice or behavior and 3 meant an exemplary teacher would strongly emphasize it. This, in turn, led to further refinement of the initial Classroom AIMS Instrument. Only items and categories that received the highest rating of 3 by at least 70% of raters were kept.

Based on these modifications, seven subcategories were identified within the Atmosphere construct, eight within the Instruction construct, two within the Management construct, and no subcategories were created within the Student Engagement construct. The subcategories within Atmosphere, which represented what the teacher does to the physical and interpersonal environment to get and keep students involved in learning, were given the following labels:

- Sense of Community Fostered,
- Interest Fostered,
- Focus on Effort Rather than Performance,
- Sense of Choice/Control Fostered,
- Value of Learning Expressed,
- High Expectations Expressed, and
- Informative Feedback Provided.

An example from Sense of Community Fostered was "Teacher expresses empathy for students-encouraging others to do so as well." An item from Sense of Choice/Control Fostered was "Teacher gives students choices in their work (e.g., encourages students to select one of a few books that are at their reading level)."

The Instruction construct, which represented the lessons, activities, and the teacher's instructional style, was divided into eight subcategories with the following labels:

- Engaging Content and Activities Used,
- High Instructional Density Achieved,
- Cross-Curricular Connections Made,
- Appropriate Challenge Level Achieved,
- Thinking Processes Modeled and Taught,
- Scaffolding Provided,
- Academic Self-Regulation Encouraged, and
- Academic Monitoring Provided.

An item from Instructional Density Achieved was "Teacher seems to teach constantly, with whole group, small group, and individual mini-lessons simply intermingled throughout the day." An item from Thinking Processes Modeled and Taught was "Teacher explicitly articulates the processes used in strategies/problem solving (e.g., explains the steps involved in brainstorming)."

The two subcategories created within Management, which represented the order, rules, routines, and procedures (i.e., what keeps the instruction moving in an orderly fashion), were

- Behavioral Self-Regulation Encouraged, and
- Behavior/Task Monitoring Provided.

The Behavioral Self-Regulation subcategory included teacher practices that lead to the development of students knowing how they are supposed to act, what they are supposed to do, and why. An item from this subcategory was "Teacher effectively uses redirection (e.g., asking students what they are doing or what they should be doing), glances, pauses to help keep students on-task." The Behavior/Task Monitoring subcategory focused on whether the teacher is on the lookout for students who are off task and quickly gets them back on the right track. An example from this subcategory was "Teacher does whole class monitoring for on-task behavior."

The Student Engagement construct had no subcategories. All four Student Engagement items concerned observable indicators of student engagement, including participation, excitement, and staying on task. These items included the following: "Students vocalize/express excitement about content/activities (e.g., lots of 'Oohs and Aahs.')," "The students eagerly raise their hands and participate," "At least 80% of students are consistently on task and highly engaged in class activities," and "Students are so self-regulated that disciplinary encounters are rarely seen."

The suggested rating scale for the items on the Classroom AIMS Instrument asked observers to evaluate instructors on a 3-point scale patterned after the three groups of teachers found in the exemplary teacher studies: exemplary/consistent use (3), typical/inconsistent use (2), or poor/rare use (1). In the initial version of the

AIMS, a 0 rating option was also available if observers believed they did not have an opportunity (or enough information) to evaluate an item. Use of the 0 option, however, was discouraged, and further observations were recommended if this was the case. In the following analyses, 0 ratings were treated as missing data except in the case of calculating rater agreement.

12.2 Method

12.2.1 Data Sources

Data were compiled from four independent studies. These studies included observations of teachers in Canada ($n = 19$), Florida ($n = 95$), Indiana ($n = 20$), and Michigan ($n = 24$). Canadian data consisted of observations of 19 first grade teachers in English-language schools in Montreal (Savage, Deault, & Burgos, 2008). Teachers varied in terms of their literacy practices, years of experience, and pedagogical approach. The researchers used the Classroom AIMS Instrument to provide a rich picture of the quality of the classroom environment and to triangulate the AIMS observations with teacher and student perceptions of the classroom environment. The Florida data were collected as part of an evaluation of a literacy reform program to provide a context of overall classroom quality (Roehrig, Turner, & Petscher, 2008). Forty-six elementary teachers and 49 secondary teachers were observed. The secondary teachers included Mathematics, English, Science, and Social Studies teachers. Further analyses of these observations are currently ongoing. The Indiana data were collected for the development of the Classroom AIMS Instrument in conjunction with two published studies about (1) more and less effective teachers (Bohn, Roehrig, & Pressley, 2004), and (2) beginning teachers and their mentors (Roehrig, Bohn, Turner, & Pressley, 2008). The 20 observed teachers taught grades K-4 primarily in private Catholic schools in one small Midwestern city. AIMS was used to evaluate the relative effectiveness of teachers as well as to evaluate change in beginning teachers' practices. The Michigan data were collected based on observations of 24 beginning teachers (teachers in their 1st or 2nd year of teaching) from a single midsized, economically depressed, urban district (Stanulis & Floden, 2009). These beginning teachers included secondary teachers in English, Mathematics, and Science as well as elementary education teachers and a special education teacher. The AIMS instrument was used as a measure of balanced effective instruction.

Data collection was similar for most of the studies. In the Canada, Florida, and Indiana studies, two people usually observed the same teacher and came to a consensus score. However, in the Michigan study, only one person observed each teacher. Agreement percentages were calculated using the data from the three studies wherein 125 teachers were observed by two people (nine teachers in these three studies were only rated by one observer). Percent agreement between raters was calculated using the items remaining after the Confirmatory Factor Analysis described below. Out of 9,350 unique observations, 95% of all ratings were exact or contiguous (i.e., contiguous $= \pm 1$); 37% of ratings reflected a 1 point discrepancy and 58% were exact matches. Only 5% of observation ratings differed by the maximum, 2 points.

Cronbach's alpha levels were calculated for the four overarching categories (Atmosphere, Instruction, Management, and Student Engagement) as well as all subcategories of items. Several subcategories were dropped from the instrument before it was used in the Florida study. Subcategories were omitted if their items were difficult for observers to rate based on only one observation (this led to the removal of most items that regularly elicited a 0 rating). Other reasons for omitting were inappropriateness of items for K-12 classrooms (this led to the removal of most beginning literacy items), as well as difficulty for observers to agree about how to rate teachers for items in the subcategories. The omitted subcategories (e.g., Cross-Curricular Connections Made) tended to be the subcategories with the lowest alphas. Alphas for the subcategories ranged from $\alpha = 0.56$ to $\alpha = 0.89$. The alphas for Atmosphere ($\alpha = 0.87$), Instruction ($\alpha = 0.90$), Management ($\alpha = 0.74$), and Student Engagement ($\alpha = 0.79$) were all high (αs above 0.70 were considered acceptable; Nunnally, 1978).

12.2.2 Confirmatory Factor Analysis (CFA) Results

The data analyzed here were pooled from the four separate prior studies. Initially inter-item correlation matrices were analyzed for the subcategories of each factor (Atmosphere, Instruction, Management, and Student Engagement). Items with no correlations above .40 with any of the other items in their subcategory were deleted. For example, the item "Teacher encourages students to participate" did not have a correlation above .40 with any other item in the Focus on Effort Rather than Performance subcategory of Atmosphere. In addition to this, three items were deleted from the Engaging Content subcategory of Instruction and one item was deleted from the High Instructional Density subcategory of Instruction because they had only one correlation above .40 with other items within their respective subcategories. In total, nine items were deleted from Atmosphere and 17 items were deleted from Instruction, including all of the Academic Monitoring items. No items were deleted from Management or Student Engagement.

Confirmatory Factor Analyses were conducted to establish the fit of the data with the original factor structures of Atmosphere, Instruction, Management, and Student Engagement (see Tables 12.1, 12.2, 12.3, and 12.4 for items, factors, and factor loadings). The original factor structures were based on the qualitative analysis resulting in the organization of items into subcategories and of subcategories into each main category: Atmosphere, Instruction, Management, and Student Engagement. Only items that had sufficient data were included in the tests of model fit (i.e., items not used in the Florida study were missing data from over half the combined sample, so those items were not included in data analyses). The model for Atmosphere was hypothesized to comprise six factors, the model for Instruction included five factors, and the model for Management had two factors. Student Engagement was hypothesized to follow a single factor model. The fit of each of the four models was individually evaluated using the chi-square test, comparative fit index (CFI), standardized root mean square residual (SRMR), and root mean square approximation (RMSEA). A non-significant chi-square suggests a good model fit, but the chi-square test is sensitive to sample size. The cutoffs used to indicate a good model fit for the other model fit indices were CFI > 0.90, SRMR < 0.10, and RMSEA < 0.10 (Weston & Gore, 2006).

Table 12.1 Factor loadings for final atmosphere model

Atmosphere factor	Factor loading	Error correlation[a]
Sense of community fostered	*0.936*	
1. Teacher expresses empathy for students—encouraging others to do so as well	0.644	
2. Teacher expresses that they value students (e.g., Teacher is attentive to the students' personal lives and needs. You can often hear "God Bless You" when someone sneezes, as well as many "Pleases" and "Thank Yous" from the teacher)	0.699	
3. Teacher has gentle, caring, inviting manner	0.623	
4. There are positive messages/tone in the classroom and throughout lessons	0.627	0.323 (w/3)
5. There is positive one-on-one teacher-student interaction	0.676	
6. Sense of community is nurtured (i.e., being helpful, respectful, and trustful toward one another)	0.802	
7. Sense of altruism is nurtured (e.g., noticing "random acts of kindness," sharing, etc.)	0.619	
8. Teacher works to move students away from self-centeredness and toward concern for others	0.560	
9. Teacher communicates to students that what they have to share is important (e.g., "Please, be active listeners for David when he reads. The story he wrote is VERY interesting")	0.582	
Democratic classroom established	*0.957*	
10. Inclusiveness and diversity are valued (e.g., teacher does not allow any students to be or feel left out)	0.665	
11. There is a high use of personal pronouns communicating a sense of community, participation, and ownership (e.g., "This is OUR class. WE will work together")	0.706	
12. It is a cooperative environment	0.713	0.189 (w/30)
13. The classroom is a democratic place (e.g., the teacher assumes an authoritative role in the classroom rather than establishing a dictatorship)	0.635	
14. Teacher communicates to students that it's ok if they didn't get the same answer as other students	0.538	

Table 12.1 (continued)

Atmosphere factor	Factor loading	Error correlation[a]
Interest fostered	*0.671*	
15. Teacher builds anticipation—getting students excited about an activity they will be doing (e.g., teacher introduces tomorrow's lesson by telling them that she'll let them know how she makes percentages on a test. She refers to tomorrow's content as "cool." "Light bulbs will go off tomorrow.")	0.793	
16. Teacher encourages curiosity/suspense—getting students excited about what they are learning/doing (e.g., "Listen carefully to the story, you'll find out the answer to our questions. Tomorrow we are going to be having a special mystery visitor!")	0.884	
17. Teacher is enthusiastic (e.g., teacher gets excited about books, reads with expression, reacts enthusiastically to student writing)	0.653	0.142 (w/3)
Focus on effort rather than performance	*0.660*	*0.284 (w/High Exp.)*
18. Teacher encourages a changeable concept of intelligence (i.e., students can get smarter by trying harder)	0.712	
19. Teacher attributes success to effort (e.g., strategies) and time. Given these, success was believed to be imminent for ALL students	0.827	
20. Teacher urges students to try hard, encouraging stick-with-it-ness (i.e., when the task is doable)	0.674	
High expectations expressed	*0.788*	
21. Teacher communicates to students that she has many high expectations of students	0.749	
22. Teacher communicates to students that she is certain students CAN learn	0.716	0.206 (w/23)
23. Teacher communicates to students that she is determined students WILL learn	0.733	
24. Teacher communicates that it is his/her responsibility that students learn (e.g., teacher explains that if students do not do well on a quiz, then he/she will try to more effectively reteach the material)	0.573	
25. Teacher signals difficult tasks that students CAN do	0.640	
26. Teacher expresses confidence in students (e.g., "I know you can do it!")	0.758	
Informative feedback provided	*0.703*	
27. Teacher uses language to cue or reorient students' attention particularly to the positive and partially correct	0.620	
28. Teacher provides feedback that is informative—teacher does NOT give much unspecific, blanket praise	0.610	
29. Teacher does NOT grade publicly (e.g., teacher does not display only "A" papers)	0.468	

Table 12.1 (continued)

Atmosphere factor	Factor loading	Error correlation[a]
30. Teacher does NOT emphasize differences between students in performance	0.649	
31. Teacher does NOT make accountability public in activities (e.g., spelling game requires that students who miss to sit so it's obvious who did not do well)	0.644	
32. Teacher does NOT embarrass students by highlighting their failures/pointing out mistakes loudly	0.713	0.141 (w/3)

Note: [a]The item/factor with a correlated error term is indicated in parentheses.

Table 12.2 Factor loadings for final instruction model

Instruction factor	Factor loading	Error correlation[a]
Engaging content and activities used	*0.915*	
33. Teacher provides rich, interesting content that is exciting to the students	0.689	
34. Tasks matched to student interests	0.741	0.142 (w/33)
35. Students' lived experience is integrated with literate practice (e.g., students encouraged to connect reading and writing with personal experiences)	0.598	
36. Teacher reviews previous content to relate it to new content	0.568	
37. Teacher frequently incorporates student questions/observations/ideas into class conversations/activities	0.625	
38. Students learn by doing (e.g., hands-on experiments and experiences, such as following recipes and cooking, taking nature hikes and collecting samples, etc.)	0.438	
39. Teacher makes learning relevant to larger life	0.669	
Instruction individualized—high instructional density achieved	*0.893*	
40. Teacher provides opportunistic mini-lessons at teachable moments	0.638	0.186 (w/49)
41. Teacher seems to teach constantly, with whole group, small group, and individual mini-lessons simply intermingled throughout the day	0.755	
42. The classroom is busy, with a high density of instruction apparent	0.840	
43. There is a high volume of reading and writing	0.514	
Instruction well planned—high instructional density achieved	*0.932*	
44. Teacher does NOT just let students sit without anything to work on	0.688	

Table 12.2   (continued)

Instruction factor	Factor loading	Error correlation[a]
45. Depth favored over breadth (i.e., fewer topics covered to provide students with a greater level of understanding)	0.664	
46. The teacher does NOT miss opportunities to explain answers	0.667	
47. Teacher uses multiple ways of teaching one skill	0.646	0.152 (w/56)
48. It is apparent that the teacher is well organized so that things run smoothly (e.g., teacher has enough copies of book to break students into groups of an appropriate size)	0.679	
Appropriate challenge level achieved	*0.980*	
49. Teacher asks questions of the class at a difficulty level that ensures a number of bidders	0.572	0.260 (w/50)
50. Teacher gives students enough time to formulate responses to questions, ensuring a number of bidders	0.558	
51. Instructional pacing is NOT so slow that students are bored or go off task	0.634	
52. Teacher provides appropriately challenging content	0.694	
53. Teacher supports appropriate risk-taking (i.e., students are encouraged to take on instructionally challenging tasks instead of ones that are too easy or too hard for them; students encouraged to try even if wrong)	0.744	
Thinking processes modeled and taught	*0.890*	
54. Teacher models thinking, problem-solving skills, and other strategies	0.561	0.265 (w/55)
55. Teacher explicitly articulates the processes used in strategies/problem solving (e.g., explains the steps involved in brainstorming)	0.483	0.223 (w/56)
56. Teacher communicates a wide range of strategies	0.726	
57. Teacher encourages use of higher order thinking skills (e.g., stimulating critical thinking by asking how and why questions rather than just who, what, or when)	0.734	
58. Teacher stimulates creative thought	0.684	

Note: [a]The item with a correlated error term is indicated in parentheses.

Table 12.3   Factor loadings for final management model

Management factor	Factor loading	Error correlation[a]
Behavioral self-regulation encouraged	*0.655*	
59. Teacher communicates importance of routines and responsibilities	0.478	
60. Teacher develops expectation that when the teacher is unavailable, everyone is to continue working	0.703	

Table 12.3 (continued)

Management factor	Factor loading	Error correlation[a]
61. The teacher expresses his/her high expectations of students to help establish student self-regulation of behavior	0.661	
62. Teacher establishes procedural routines that students have automatized	0.732	
63. Teacher makes expectations for behavior clear	0.633	
64. Teacher effectively uses redirection (e.g. asking students what they are doing or what they should be doing), glances, pauses to help keep students on-task	0.649	
65. Teacher does whole class monitoring for on-task behavior	0.612	
66. Teacher does NOT allow off-task disruptions	0.554	
Behavior/Task monitoring provided	*0.585*	
67. Teacher does NOT scapegoat students	0.689	
68. Teacher does NOT threaten students (i.e., to take away recess time or snacks, to tell parents about the child's misbehavior, etc.)	0.876	
69. Teacher does NOT use punishment to keep students on task	0.869	
70. Teacher does NOT use public punishment	0.842	
71. Teacher does NOT use punishment that distracts students from their work	0.634	

Note: [a]The item with a correlated error term is indicated in parentheses.

Table 12.4 Factor loadings for Student Engagement model

Student Engagement factor	Factor loading	Error correlation[a]
72. Students vocalize/express excitement about content/activities (e.g., lots of "Oohs and Aahs")	0.576	
73. The students eagerly raise their hands and participate	0.591	0.329 (w/72)
74. At least 80% of students are consistently on task and highly engaged in class activities	0.898	
75. Students are so self-regulated that disciplinary encounters are rarely seen	0.674	

Note: [a]The item with a correlated error term is indicated in parentheses.

The factor structure for Management ($\chi^2 = 90.24$, $df = 64$, $p < 0.001$, $CFI = 0.958$, $SRMR = 0.063$, $RMSEA = 0.059$ (0.026–0.086)) showed a reasonable fit. However, the factor structures within Atmosphere ($\chi^2 = 757.96$, $df = 449$, $p < 0.001$, $CFI = 0.85$, $SRMR = 0.08$, $RMSEA = 0.07$ (0.06–0.08)), Instruction ($\chi^2 = 646.33$, $df = 345$, $p < 0.001$, $CFI = 0.83$, $SRMR = 0.07$, $RMSEA = 0.08$ (0.07–0.09)), and Student Engagement ($\chi^2 = 25.25$, $df = 2$, $p < 0.001$, $CFI = 0.89$, $SRMR = 0.07$, $RMSEA = 0.28$ (0.19–0.39)) initially all showed a poor fit. As a result, modifications were made to the relationships between items based on the suggested modification indices. These modifications included creating error correlations between multiple pairs of items and deleting items which had low loadings on their respective subcategories. After the modifications were made, the factor structures for Atmosphere ($\chi^2 = 654.95$, $df = 452$, $p < 0.001$, $CFI = 0.90$, $SRMR = 0.08$, $RMSEA = 0.06$ (0.05–0.07)), Instruction ($\chi^2 = 429.37$, $df = 288$, $p < 0.001$, $CFI = 0.91$, $SRMR = 0.06$, $RMSEA = 0.06$ (0.05–0.07)), and Student Engagement ($\chi^2 = 0.86$, $df = 1$, $p = 0.354$, $CFI = 1.00$, $SRMR = 0.01$, $RMSEA = 0.00$ (0.00–0.21)) all showed a good or reasonable fit.

12.2.3 Further Evidence of Construct Validity

Based on the revised models for each of the AIMS factors described above, scores for each teacher in the dataset were created by taking the average of all ratings (on the scale of 1 poor/rare use to 3 for exemplary/consistent use) received by a teacher for items representing each of the four factors. Skewness and kurtosis statistics for the total sample were all within normal range.

Large, significant, positive correlations were found between each of the classroom practice categories (Atmosphere, Instruction, Management) and Student Engagement. Student Engagement had the highest correlation with Instruction ($r = 0.73$, $n = 158$, $p < 0.001$), followed by Atmosphere ($r = 0.67$, $n = 158$, $p < 0.001$) and Management ($r = 0.67$, $n = 158$, $p < 0.001$). Significant correlations also were found between the classroom practice categories. Atmosphere was significantly correlated with Instruction ($r = 0.84$, $n = 158$, $p < 0.001$) and Management ($r = 0.62$, $n = 158$, $p < 0.001$). Instruction was also significantly correlated to Management ($r = 0.57$, $n = 158$, $p < 0.001$), though moderately.

An analysis of AIMS scores by teachers' demographics (see Table 12.5) showed that teachers with 6 or more years of experience ($n = 27$) had descriptively higher average scores on each of the four overarching categories than did the teachers with 1–5 years of experience ($n = 18$). We hypothesized that teachers with more experience would score higher on these categories than novice teachers, but none of these differences was significant. Though comparing novice teachers to experienced teachers is common in the literature, we also examined the relationship of experience to effectiveness correlationally to take advantage of the continuous nature of the years of teaching experience data. The only significant correlation was a small positive one between experience and Student Engagement ($r = 0.35$, $p < .05$). Because we did not have experience data for the majority of teachers in our sample, these analyses were based on small samples and may be underpowered. The results might be different with a larger sample.

Elementary teachers ($n = 158$) scored descriptively higher on Management while secondary teachers ($n = 85$) scored higher on Atmosphere, Instruction and Student Engagement. None of these differences, however, was significant. This is promising in that the AIMS items were developed with elementary teachers in mind but also seem relevant to secondary teachers. We did not have a large enough sample to do

Table 12.5 Descriptive statistics (M, SD, Range) on AIMS for total sample and by teacher demographics (Grade level, years experience)

Factor		Total Sample[a,b,c,d]	Grade level		Level of experience[a,b,c]	
			Elementary[a,b,c] K-5	Secondary[b] 6-12	Novice 1–5 years	Experienced 6+ years
	N	158	85	49	18	27
Atmosphere	M(SD)	2.15 (0.387)	2.16 (0.432)	2.19 (0.379)	2.04 (0.59)	2.13 (0.45)
	Range	1.14–2.94	1.14–2.94	1.35–2.88	1.15–2.94	1.14–2.94
Instruction	M(SD)	2.18 (0.413)	2.23 (0.434)	2.12 (0.448)	2.18 (0.559)	2.22 (0.442)
	Range	1.06–3.00	1.29–3.00	1.06–2.90	1.33–2.96	1.37–3.00
Management	M(SD)	2.32 (0.449)	2.31 (0.476)	2.46 (0.355)	2.08 (0.559)	2.35 (0.425)
	Range	1.07–3.00	1.07–3.00	1.26–2.94	1.07–3.00	1.21–2.94
Student Engagement	M(SD)	2.22 (0.558)	2.31 (0.523)	2.19 (0.614)	2.074 (0.599)	2.25 (0.548)
	Range	1.00–3.00	1.00–3.00	1.00–3.00	1.00–3.00	1.50–3.00

Note: Superscripts indicate source of sample included in analyses: [a]Canadian, [b]Florida, [c]Indiana, [d]Michigan. The sum of Ns by demographic do not equal the total N; demographic data were either missing or (in the case of the Michigan dataset) the authors' did not have access to these data.

multi-group CFAs that would allow us to compare the similarity of the factor structures across elementary and secondary teachers, but future research could explore this issue.

We also found it promising that preliminary findings from the work of Savage et al. (2008) provide further evidence of construct validity. Not only did Savage et al. find positive correlations between AIMS observations and teacher interviews, but they also found classroom-level variance in listening comprehension was well-explained by the AIMS observations and interviews. We caution, however, that further evidence of a positive association between scores based on AIMS observation and student achievement, controlling for students' initial achievement status, is needed.

12.3 Discussion

The evidence described in this chapter suggests that the Classroom AIMS Instrument is a potentially valid and reliable tool for evaluating the effectiveness of K-12 teachers who are observed for as little as one class period. Only minor changes to the theoretical constructs of the Classroom AIMS Instrument were needed to confirm a fairly simple factor structure, and the scores from a sample drawn from four independent studies were normally distributed. In addition, large positive correlations were found between scores of Student Engagement and scores on Atmosphere, Instruction, and Management, indicating that teachers who more consistently pattern instruction after exemplary teachers are more likely to have students who are academically engaged. The causal direction of these findings is not clear, and experimental research that could provide evidence of the impact of teacher practices (as rated on the AIMS) on student engagement as well as achievement is warranted.

In addition, while the percent agreement between raters was reasonable, with only 5% of ratings not exact or contiguous, it was not ideal. We strongly recommend that each teacher be observed by at least two people or, at a minimum, by the same person more than one time. The initial training and practice of potential observers is important when establishing a basis for comparison when rating teachers (Pearlman, 2008a, 2008b). Furthermore, our results suggest that having a discussion to come to a consensus after two observers have independently completed an AIMS protocol for one teacher may be useful, particularly given that 37% of ratings differed by 1 point. Evidence from each observer's observational field notes should be shared and considered in selecting a final rating (particularly if they observed the teacher at two different times). In at least the Indiana and Florida studies, it was common for raters to observe teachers at different times. While we strove to have at least 1 hour of common observation time per teacher, the practicality of scheduling 90-min minimum length observations with multiple teachers and observers made this difficult. We estimate that at least half of the total observation time spent collecting the data used in interrater reliability calculations was conducted by raters who visited the same teachers at different times. Given this, the robustness of AIMS for capturing the essence of teachers' classrooms regardless of incongruous observation times and different observers is promising.

12.3.1 Implications

Research conducted on AIMS, and the observation tools developed contemporaneously with AIMS, provide strong converging evidence about the nature of effective teaching. That is, effective teachers are masters not only of instructional techniques, but also of methods and means of establishing classroom management systems and positive climates that are mutually supportive of engaging instruction.

While the constructs captured in AIMS were developed primarily using qualitative research methods, recent quantitative research has led to the identification of similar observable classroom practices that set apart more and less effective teachers (Stronge, Tucker, & Ward, 2003). Stronge et al. identified more and less effective grade 3 teachers based on student achievement, with effective teachers being those whose students achieved at higher than expected rates on the Virginia Standards of Learning (SOL) Assessments in English, Mathematics, Social Studies, and Science. The value added achievement gains, or achievement gains beyond those expected based on past achievement, were calculated from statistical models with student gender, age, race, SES, English proficiency, days absent, school mobility, grade 1 reading proficiency, grade 2 reading proficiency, and class size as predictors. The effective teaching behaviors they identified after observing these more and less effective teachers were remarkably similar to ones included in the Classroom AIMS Instrument, including such practices as "notably broader range of instructional strategies, using a variety of materials and media to support curriculum" (similar to AIMS item: *Teacher uses multiple ways of teaching one skill*), "differentiated assignments for students at a higher rate" (similar to AIMS item: *Teacher makes formative assessments/notes of students, which allows adjustment of instruction to improve learning outcomes*), "behavioral expectations for students... much higher" (similar to AIMS item: *The teacher expresses his/her high expectations of students to help establish student self-regulation of behavior*) and "more respect for and demonstrated notable fairness toward all students" (similar to AIMS item: *Sense of community is nurtured—being helpful, respectful, and trustful toward one another*) (Stronge et al., p. 9).

While Stronge et al. (2003) have not yet organized the practices that differentiated their more and less effective teachers into a formalized observation instrument, LaParo, Pianta, and Stuhlman (2004) have developed the Classroom Assessment Scoring System (CLASS), which captures a number of classroom climate constructs in addition to managerial and instructional constructs that overlap with AIMS. Validity and reliability evidence supports using CLASS with prekindergarten through grade 5 teachers (LaParo et al., 2004; Pianta, LaParo, & Hamre, 2008), and there is also a version available for secondary classroom observations.

12.3.2 Applications

As a schema for organizing our understanding of effective teaching in elementary and secondary schools, the Classroom AIMS Instrument has a number of potential applications. It has already been utilized in several ways beyond its primary function as an observation tool. As a comprehensive instrument (i.e., incorporating social, motivational, instructional, and managerial aspects of classroom contexts) and one that sets high standards for excellence in teaching, the Classroom AIMS Instrument can be used diagnostically. For example, it may be used to identify teachers who are exemplary in some or all key areas of classroom practice, and also to identify particular areas of improvement for teachers. The tool may also be used to guide the formation of professional development programs. For instance, in a professional development context, the Classroom AIMS Instrument can be used to guide teachers' reflections about a number of specific practices in their own teaching or in the teaching they observe others do. To conclude this chapter, we describe the use of AIMS in three studies along with some key findings.

Bohn et al. (2004): These authors explored differences between more and less effective teachers in how they start the school year. Bohn et al. used AIMS to evaluate the quality of the classrooms nominated by principals for observation. Effective teachers were found to do more to establish routines and procedures at beginning of the year than less effective teachers. Notably, they provided highly engaging activities more often, indicated higher expectations, and encouraged student self-regulation.

Roehrig, Bohn et al. (2008): In this study the potential for mentoring to support novice teachers' use of effective teaching practices was explored. In this research, the constructs of AIMS were used to (a) guide beginning teacher induction, (b) evaluate the teaching effectiveness of mentors, and (c) evaluate whether beginning teachers changed their classroom practices over time. Mentoring activities were structured around discussion of atmosphere, instruction, and management, with opportunities for beginning teachers to observe the associated practices in their mentor teachers' classrooms and to reflect on their own attempts to use exemplary practices. Mentors of effective beginning teachers, compared to mentors of less effective beginning teachers, had more experience as mentors; they also were more effective teachers than other mentors. In addition, effective beginning teachers communicated more often with their mentors, more accurately self-reported use of effective teaching practices, and were more open to mentoring.

Roehrig, Guidry et al. (2008): This study explicitly examined the use of AIMS to guide the reflection and classroom observations of those learning to teach. Specifically, AIMS was used to guide preservice teachers' observations of their supervising teachers. In this correlational study, AIMS was used to guide preservice teachers' field observations and to code beginning teachers' concept maps representing their understanding of effective beginning reading practices. The following relationships between preservice teachers' guided field observations of primary literacy instruction and knowledge about effective beginning reading practices were found. The greater the number of effective motivating practices a preservice teacher observed, the more likely he or she was to reflect these practices in a concept map representing effective beginning literacy instruction. Correctly identifying ineffective practices, however, was not related to representation of effective practices in the concept map. That is, it seemed to be most important for these preservice elementary teachers to have the opportunity to observe effective practices in their cooperating teachers' classrooms. While finding enough cooperating teachers to work with every teacher candidate in a large teacher education program can be daunting, it may not be enough to have preservice teachers observe ineffective teaching practices and hope that discussions of such examples of poor practice in university courses will be an adequate substitute for models of effective practice.

12.3.3 Conclusion

In conclusion, the Classroom AIMS Instrument was created to capture the complexity of the practices characterizing effective teaching. It has strong face validity, as it has been created from the results of a wealth of richly descriptive qualitative studies of exemplary teaching. Moreover, the factors in AIMS converge with the qualitatively and theoretically derived categories of other recent studies and instruments. Quantitative evidence also supports the appropriateness and usefulness of the AIMS instrument.

AIMS can be used in various ways, in addition to evaluating the effectiveness of teaching based on classroom observations. As we have described in this chapter, it can be used to identify the professional development needs of teachers, and it has already been used in several studies to organize and facilitate professional development. While further research is needed to establish a relationship between student academic achievement outcomes and their teachers' AIMS scores, the preliminary validity evidence presented here suggests that AIMS captures many elements important to engaging students in learning across grades K-12.

References

Allington, D. L., & Johnston, P. H. (2002). *Reading to learn: Lessons from exemplary fourth-grade classrooms*. New York: Guilford Press.

Anderson, L. M., Evertson, C. M., & Brophy, J. E. (1979). An experimental study of effective teaching in first-grade reading groups. *Elementary School Journal, 79*, 193–223.

Berliner, D. C. (1988). Implications of studies on expertise in pedagogy for teacher education and evaluation. In J. Pfleiderer (Ed.), *New directions for teacher assessment* (Proceedings of the 1988 ETS Invitational Conference, pp. 39–68). Princeton, NJ: Educational Testing Service.

Bogner, K., Raphael, L. M., & Pressley, M. (2002). How grade 1 teachers motivate literate activity by their students. *Scientific Studies of Reading, 6*, 135–165.

Bohn, C. M., Roehrig, A. D., & Pressley, M. (2004). The first days of school in effective and less effective primary-grades classrooms. *Elementary School Journal, 104*, 269–287.

Burry-Stock, J. A., & Oxford, R. L. (1993). *Expert science teaching educational evaluation model (ESTEEM) for measuring excellence in science teaching for professional development.*

Washington, DC: Office of Educational Research and Improvement (ERIC Document Reproduction Service No. ED 336 633).

Cloud-Silva, C., & Denton, J. J. (1988, April). *The development of a low-inference observation instrument to assess instructional performance of teaching candidates.* Paper presented at the annual meeting of the American Educational Research Association, New Orleans, LA (ERIC Document Reproduction Service No. ED 293 876).

Day, J. P., Boothroyd, K., Johnston, P., & Cedeno, M. (1999, December). *Larger fourth grade study findings in exemplary teaching practices.* Paper presented at the National Reading Conference, Austin, TX.

Day, J. P., Woodside-Jiron, H., & Johnston, P. (1999). *Principles of practice – the common and unique.* Paper presented at the National Reading Conference, Austin, TX.

Dolezal, S. E., Welsh, L. M., Pressley, M., & Vincent, M. M. (2003). How nine third-grade teachers motivate student academic engagement. *Elementary School Journal, 103*(3), 239–267.

Harms, T., Clifford, R. M., & Cryer, D. (1998). *Early childhood environment rating scale* (Rev. ed.). New York: Teachers College Press.

Hemmeter, M. L., Maxwell, K. L., Ault, M. J., & Schuster, J. W. (1998). *Assessment of practices in early elementary classrooms (APEEC).* New York: Teachers College Press.

Johnston, P., Powers, S., & Costello, P. (1999, December). *The genesis of democratic literacy: Discourse requirements for a democratic society.* Paper presented at the National Reading Conference, Austin, TX.

Kennedy, M. M. (1999). Approximations to indicators of student outcomes. *Educational Evaluation and Policy Analysis, 21*, 345–363.

LaParo, K. M., Pianta, R. C., & Stuhlman, M. (2004). The classroom assessment scoring system: Findings from the prekindergarten year. *The Elementary School Journal, 104*, 409–426.

Lavely, C., Berger, N., Blackman, J., Follman, J., & McCarthy, J. (1994). Contemporary teacher classroom performance observation instruments. *Education, 114*(4), 618–624.

Morrow, L. M., Tracey, D., Woo, D., & Pressley, M. (1999). Characteristics of exemplary first-grade instruction. *The Reading Teacher, 52*, 462–476.

Muijs, D., & Reynolds, D. (2002). Teachers' beliefs and behaviors: What really matters? *Journal of Classroom Interaction, 37*(2), 3–15.

No Child Left Behind Act of 2001, PL 107–110, 115 Stat. 1425, 20 U.S.C. §§ 6301 *et seq.*

Nunnally, J. C. (1978). *Psychometric theory* (2nd ed.). New York: McGraw-Hill.

Pearlman, M. (2008a) The design architecture of NBPTS certification assessments. In L. Ingvarson & J. Hattie (Eds.), *Assessing teachers for professional certification: The first decade of the National Board for Professional Teaching Standards* (pp. 55–91). Bingley, UK: Emerald.

Pearlman, M. (2008b) The evolution of the scoring system for NBPTS assessments. In L. Ingvarson & J. Hattie (Eds.), *Assessing teachers for professional certification: The first decade of the National Board for Professional Teaching Standards* (pp. 177–209). Bingley, UK: Emerald.

Pianta, R. C., LaParo, K. M., & Hamre, B. (2008). *CLASS Pre-K: Technical appendix.* Available from CLASS Web site, http://www.brookespublishing.com/class2007/CLASS_Pre-K.pdf

Pressley, M., Allington, R. L., Wharton-McDonald, R., Block, C. C., & Morrow, L. M. (2001). *Learning to read: Lessons from exemplary first-grade classrooms.* New York: Guilford.

Pressley, M., Roehrig, A. D., Raphael, L. M., Dolezal, S. E., Bohn, C., Mohan, L., et al. (2003) Teaching processes in elementary and secondary education. In W. M. Reynolds & G. E. Miller (Eds.), *Handbook of psychology, Volume 7: Educational psychology* (pp. 153–175). New York: Wiley.

Pressley, M., Wharton-McDonald, R., Allington, R., Block, C. C., Morrow, L., Tracey, D., et al. (2001). A study of effective first-grade literacy instruction. *Scientific Studies of Reading, 5*(1), 35–58.

Pressley, M., Wharton-McDonald, R., Raphael, L. M., Bogner, K., & Roehrig, A. D. (2002) Exemplary first grade teaching. In B. M. Taylor & P. D. Pearson (Eds.), *Teaching reading:*

Effective schools, accomplished teachers (pp. 73–88). Mahwah, NJ: Lawrence Erlbaum & Associates.

Roehrig, A. D., Bohn, C. M., Turner, J. E., & Pressley, M. (2008). Mentoring beginning primary teachers for exemplary teaching practices. *Teaching and Teacher Education, 24*, 684–702.

Roehrig, A. D., Dolezal, S., Welsh, L. M., Bohn, C. M., & Pressley, M. (2002, December). *Assessing the quality of early-primary grade teachers' classroom behaviors.* Paper presented at the meeting of the National Reading Conference, Miami, FL.

Roehrig, A. D., Guidry, L. O., Bodur, Y., Guan, Q., Guo, Y., & Pop, M. (2008). Guided field observations: Variables related to preservice teachers' knowledge about effective primary reading instruction. *Literacy Research and Instruction, 47*(2), 76–98.

Roehrig, A. D., Pressley, M., & Sloup, M. (2001). Reading strategy instruction in regular primary-level classrooms by teachers trained in reading recovery. *Reading & Writing Quarterly, 17*, 323–348.

Roehrig, A. D., Turner, J. E., & Petscher, Y. (2008). *Evaluation of the Florida reading initiative for the North East Florida education consortium (Tech. Rep. No. 1).* Tallahassee, FL: Department of Educational Psychology and Learning Systems and the Florida Center for Reading Research, Florida State University.

Savage, R., Deault, L., & Burgos, G. (2008, February). *Effective literacy instruction: A (Quebec) Canadian perspective.* Paper presented at the FCRR Research Symposium, Tallahassee, FL.

Shulman, L. S. (1986). Those who understand: Knowledge growth in teaching. *Educational Researcher, 15*, 4–14.

Stanulis, R. N., & Floden, R. E. (2009). Intensive mentoring as a way to help beginning teachers develop balanced instruction. *Journal of Teacher Education, 60*(2), 112–122.

Sternberg, R. J. (1998). Abilities are forms of developing expertise. *Educational Researcher, 3*, 22–35.

Stipek, D. J. (1996) Motivation and instruction. In D. C. Berliner & R. C. Calfee (Eds.), *Handbook of educational psychology* (pp. 85–113). New York: Macmillan.

Strauss, A., & Corbin, J. (1998). *Basics of qualitative research: Techniques and procedures for developing grounded theory.* Thousand Oaks, CA: Sage.

Stronge, J. H., Tucker, P. D., & Ward, T. J. (2003, April). *Teacher effectiveness and student learning: What do good teachers do?* Paper presented at the annual meeting of the American Educational Research Association, Chicago, IL.

Stulac, J. F., Stone, J. W., Woods, D. G., Worthy, D. H., Maiden, M. L., & Thompson, S. A. (1982). *Assessments of performance in teaching: Observation instrument and training manual.* Columbia, SC: South Carolina Educator Improvement Task Force (ERIC Document Reproduction Service No. ED 218 349).

Weston, R., & Gore, P. A., Jr. (2006). A brief guide to structural equation modeling. *The Counseling Psychologist, 34*, 719–751.

Wharton-McDonald, R., Pressley, M., & Hampston, J. M. (1998). Literacy instruction in nine first-grade classrooms: Teacher characteristics and student achievement. *Elementary School Journal, 99*, 101–128.

Chapter 13
Epilogue: Achieving Quality 21st Century Assessment

Betsy Jane Becker and Valerie J. Shute

Abstract In this chapter we describe three themes drawn from the chapters in our book. We first point out how our authors describe ways for assessment to capitalize on advances in technology. Then we discuss how assessment is a contextualized, social activity which creates both challenges and exciting opportunities for research and practice. Last, we argue that assessment must serve teaching and learning.

Keywords Assessment · Learning · Teaching · Social context · Technology

Writing a chapter to summarize all of the contents of this multifaceted book presents a challenge. Rather than create a laundry list of the conclusions drawn by our authors, we have tried to draw out three themes that appear across the works herein. These themes represent ideas that we believe will need careful attention from assessment experts, measurement professionals, teachers, principals, learning scientists and many others if the field is to move forward to develop better assessments that promote learning as well as provide fair means of accountability for students, teachers, and schools. We argue that

- Assessment must capitalize on advances in technology,
- Assessment is a contextualized, social activity, and
- Assessment must serve teaching and learning.

We discuss in turn how each of these themes is raised by the authors of our book, and also touch on potential areas for research suggested by their work. We do not, however, mention every instance in which every author touches on these themes. We apologize if we have omitted points on these themes that are important to our authors.

B.J. Becker (✉)
Department of Educational Psychology and Learning Systems, Florida State University, Tallahassee, FL, USA
e-mail: bbecker@fsu.edu

V.J. Shute, B.J. Becker (eds.), *Innovative Assessment for the 21st Century*,
DOI 10.1007/978-1-4419-6530-1_13, © Springer Science+Business Media, LLC 2010

13.1 Assessment Must Capitalize on Technology

Technological advances have already clearly affected the world of assessment in many ways. Even mundane components of assessment, such as the scoring of multiple choice questions, were long ago made easier by Scantron machines and other scanning devices (Clarke, Madaus, Horn, & Ramos, 2000). However, while such devices enabled the rapid increase and widespread use of testing in the schools in the 1960s and 1970s, they did not always lead to improvements in what we know about students, or in what students learn (e.g., Epstein, Epstein, & Brosvic, 2001). Indeed, while modern technologies clearly have made an impact on how testing is done, it is clear they present both new challenges and new possibilities for assessment in the twenty-first century (e.g., Naglieri et al., 2004).

Hickey, Honeyford, Clinton and McWilliams examine a context where technology is inherently part of the assessment—the assessment of competence with new media. New media literacies include activities as diverse as social networking, creation of fan fiction, music remixing, and blogging. Because nearly all new media are based in technology, to assess competencies in these domains requires that technology be embedded in the assessment process. However, it is also true that traditional literacy skills—in writing, reading and spoken communication—are both needed for and enhanced by use of new media (see also Leu, O'Bryne, Zawilinski, McVerry, & Everett-Cacopardo, 2009). While endorsing the idea of assessing new media competencies, Hickey and his colleagues raise considerable concerns about whether the advent of accountability in this domain will narrow views of "proficiencies" to what is easily measured. Indeed, since many new media skills are inherently social (see our next theme), but most existing assessment systems are fundamentally individualized, clear tensions and conflicts will play out as assessment of these new skills moves forward. Given the view of many scholars that media literacy is (and must be) entwined with a participatory culture, such tensions will be a key concern for the field. But as with many challenges, we also see interesting possibilities for research. For example, how should we best assess media literacy? Is it ever possible to gauge individual contributions to fully participatory activities? Many interesting research questions will emerge in relation to this context.

Several authors in our volume attend to the role technology must play in the future of assessment. An argument for an elegant system of evidence centered design (ECD) for assessment is given by Russell Almond. Almond lays out key aspects of the ECD philosophy he has developed with collaborators Robert Mislevy and Linda Steinberg. His chapter makes concrete how a complex mathematical modeling framework can be combined with thoughtful consideration of the skills desired of an examinee population to produce both improved learning and quality assessment all in one comprehensive system. The system relies on technology in its fundamental use of a Bayesian framework for evaluating student capacities. Information based on prior knowledge of examinee capabilities, along with data from observable events associated with a collection of tasks is fed back into a system to create posterior distributions of (hopefully changed) student skill levels. Almond also points out that an ECD system could aim at tracking growth in multiple competencies, based on related process or product observables, and can even interface with automated scoring systems (like those described by Shermis for essay scoring). Almond argues that eventually ECD, combined with modern technologies could support "seamless" collection of observables embedded in ongoing work—assessment that would seem so natural students would not realize that it had even occurred (see also Shute, in press for more on this topic). Clearly such assessment would not cause the stress and disruptions present in so much high-stakes testing (e.g., Cizek & Burg, 2005; Suen & Yu, 2006).

While they endorse many of Almond's ideas, commenters Ellington and Verges point out that currently schools do not have the infrastructure to support these innovations. For example, problems and incompatibilities in hardware and software could lead to glitches with data collection from diverse sources. Also while they acknowledge the benefits of using complex tasks in assessments, they raise several practical problems (such as cost and extensive field test requirements) that would limit implementation especially in the current economic climate. Clearly such a system for assessment does not currently exist, but the goal of realizing it presents another set of fascinating possibilities for research.

A more conventional take on technology and assessment comes from Mark Shermis. His chapter describes how technology can assist with improved student learning of writing skills when the electronic scoring of essays is built into a system of writing improvement, along with revision, feedback, and teacher participation. Shermis describes how automated essay scoring or AES works, from the development of "proxes" or features used to represent the quality of a writing sample, to the evaluation of the statistical models used in algorithmic scoring. Shermis cites evidence that with careful development and good rubrics, an AES system is at least as reliable as human raters, and can in some cases help avoid biases that human raters cannot seem to eliminate from their rating behavior. One goal of this chapter is to simply describe how AES works, and Shermis further illustrates that by way of a detailed description of the "Intellimetric" system. However Shermis goes farther, and makes the controversial claim that automated essay scoring (and the teaching structures associated with its ongoing use) can replace high-stakes writing assessments. Consistent with Almond's arguments for incorporating multiple pieces of evidence in ongoing assessment systems, Shermis argues that an assessment based on multiple instances of writing (such as essays produced throughout the year) would provide a more useful and valid evaluation of student writing than a single-occasion high stakes test. He describes how an integrated writing assessment system could also support instruction by providing feedback aimed at each essay produced by a student. In addition, the release of "used" writing prompts could provide materials for ongoing instruction. Finally he argues that all of this can be accomplished at costs lower than those incurred with human scoring of similar writing products. This is an excellent example of how capitalizing on technology can enhance not only the assessment itself but also student learning. And as with our other chapters that touch on technology, various ideas for research arise from Shermis's work. For example, what measurement models best suit this kind of assessment system? How often would one need to take samples of writing throughout the year to get solid information about change in writing competence? Could an AES system have a built-in way to assess the impact of particular kinds or amounts of teacher (or system) feedback? How would we assess whether the system is providing appropriate feedback to students (i.e., what kinds of "quality control" would be needed)? These and other practical and theoretical questions provide a rich set of ideas for those interested in the future of assessment.

13.2 Assessment is a Contextualized, Social Activity

The strongest advocate of the social view of assessment in our collection of authors is James Gee. Gee lays out the case for assessment of twenty-first century skills in domains as part of social "appreciative systems". Loosely these are sets of conventions, values—perhaps even rules—for what is acceptable or valuable in a certain domain. He argues that appreciative systems are shared across people, and gives quite a few examples of how such systems develop. He also argues that most assessment goes on as a part of ongoing human interactions and activity, and is not—and does not need to be—formalized. King Beach, who comments on Gee's chapter, provides several examples of such real-life assessment in out-of-school settings in western Nepal.

Gee also contends that groups themselves can formalize assessment in a quite natural way. He argues that this often occurs via "Pro-Am" communities, or groups of " … innovative, committed and networked amateurs working to professional standards" (Leadbeater & Miller, 2004, p. 9). A compelling example comes from his research on online communities (Gee & Hayes, 2010) where a young girl learned to create virtual clothing for the virtual world *Second Life*. Eventually various discoveries led her to provide clothes to virtual people on the Internet, first for free then later at a price, after she realized that the "appreciative" community of virtual shoppers highly valued her product. More controversially, Gee goes on to argue that schools could promote twenty-first century skills by encouraging and equipping students to become high-status members of Pro-Am communities that value and promote such skills.

Gee notes that society has in some cases formalized assessment by removing it from such Pro-Am communities. Institutions, including schools, have been created in support of this formalization. But Gee believes this kind of assessment is "backwards" (Section 2.11) because it occurs at such an abstract, disembedded level, removed from real problems. His arguments for authentic assessments echo in part those of measurement scholars (e.g., Wiggins, 1990) and others (e.g., Darling-Hammond & Snyder, 2000) who called for more realism and context in assessment years ago.

Finally, Gee raises the radical idea that formalized assessments may not be needed if existing communities (like the online buyers of simulated clothing) have already assessed and accepted someone's skills. He states that, "The job of twenty-first century educators ought to be designing such social organizations and then letting them run." (Section 2.11) Again we see plenty of possible research avenues in this work, and Beach's commentary raises one interesting question—what is the appropriate unit of assessment in such circumstances? Could we find a way to examine the developmental relationship between a learner and the domain to be assessed, over time? Could such a complex entity be assessed by the "indigenous workings" (Section 2.11) of the group, as advocated by Gee? It is intriguing to consider how one could study and obtain empirical evidence on such a system of assessment.

Hickey and colleagues also deal with the social context for learning, which is fundamentally a part of examining competencies with "new media". They begin by examining the positions of groups like the National Council of Teachers of English and the National Writing Project, which argue that writing is an inherently social activity. This is a launching point for the efforts of Hickey and his colleagues to create a cohesively designed assessment framework for language arts. Their efforts have used not only a classic text (Moby-Dick) but also new media sources such as related music videos and theatre "re-mixes". They argue that by using multiple levels of assessment (designed after the five levels of Ruiz-Primo et al. 2002) the teacher can focus initially and closely on social and interactive aspects of writing, with a quick time frame for feedback and a very informal assessment context. The assessments and classroom activities then move to more individualized, but distant aspects at other levels. Their chapter gives many examples of assessment activities at their five levels, but the contextualized nature of assessment is most evident at their first two levels. Only at the highest level would fully individualized assessments (e.g., external tests with essay items) be used to tap into an abstract context, and might, for instance, measure performance on content standards such as those at a state level.

We consider one example from their second level—"close-level activity-oriented reflections" (Section 8.4.3.2). Here the focus is on discussion questions presented to the class, either orally, in written form, or online. The authors found that the informal nature of these assessments and an attendant emphasis on "communal discussion" of ongoing classroom activities enhanced broader student participation. The teacher then could consider the nature of the discussion, and focus further discussion in ways that led students ". . .to create more compelling and creative artifacts" (Section 8.4.4.2). This is an interesting example of how a teacher can assess student understanding in a group context, and provide feedback based on questions that are less formal, but very targeted to the activities of the learners.

Allan Jeong's work in examining conceptual causal maps provides a nice example of how learning can be enhanced by the use of social interactions and by assessments that provide a window on the understandings of experts and of other learners. Jeong describes the use of jMAP, a program that enables learners to create and evaluate causal maps, and also allows for the assessment of changes in maps over time. Students use jMAP to identify critical components of a causal system, to draw interconnections among those components, and to identify the strength of those connections. The connection to "others" is embedded in the structure and use of jMAP. Specifically, after creating their own maps, students can be exposed to the maps of experts, to discussions about the nature of the causal connections (as was the case in Jeong's studies), and to composite maps made by aggregating the maps of various subsets of learners or all learners in a class. Subsequent rounds of maps can be drawn and changes in the maps of learners can be examined. Jeong shows how comparisons of individual versus aggregate maps can lead to changes in subsequent maps of individual learners. Also the nature of discussions held (e.g., whether links in the maps are supported or challenged by others, whether explanations are provided, etc.) can impact how learners change their maps on subsequent drawings.

For those interested in how learner interactions can impact learning, jMAP provides intriguing tools for analysis of causal maps. We challenge those interested in such phenomena to consider how learning in other domains of understanding (i.e., other than causal maps) might be represented (using technology) and then examined for changes due to exposure to the knowledge and ideas of others. Domains suggested by the work of our other authors might include writing, where automated scoring systems like those described by Shermis could produce indices of change following peer or teacher feedback of different sorts, or Gee's "Pro-Am skills" where changes in the products or skill sets of members of Pro-Am communities might be evaluated for evolution as individuals receive feedback from relevant community members. Roehrig and Christesen's Classroom AIMS is another assessment device where modal (typical) or expert performance ratings could be shared with teachers, and then further measurement instances could be evaluated for change due to those different kinds of feedback.

13.3 Assessment Must Serve Teaching and Learning

Mari Pearlman views assessment as integral to the educational enterprise. In her chapter she argues that we must "...ally assessment with instruction" (Section 4.3) and she makes a provocative case for using an assessment based on the vast architecture of the National Assessment of Educational Progress or NAEP as a vehicle to accomplish this goal. Pearlman outlines a variety of problems in our educational system, and among them she lists a need to align all components of the system— curriculum, teacher practice, teacher preparation and assessments—in concert to move student learning ahead. She argues that to date these components have been manipulated by the states, but mainly in efforts to achieve "AYP" or adequate yearly progress, not in efforts to increase learning of content identified as important (See for example Kane, Staiger, & Geppert's, 2002 views on gaming the AYP system so states can look most successful). Pearlman endorses the move towards national standards, and argues that having clear frameworks could lead to national "conversations" about content, curriculum and most importantly equity across states. Equity is an issue conveniently (but sadly) avoided in the current context, where each state can use its own distinct tests to assess progress, and also can set different goals. In such a context, it is not hard to see that all states could theoretically measure up as "adequate" while in fact being quite different in terms of what their students actually learn. Initial examinations however showed that some states did the opposite—setting such high standards that they were virtually unreachable (Linn, Baker, & Betebenner, 2002).

In terms of the theme of assessment in support of learning, Pearlman challenges us to find ways to use the many items developed as part of the NAEP assessments in support of learning. Indeed, thousands of released NAEP items are currently available for public use via the NAEP Questions Tool (see http://nces.ed.gov/nationsreportcard/itmrlsx/landing.aspx), and can be used by teachers and others in a variety of ways. Much like the position taken by Almond, Pearlman argues that we must first know what we want students to learn, then what we want to measure, then only last can we design lessons and activities to support those goals. Pearlman argues that if benchmarks such as those set for NAEP were used as goals, and NAEP's current plan of sampling students were replaced with every-pupil-testing, we would soon move towards better outcomes and towards equity across states in terms of student learning.

In her response to Pearlman, Lynn Wicker emphasizes a point made by Pearlman. That is, both agree that the culture of schools relative to assessment must change so that a stronger link to learning can be achieved. Wicker argues that the use of multiple ongoing assessments tied with targeted interventions "should be viewed as a non-negotiable in the learning process" (Section 5.4). We also strongly endorse this view.

Martineau and Dean give perhaps the most comprehensive proposal in our volume for how assessment, in many forms and at many levels, can serve instruction and learning. They draw on the idea of balanced assessment (Redfield, Roeber, Stiggins, & Philip, 2008) and elaborate it to describe how formative, summative and interim assessments can be used to provide both indices for accountability as well as detailed input to teachers in support of their instruction. Their system begins with clear and focused K-12 content standards, aimed at supporting students' progression towards specified high-school outcomes. They argue that curriculum materials ("model curriculum units", as in Section 9.5.1) can then be developed in support of these standards, and be made available to all teachers (but not mandated as a required curriculum). This set of content standards and materials would be paired with professional development for teachers aimed at helping them to understand the content standards and how they can be used, but more critically how to use data from assessments—both classroom assessments and more formalized "secure" assessments—to modify their instruction.

A requirement that teachers receive instruction in classroom assessment is already a part of the Florida Department of Education's preservice teaching requirements. Martineau and Dean want continued support in the form of professional development for both teachers and other administrators. They also argue that accountability purposes can also be served by their system, but only with a multifaceted system in which teachers, teacher preparation institutions, administrators and students are all held to account.

Working from a very different perspective, Hickey and colleagues also describe a system of assessment that focuses on different kinds and levels of assessment in the context of new media literacy. Based in the technological context discussed earlier, the first three of their five levels of assessment—the immediate, close and proximal levels—are completely entwined with student products (artifacts) and interactions with teachers and other students as they create those products in the classroom. At the third (proximal) level the assessment tasks move towards more individualization, but even at this level reflection questions and student products together allow for targeted teacher feedback. Their system illustrates how assessment can be tied directly into ongoing instruction.

A more targeted approach to both assessing and supporting instruction is described by Roehrig and Christesen. They describe the development and use of the Classroom AIMS instrument, which examines how teachers create a positive classroom atmosphere, implement instruction and classroom management, and engage students in learning. Roehrig and Christesen start with the premise that teachers' behaviors and activities are more likely to predict student outcomes than teacher characteristics such as teacher knowledge. They describe how a set of exemplary behaviors were identified by observing teachers who had produced students with strong learning gains in reading and writing performance. More importantly for this "theme" of our book, the authors go on to describe how the AIMS instrument can be used not just to observe the current behaviors of teachers, but also to diagnose possible areas for teachers to improve. They describe the use of AIMS with pre-service teachers as well as practicing teachers working with mentors. Other research questions could be asked about the Classroom AIMS instrument. How does AIMS function as a measure of the effects of professional development for practicing teachers? Can it differentiate between more and less effective interventions? How well does it work across different subject areas? These and other questions may be fertile areas for future research.

13.4 Conclusion

As mentioned in the Prelude, our goal for the symposium and this book was to bring together groups of individuals who normally do not converse, but who we believe should communicate—researchers from different areas, policymakers, and educational professionals. In all chapters, the call for educational reform is clear and there is no shortage of problems to be addressed with innovative thinking and high-quality research. The linchpin for such reform—reform that aims to fully support students' success in the twenty-first century—is assessment.

The chapters in this book present a broad swath of assessment issues and possible solutions, and embrace three main theses: (a) assessment must capitalize on advances in technology, (b) assessment is a contextualized, social activity, and (c) assessment must serve teaching and learning. Each of these alone can move the assessment conversation and ensuing research forward, but we contend that when these issues are considered collectively, important breakthroughs in assessment and educational reform will surely follow.

References

Cizek, G. J., & Burg, S. S. (2005). *Addressing test anxiety in a high-stakes environment: Strategies for classrooms and schools.* Thousand Oaks, CA: Corwin Press.

Clarke, M. M., Madaus, G. F., Horn, C. L., & Ramos, M. A. (2000). Retrospective on educational testing and assessment in the 20th century. *Journal of Curriculum Studies, 32*(2), 159–181.

Darling-Hammond, L., & Snyder, J. (2000). Authentic assessment of teaching in context. *Teaching and Teacher Education, 16*(5–6), 523–545.

Epstein, M. L., Epstein, B. B., & Brosvic, G. M. (2001). Immediate feedback during academic testing. *Psychological Reports, 88*(3), 889–894.

Kane, T. J., Staiger, D. O., & Geppert, J. (2002). Randomly accountable. *Education Next, 2*(1), Downloaded 12/16/09 from http://educationnext.org/randomly-accountable/

Leadbeater, C., & Miller, P. (2004). *The Pro-Am Revolution: How enthusiasts are changing our economy and society.* Demos. Downloaded on January 12, 2010 from http://www.demos.co.uk/files/proamrevolutionfinal.pdf?1240939425

Leu, D. J., O'Bryne, I., Zawilinski, J., McVerry, J. G., & Everett-Cacopardo, H. (2009). Expanding the new literacies conversation. *Educational Researcher, 38*(4), 264–269.

Linn, R. L., Baker, E. L., & Betebenner, D. W. (2002). Accountability systems: Implications of requirements of the No Child Left Behind Act of 2001. *Educational Researcher, 31*(6), 3–16.

Naglieri, J. A., Drasgow, F., Schmit, M., Handler, L., Prifitera, A., Margolis, A., et al. (2004). Psychological testing on the Internet: New problems, old issues. *American Psychologist, 59*(3), 150–162.

Redfield, D., Roeber, E., Stiggins, R., & Philip, F. (2008). *Building balanced assessment systems to guide educational improvement.* A background paper for the keynote panel presentation at the National Conference on Student Assessment, June 15, 2008, Orlando, FL. Downloaded on December 15, 2009, from http://www.ccsso.org/content/PDFs/OpeningSessionPaper-Final.pdf

Ruiz-Primo, M. A., Shavelson, R. J., Hamilton, L., & Klein, S. (2002). On the evaluation of systemic science education reform: Searching for instructional sensitivity. *Journal of Research in Science Teaching, 39*(5), 369–393.

Suen, H. K., & Yu, L. (2006). Chronic consequences of high-stakes testing? Lessons from the Chinese Civil Service Exam. *Comparative Education Review, 50*(1), 46–65.

Wiggins, G. (1990). *The case for authentic assessment.* ERIC Digest. ERIC Document Reproduction Service Number ED328611. Washington, DC: ERIC Clearinghouse on Tests Measurement and Evaluation.

Gee, J. P., & Hayes, E. R. (2010). *Women and gaming: The Sims and 21st century learning.* New York: Palgrave/McMillan.

Shute, V. J. (in press). Stealth assessment in computer-based games to support learning. To appear in S. Tobias & J. D. Fletcher (Eds.), *Computer games and instruction.* Charlotte, NC: Information Age Publishers.

Subject Index

Note: The letters 'f' and 't' following the locators refer to figures and tables respectively.

Breinigsville, PA USA
06 September 2010
244751BV00003B/20/P